The Apocryphal Acts of Peter:
Magic, Miracles and Gnosticism

STUDIES ON THE APOCRYPHAL ACTS OF THE APOSTLES

In recent years the Apocryphal Acts of the Apostles have increasingly drawn the attention of scholars interested in early Christianity and/or the history of the ancient novel. New editions of the most important Acts have appeared or are being prepared. We are therefore pleased to announce an new series, *Studies on the Apocryphal Acts of the Apostles* (edited by Jan N. Bremmer), which will contain studies of individual aspects of the main Acts: Those of John, Paul, Peter, Andrew, and Thomas. Initially, five volumes are scheduled.

Edited by:
T. Adamik, J. Bolyki, J.N. Bremmer (*editor-in-chief*),
P. Herczeg, A. Hilhorst, G. P. Luttikhuizen and J. Roldanus.

1. *The Apocryphal Acts of John*, J.N. Bremmer (ed.), Kampen 1995
2. *The Apocryphal Acts of Paul en Thecla*, J.N. Bremmer (ed.), Kampen 1996
3. *The Apocryphal Acts of Peter: Magic, Miracles and Gnosticism*, J.N. Bremmer (ed.), Leuven 1998
4. *The Acts of John: a Two-stage Initiation into Johannine Gnosticism*, P.J. Lalleman, Leuven 1998

The Apocryphal Acts of Peter

JAN N. BREMMER (ED.)

Magic, Miracles and Gnosticism

PEETERS

© 1998, Uitgeverij Peeters, Bondgenotenlaan 153, 3000 Leuven
   ISBN 90-429-0019-9
   D. 1998/0602/36

All rights reserved. No part of this book may be reproduced or transmitted in any form or by any means, electronic or mechanical, including photocopying, recording, or by any information storage and retrieval system, without permission in writing from the publisher.

Contents

Preface		i
Notes on contributors		iii
List of abbreviations		vii
I	J.N. Bremmer, *Aspects of the Acts of Peter: Women, Magic, Place and Date*	1
II	I. Karasszon, *Agrippa, King and Prefect*	21
III	P. Herczeg, *Theios Aner Traits in the Apocryphal Acts of Peter*	29
IV	G. P. Luttikhuizen, *Simon Magus as a Narrative Figure in the Acts of Peter*	39
V	T. Adamik, *The Image of Simon Magus in the Christian Tradition*	52
VI	C.M. Thomas, *... Revivifying Resurrection Accounts: techniques of composition and rewriting in the Acts of Peter cc.25-28*	65
VII	I. Czachesz, *Who is Deviant? Entering the Story-world of the Acts of Peter*	84
VIII	M. Misset-van de Weg, *'For the Lord always takes Care of his own'. The Purpose of the Wondrous Works and Deeds in the Acts of Peter*	97

CONTENTS

IX	J. Bolyki, *'Head Downwards': The Cross of Peter in the Lights of the Apocryphal Acts, of the New Testament and of the Society-transforming Claim of Early Christianity*	111
X	M. Pesthy, *Cross and Death in the Apocryphal Acts of the Apostles*	123
XI	L. H. Westra, *Regulae fidei and Other Credal Formulations in the Acts of Peter*	134
XII	A. Hilhorst, *The Text of the Actus Vercellenses*	148
XIII	P.J. Lalleman, *The Relation between the Acts of John and the Acts of Peter*	161
XIV	W. Rordorf, *The Relation between the Acts of Peter and the Acts of Paul: State of the Question*	178
XV	G. Poupon, *L'Origine africaine des Actus Vercellenses*	192
XVI	P.J. Lalleman and J.N. Bremmer, *Bibliography of the Acts of Peter*	200
Index of names, subjects and passages		203

Preface

After the fall of the Berlin Wall the Rijksuniversiteit Groningen decided to intensify contacts with universities in Eastern Europe. In 1991 the then Head of the Department of Church History, Professor Hans Roldanus, took this opportunity to forge links with the Károli Gáspár University of Budapest. In the search for a common research project, which would also prove to be attractive to classicists of the Loránd-Eötvös University of Budapest, it was decided to focus on the Apocryphal Acts of the Apostles. This particular choice hardly needs to be defended. The world of early Christianity is currently receiving an ever increasing attention from New Testament and patristic scholars as well as from ancient historians. Various Apocryphal Acts have recently been re-edited or are in process of being re-edited, but the contents of these Acts are still very much under-researched.

It is the object of the Dutch-Hungarian cooperation to study the major Apocryphal Acts in a series of yearly conferences, of which the proceedings are published in the series, *Studies in the Apocryphal Acts of the Apostles*. The editors in principle envisage the publication of five volumes, but they are open to further suggestions.

Following the first two volumes of the new series on the *Acts of John* (1995) and the *Acts of Paul and Thecla* (1996), this new volume is devoted to the *Acts of Peter*. The major part of the book studies various persons, aspects and passages of the *Acts*: women, magic, Agrippa, Simon Magus, resurrection accounts, invectives, miracles, the cross, and credal formulations. After a study of their Latinity, there follow two chapters studying the relation of the *Acts of Peter* to those of *John* and *Paul*. The penultimate chapter succeeds in locating the *Actus Vercellenses*, the surviving part of the *Acts of Peter* in Latin, in Africa. As has become customary, the volume is rounded off by a bibliography and an index.

PREFACE

The conference which formed the basis of this book took place at the Rijksuniversiteit Groningen in the autumn of 1996. I am grateful to the Faculty of Theology and Science of Religion of the Rijksuniversiteit Groningen and the Rudolf Agricola Instituut, the Groningen Institute for the Humanities, for its financial support towards the conference. Pieter Lalleman most helpfully assisted with the editing of the proceedings. Ken Dowden, Christine Thomas and Phil Sellew, especially, helped to correct the English. Without the generous help of all these colleagues it would have been impossible to prepare this volume in such a speedy manner.

Jan N. Bremmer   Groningen, 31 October 1997

Notes on Contributors

Tamás Adamik b. 1937, is Professor of Latin at the Loránd-Eötvös University of Budapest. He is the author of the following studies in Hungarian: *A Commentary on Catullus* (1971), *Martial and His Poetry* (1979), *Aristotle's Rhetoric* (1982), *Jerome's Selected Works* (1991), *A History of Roman Literature* I-IV (1993-96). He is also the editor of new Hungarian translations of the *Apocryphal Acts of the Apostles* (1996), the *Apocryphal Gospels* (1996) and the *Apocryphal Apocalypses* (1996).

János Bolyki b. 1931, is Professor Emeritus of New Testament Studies at the Károli Gáspár University of Budapest. He is, in Hungarian, the author of *The Questions of the Sciences in the History of Theology in the 20th Century* (1970), *Faith and Science* (1989), *Principles and Methods of New Testament Interpretation* (1990) and *The Table Fellowships of Jesus* (1992), and co-author of *Codex D in the Book of Acts* (1995).

Jan N. Bremmer b. 1944, is Professor of History and Science of Religion at the Rijksuniversiteit Groningen. He is the author of *The Early Greek Concept of the Soul* (1983) and *Greek Religion* (1994), co-author of *Roman Myth and Mythography* (1987), editor of *Interpretations of Greek Mythology* (1987), *From Sappho to de Sade: Moments in the History of Sexuality* (1989), *The Apocryphal Acts of John* (1995), *The Apocryphal Acts of Paul and Thecla* (1996) and co-editor of *A Cultural History of Gesture* (1991), *Between Poverty and the Pyre. Moments in the history of widowhood* (1995) and *A Cultural History of Humour* (1997).

István Czachesz b. 1968, is Research Fellow at the Centre for Hermeneutical Research in Budapest. He is, in Hungarian, the author of *Gaia's Two Faces* (1996), co-author of *Codex D in the Book of Acts* (1995), editor of *Disciples, Wonderworkers, Martyrs* (1997: a volume of essays on the Apocryphal Acts of the Apostles), and translator of *Tyconius' Book of Rules* (1997).

Pál Herczeg b. 1939, is Professor of History of Religion at the Károli Gáspár University. He is the author of the following studies in Hungarian: *The History of the New Testament* (1979), *The Plot of the Theology of the New Testament* (1986), *"Do you understand what you are reading?"* (1990) and *History of Religions* (1993).

A. Hilhorst b. 1938, is Associate Professor of Early Christian Literature and New Testament Studies at the Rijksuniversiteit Groningen. He is the author of *Sémitismes et latinismes dans le Pasteur d'Hermas* (1976) and co-author of *Apocalypse of Paul: a new critical edition of three long Latin versions* (1997), editor of *De heiligenverering in de eerste eeuwen van het Christendom* (1988), and co-editor of *Fructus Centesimus. Mélanges G.J.M. Bartelink* (1989), *The Scriptures and the Scrolls. Studies A.S. van der Woude* (1992), *Early Christian Poetry* (1993) and *Evangelie en beschaving. Studies Hans Roldanus* (1995).

István Karasszon b. 1955, is Professor of Old Testament Studies at the Károli Gáspár University of Budapest. He is the author of the following studies in Hungarian: *The Methodology of Old Testament Interpretation* (1991), *The History of Ancient Israel* (1992) and *Religion in Ancient Israel* (1995).

Pieter J. Lalleman b. 1960, was Research Associate at the Rijksuniversiteit Groningen and has almost completed a dissertation on the *Acts of John*.

Magda Misset-van de Weg b. 1943, is Research Associate at the Rijksuniversiteit Utrecht and prepares a dissertation on women as models of faith in *1 Peter* and the *Acts of Thecla*.

Gerard P. Luttikhuizen b. 1940, is Professor of Early Christian Literature and New Testament Studies at the Rijksuniversiteit Groningen. He is the author of *The Revelation of Elchasai* (1985) and *Gnostische Geschriften* I (1986).

Monika Pesthy b. 1954, teaches Classical Greek and Patristics at the Loránd-Eötvös University of Budapest. She is the author of the following studies in Hungarian: *Origen: Commentary on the Songs of Songs* (1993); *Origen, Interpreter of the Bible* (1996).

Gérard H. Poupon b. 1942 is presently free-lance translator after having taught Latin at the University of Geneva. He is preparing the edition of the *Acts of Peter* for the *Corpus Christianorum*. His annotated translation of the *Acts of Peter* has appeared in *Ecrits apocryphes chrétiens* (Collection de la Pléiade, 1997).

Willy Rordorf b. 1933, is Professor Emeritus of Early Church History and Patristic Studies at the University of Neuchâtel, Switzerland, and the editor-in-chief of the series *Traditio Christiana*. He is the author of *Sunday. The History of the Day of Rest and Worship in the Earliest Centuries of the Christian Church* (1968; also in German and Spanish) and of a collection of texts on the same subject: *Sabbat und Sonntag in der Alten Kirche* (1972; also in French and Italian). He is co-editor of *Didache* (1978, 1998²) and co-author of *L'evolution du concept de tradition dans L'Eglise ancienne* (1982; also in German). Two volumes of his collected studies have been printed: *Liturgie, foi et vie des premiers chrétiens* (1988²) and *Lex orandi – lex credendi* (1993).

Christine M. Thomas b. 1963, is Assistant Professor of Religious Studies at the University of California, Santa Barbara. She is the author of *The Beginnings of Christian Romance: The Acts of Peter, the Ancient Novel, and Early Christian History* (1998).

Liuwe Westra b. 1966, is a minister of the Dutch Reformed Church. He is the author of *The Apostles' Creed. Origin, history and some early commentaries* (1998).

List of abbreviations

AAA	*Apocryphal Acts of the Apostles*
ANRW	*Aufstieg und Niedergang der römischen Welt*
Bremmer, *AAJ*	Jan N. Bremmer (ed), *The Apocryphal Acts of John* (Kampen, 1995)
Bremmer, *AAP*	Jan N. Bremmer (ed), *The Apocryphal Acts of Paul and Thecla* (Kampen, 1996)
CIL	*Corpus Inscriptionum Latinarum*
JAC	*Jahrbuch für Antike und Christentum*
JTS	*Journal of Theological Studies*
NTA	W. Schneemelcher, *New Testament Apocrypha*, tr. and ed. R. McL. Wilson, 2 vols (Cambridge, 1992²)
PG	*Patrologia Graeca*
PL	*Patrologia Latina*
RAC	*Reallexikon für Antike und Christentum*
RE	*Realencyclopädie der classischen Altertumswissenschaft*
SBL	*Society of Biblical Literature*
SEG	*Supplementum Epigraphicum Graecum*
TRE	*Theologische Realenzyklopädie*
TWNT	*Theologisches Wörterbuch zum Neuen Testament*
VigChris	*Vigiliae Christianae*
ZNW	*Zeitschrift für die neutestamentliche Wissenschaft*
ZPE	*Zeitschrift für Papyrologie und Epigraphik*

All translations, if not otherwise indicated, are from *NTA* II (by W. Schneemelcher).

I. Aspects of the *Acts of Peter*: Women, Magic, Place and Date

JAN N. BREMMER

Around the turn of the century, after the discovery of various new texts, the *Acts of Peter* (*APt*) received much scholarly attention. This attention, as exemplified by scholars such as Carl Schmidt, Gerhard Ficker and Jean Flamion, focussed on the date, composition and place of origin of the *APt* but paid little attention to the interpretation of the text in general[1]. It is only in the last decade that the *APt* have, so to speak, re-emerged from oblivion. This renewed interest is especially due to the preparation of new texts of the *Apocryphal Acts of the Apostles* (*AAA*) by a Swiss équipe and the work towards a new translation of the *AAA* by an American group[2]. There is therefore plenty of scope for investigation into specific aspects of the text. In this contribution I will first discuss the 'new' subjects of women, demons and magic, and conclude with the 'traditional' subjects of the place and date of composition.

1. *Women*

The *APt* lack striking female figures, such as Drusiana in the *Acts of John* (*AJ*) or Thecla in the *Acts of Paul* (*AP*), but women are certainly

---

[1] For their work see the bibliography at the end of this volume. Regarding commentaries, the only exception is Ficker's very useful 'Petrusakten', in E. Hennecke (ed), *Handbuch zu den neutestamentlichen Apokryphen* (Tübingen, 1904) 395-491.

[2] See especially J.B. Perkins, *The Suffering Self* (London, 1995) 124-41; R.F. Stoops, Jr., 'Patronage in the *Acts of Peter*', *Semeia* 38 (1986) 91-100; 'Christ as Patron in the *Acts of Peter*', *Semeia* 56 (1992) 143-57 and 'Departing to Another Place: The *Acts of Peter* and the Canonical Acts of the Apostles', in E.H. Lovering (ed), *SBL 1994 Seminar Papers* (Atlanta, 1994) 390-404.

not absent. In fact, we find a rich variety of ages and classes in the *Acts*, whose importance for the church is heavily stressed: when most brothers defected from the faith, impressed as they were by the miracles of Simon Magus, only a few kept the faith, amongst whom 'two women in the lodging-house of the Bithynians (see below §3) and four who could no longer go out of their house' (4).

Let us start our discussion with virgins. Due to a happy identification by Carl Schmidt, a scene in a Coptic papyrus is now generally accepted as being part of the *APt*[3]. It relates how the crowd reacted to Peter's healing activities by asking him to heal his own, beautiful daughter, who was paralysed on one side. Peter immediately gave in to the request and cured his daughter, but then asked her to return to her place and lie down again. The reason for her illness, as he explained, was that a certain Ptolemaeus had fallen in love with her, when she was bathing with her mother at the age of ten. Vouaux thought of a bathe in the sea, but the scene is situated in Jerusalem and it seems more likely that the author had in mind one of the baths which were widespread in Asia Minor. Baths were haunted by voyeurs and typical places for picking up boys and girls. It is therefore not surprising that later Christians often objected to them[4]. The age of ten may be suspect, since for Greek girls menarche probably started some years later and they do not seem to have married before the age of about fifteen[5], but it may perhaps stress the evil nature of the man's desire.

---

[3] See now J. Brashler and D. Parrott, *Nag Hammadi Codices V 2-5 and VI with Papyrus Berolinensis 8502.1 and 4* (Leiden, 1979) 473-93; M. Tardieu, *Écrits gnostiques. Codex de Berlin* (Paris, 1984) 217-22, 403-10.

[4] Petronius 92.7f; Martial 1.23, 11.63 (with N.M. Kay ad. loc.); R.W. Daniel and F. Maltomini, *Supplementum Magicum II* (Opladen, 1992) 143f; J. Zellinger, *Bad und Bäder in der altchristlichen Kirche* (Munich, 1928); K. Dunbabin, '*Baiarum grata voluptas*: pleasures and dangers of the baths', *Papers of the British School at Rome* 57 (1989) 6-46; F. Yegül, *Baths and Bathing in Classical Antiquity* (New York, 1992) 250-313; G. Charpentier, 'Les petits bains proto-byzantins de la Syrie du Nord', *Topoi* 5 (1995) 219-47.

[5] For the age of a girl's marriage compare *Ninos*, Col. A.III.1 (15); Longus, *Daphnis and Chloe* (14). For menarche see H. King, 'Medical Texts as a Source for Women's History', in A. Powell (ed), *The Greek World* (London, 1995) 199-218, esp. 210f.

The paralysed girl is one more indication of the encratitic tendencies of the *APt*. Not only is the apostle the cause of four (!) concubines deserting their lover, the prefect Agrippa[6], but Peter also causes the breakdown of the marriage of a certain Xanthippe, which will mean his death. The message of the *APt* is therefore clear: serious illness and death are less harmful than sexual relationships with people who refuse to follow Christ. This message is even stressed right at the beginning of the *APt*, since Paul sternly addressed Rufina, a woman who lived with an adulterer and who instantly 'fell down, being paralysed on the left side from her head to her toe-nails' (2).

The message is also stressed through a scene, known only via the eighth-century Pseudo-Titus, *De dispositione sanctimonii* (lines 83-4), which mirrors that of Peter's daughter in a negative way. After Peter had been requested by someone to pray for the good of his only daughter's soul, he did so and she immediately fell down dead. Understandably, the father asked Peter to raise his daughter again, but some days later she eloped with a man who had posed as a believer. Considering the often hostile attitude towards the country in most Greek novels[7], we may notice that the girl was the daughter of a peasant.

The cases of these virgins are relatively straightforward, but other virgins are much harder to place. After Peter had healed various widows in the house of Marcellus (below), he began 'to attend the virgins of the Lord' (22), who are also mentioned later when the mother of the senator (see below §3) brought Peter two thousand pieces of gold (29). These maidens were evidently unable to support themselves and may well have deserted their families. They also seem already to form a separate category among the faithful – a development which would accelerate in subsequent centuries[8].

Our next category are the widows who are prominent in the *APt*[9]. They were clearly dependent on the charity of the richer members of

---

[6] On Agrippa see also Karasszon, this volume, Ch. II.
[7] E.L. Bowie, 'The novels and the real world', in B. Reardon (ed), *Erotica Antiqua* (Bangor, 1976) 91-6, esp. 94f.
[8] R. Metz, *La consécration des vierges dans l'église romaine* (Diss. Strasbourg, 1954).
[9] For Christian widows see now, with extensive bibliographies, J.-U. Krause, *Witwen und Waisen im frühen Christentum* (Stuttgart, 1995); Bremmer, 'Pauper or Patroness: the widow in the early Christian Church', in Bremmer and L.P. van den Bosch (eds), *Between Poverty and the Pyre. Moments in the*

the congregation, such as the senator Marcellus (8, 19-21). There were widows of various ages and the *APt* regularly combine *viduae et seniores* (19, 21, 27), the latter being clearly particularly dependent: one of them is blind and has to be guided by her daughter (20) and another has only a son to help her (27)[10]. Many of these widows were despondent, ill or blind and Peter assisted them in various ways, by charity (28-9), healing or raising a son (27). It is no wonder, then, that they were singled out among the Christians who tried to save Peter from the cross (36).

Having healed the blind widow, Peter entered Marcellus' dining-room, where men and old blind widows were listening to the reading of the gospel. The apostle 'rolled up (the book)' (*involvens*) and started a long theological exposition (20). The reference to a scroll is rather surprising, since virtually all early Christian papyri have come to us in the form of a *codex*[11]. On the other hand, Jan den Boeft and I have drawn attention to a passage in the *Acta Scillitanorum* (12), where one of the future martyrs, Speratus, carries 'books and epistles of Paul' in a *capsa*, normally a container of scrolls. We concluded that this passage seems to suggest a continuing use of the scroll in some parts of the Christian church and pointed out that *codex* was also absent from Tertullian, despite his rich terminology for Christian scripture[12]. This passage of the *APt*, then, might be a

history of widowhood (London, 1995) 31-57; G. Dönni, *Der alte Mensch in der Antike. Ein Vergleich zwischen christlicher und paganer Welt anhand der Aussagen von Hieronymus, Augustinus, Ambrosius und Cicero* (Diss. Basel 1995; Bamberg, 1996) 175-94.

[10] J.-D. Kaestli, 'Fiction littéraire et réalité sociale: que peut-on savoir de la place des femmes dans le milieu de production des Actes apocryphes des apôtres?', *Apocrypha* 1 (1990) 279-302, esp. 300, persuasively argues that the *seniores* in cc.19-21 are not 'old men' but 'older widows'. For old women in patristic literature see now Dönni, *Der alte Mensch*, 165-75.

[11] For this phenomenon and possible explanations see most recently G.H.R. Horsley, 'Classical Manuscripts in Australia and New Zealand, and the Early History of the Codex', *Antichthon* 27 (1993) 60-83; T.C. Skeat, 'The Origin of the Christian Codex', *ZPE* 102 (1994) 263-8; J.L. de Miguel Jover, 'El humilde nacimiento del Códice', *Myrtia* no. 10 (1995) 157-76; especially, H.Y. Gamble, *Books and Readers in the Early Church* (New Haven and London, 1995) 42-81.

[12] J. den Boeft and J. Bremmer, 'Notiunculae Martyrologicae IV', *VigChris* 45 (1991) 105-22, esp. 116-17.

further illustration of the continuing use of the scroll in some Christian circles.

Whereas the first part of our argument has been well received and gains some force from the observation that scrolls also appear in some early Christian art[13], Gamble has objected that our comment on Tertullian 'carries no more weight than any argument from silence'[14]. However, he has overlooked the fact that Tertullian's oeuvre is not particularly a small one and consistently uses *volumen* not *codex*[15].

Widows were not only members of the church because of their expectation of charity or healing, but they also fulfilled certain functions, although we do not yet hear of the *ordo viduarum* in the *APt*. However, Marcellus gave orders to bring the *viduae et seniores* into his house 'in order to pray with us' (19). In the Jewish tradition, which is still visible in the New Testament, widows were valued for their prayer because God was thought to have pity on them in particular. It may well be that we still find this tradition alive in our *Acts*[16]. Their special position, especially that of the *seniores*, also appears from the fact that they alone, even though they did not yet believe, saw Jesus in a number of ways: old, young and as a child (21)[17].

In addition to poor women, the *APt* also pay much attention to those of the upper classes. Right at the beginning of the *APt* 'a large crowd of women' (3) accompanied Paul to the harbour; amongst them were two *matronae* 'from the house of Caesar', Berenice and Philostrate, clearly freedwomen. In a way, they set the tone for the *APt*, which seem to mention more women of the upper classes than any other of the major *AAA*.

---

[13] As is observed by W.V. Harris, 'Why Did the Codex Supplant the Book-Roll?', in J. Monfasani and R.G. Musto (eds), *Renaissance Society and Culture: Essays in Honor of Eugene F. Rice, Jr.* (New York, 1991) 71-85, esp. 77.
[14] R. Lane Fox, 'Literacy and power in early Christianity', in A.K. Bowman and G. Woolf (eds), *Literacy and Power in the Ancient World* (Cambridge, 1994) 126-48, esp. 142; Gamble, *Books*, 279 note 138 (quotation).
[15] J.E.L. van der Geest, *Le Christ et l'Ancien Testament chez Tertullien* (Nimwegen, 1972) 56-7, 60.
[16] K. van der Toorn, 'The Public Image of the Widow in Ancient Israel', in Bremmer and Van den Bosch, *Between Poverty and the Pyre*, 19-30, esp. 25.
[17] Cf. P.J. Lalleman, 'Polymorphy of Christ', in Bremmer, *AAJ*, 97-118.

These rich women are especially mentioned at the beginning of the *Martyrium Petri* (30), where the apostle preaches to 'many senators, more knights, and rich aristocratic women' (*matronae*). Some of these women did even leave their husbands, such as Xanthippe, the wife of Albinus, 'the friend of the Emperor' (*tou Kaisaros philou*: 34). Incidentally, we may observe that this qualification points to Asia Minor rather than to Rome, since the Emperor frequently used this title in letters referring to provincial governors or other high officials: the mode of address stressed their authority and access to the Emperor. Illustrative of this is a letter from Trajan to Smyrna, which has recently been found in Aphrodisias and which mentions 'Iulius Balbus (see below §3), my friend and proconsul'[18]. Other women were Agrippina, Nicaria, Euphemia and Doris, the four concubines of the praefect Agrippa, surely the *praefectus urbi*, who acted as a judge in Rome (33). Not all women, though, were as chaste as these. One wealthy woman, Chryse, apparently had liaisons with her younger slaves, a not unusual practice in ancient Rome: Trimalchio relates that he gave sexual favours to his boss but did not neglect his mistress either[19].

Aristocratic women also occur earlier in the narrative. We have already heard about the mother of the young senator, whose wealth is illustrated by her gift of two thousand pieces of gold. She clearly also owns a number of slaves, and it is highly interesting that Peter stresses that they, even though freed before the resurrection of her son, must remain free but also employed. We have here a hint of the excitement which slaves must have felt at the thought of being freed, but also of the concomitant anxiety of being turned out on the street at the same time. To my knowledge there is not a single classical passage which informs us about the experiences of freedmen being suddenly on their own, but reports from the aftermath of the American Civil War can give us some idea of the shock that sudden manumission gave to slaves[20].

---

[18] Schneemelcher, *NTA* II, 313 wrongly translates with 'the friend of Caesar'. *Amici*: F. Millar, *The Emperor in the Roman World* (London, 1977) 110-22. New example: *SEG* 32.1202 = G. Petzl, *Die Inschriften von Smyrna* II.1 (Bonn, 1987) no. 593.
[19] Petronius 75.11; note also Herodas 5; Pliny, *NH* 34.11f; Martial 1.84; Juvenal 6.279, 331; Suetonius, *Vitellius* 12.
[20] K. Hopkins, *Conquerors and Slaves* (Cambridge, 1978) 148f. For the Christian manumission of slaves see now J.A. Harrill, *The Manumission of Slaves in Early Christianity* (Tübingen, 1995).

A more interesting case, though, is that of the Judaean Eubola, who seems to be typical of the wealthy women of that time, who were regularly the target of heretics and founders of new religions (17)[21]. Simon and his accomplices had robbed this woman of her gold, but they also planned to rob her of a statuette, a satyriskos, of gold, 'with a precious stone set in it' and to hand it over to a goldsmith, presumably to be smelted down. Satyriskoi are not often mentioned or depicted, but they start to appear in the Hellenistic period[22]. Eubola's satyriskos also was the object of worship, since Peter mentions that she put up her idol and veiled it, when she meant to celebrate a festival. In other words, the statuette was the object of private devotion.

Eubola's statuette must have been quite small, since it was of gold but weighed only two pounds. Such portable statues of gods were not unusual in the period of our *Acts*. In recent times, examples have become known of small statues of Glykon, the god created by Alexander of Abunoteichos, measuring between 6 and 7 centimetres. The famous French epigraphist Louis Robert has dedicated an excellent article to these statuettes, building also on earlier work done by Franz Joseph Dölger[23]. The latter had drawn attention to a passage in Philostratus' biography of Apollonius of Tyana, in which the sage berated people who wore small statuettes of Demeter and Dionysos around their necks (5.20). He had also drawn attention to a passage in Apuleius' *Apology* in which the philosopher admitted that 'wherever I

---

[21] See my 'Why Did Christianity Attract Upper-Class Women?', in A.A.R. Bastiaensen *et al.* (eds), *Fructus centesimus: Mélanges G.J.M. Bartelink* (Steenbrugge and Dordrecht, 1989) 37-47.

[22] Theocritus, 27.3, 49f; Hero, *Spir.* 1.37, cf. H. von Hesberg, 'Mechanische Kunstwerke und ihre Bedeutung für die höfische Kunst des frühen Hellenismus', in *Marburger Winckelmannprogramm* 1987, 47-72, esp. 55; Anth. Pal. 16.244; B. Andreae, 'Schmuck eines Wasserbeckens in Sperlonga. Zum Typus des sitzenden Knäbleins aus dem Schiffsfund von Mahdia', *Röm. Mitt.* 83 (1976) 287-309 and 'Statuetten eines sitzenden Knäbleins', in G. Hellenkemper-Salies *et al.* (eds), *Das Wrack. Der antike Schiffsfund von Mahdia* (Cologne, 1994) 365-74; *P.Oxy.* 64.4432.

[23] L. Robert, *Opera Minora Selecta* V (Amsterdam, 1989) 747-69 (= *CRAI* 1981, 513-35); F.J. Dölger, *Antike und Christentum* IV (Münster, 1934) 67-72, 277-9; E. Bartman, *Ancient Sculptural Copies in Miniature* (Leiden, 1992) 43-8.

go, I carry an image of a god hidden among my books and on festive days (like Eubola!) I supplicate it with incense, wine and sometimes a victim' (63). This god, Hermes, was therefore a portable god, just like the image belonging to Eubola[24]. Louis Robert was able to add various inscriptions which all went to show that in the time of our *Acts* there was a lively trade of these small, often very precious statuettes of divinities. In this respect, then, Eubola was a typical religious product of her time.

The final woman I want to discuss is only a dream woman. On the day preceding the great contest of Peter and Simon Magus, the senator Marcellus had a short sleep. In his dream he saw a 'most evil-looking woman, who looked like an Ethiopian, not an Egyptian, but was all black, clothed in filthy rags, dancing with an iron collar about her neck and chains on her hands and feet'. Although the Greeks generally considered the Egyptians to be black, they could, if necessary, also distinguish them from their neighbours. For example, Achilles Tatius calls the Boukoloi black but 'not deep black like Indians but as black as, say, a half-Ethiopian might be' (2.9, tr. J. Winkler) and according to Philostratus (*V. Apoll.* 6.2), those who inhabited the border regions between Egypt and Ethiopia were 'less black than the Ethiopians but more black than the Egyptians'[25]. The message is clear: the woman is terribly black and as such disgusting; not surprisingly, black was a regular colour for demons in antiquity[26]. Her low status is further

---

[24] On this passage of Apuleius see most recently F. Graf, *Gottesnähe und Schadenzauber. Die Magie in der griechisch-römischen Antike* (Munich, 1996) 75f; V. Hunink, *Apuleius of Madaurus, Pro se de magia*, 2 vls (Amsterdam, 1997) II.162-74.

[25] For the colour of the Egyptians and Ethiopians see especially A. Cameron, *Callimachus and His Critics* (Princeton, 1995) 233-6; add J. den Boeft and J. Bremmer, 'Notiunculae martyrologicae II', *VigChris* 36 (1982, 383-402) 390; J. den Boeft *et al.*, *Philological and Historical Commentary on Ammianus Marcellinus XXII* (Groningen, 1995) 310; S. Walker and M. Bierbrier, *Ancient Faces. Mummy Portraits from Roman Egypt* (London, 1997).

[26] B. Steidle, 'Der kleine schwarze Knabe in der alten Möncherzählung', *Bened. Monatsschr.* 34 (1958) 339-50; P. du Bourguet, 'La couleur noire de la peau du démon dans l'iconographie chrétienne à-t-elle une origine précise?, in *Actas del VIII Congreso Internacional de Arqueología Cristiana* (Vatican City, 1972) 271-2; L. Cracco Ruggini, 'Il negro buono e il negro

stressed by the signs of her being a prisoner: her chains and the collar about her neck, which probably suggests a member of a chain gang; the martyr Pionius also made collars for himself and his followers[27]. Marcellus twice rejected Peter's exhortation to kill the woman, but suddenly a man appeared who closely resembled Peter and who cut the woman into pieces. Refreshed and encouraged by the dream, Peter went to face his magician opponent (22).

There is a striking parallel to this dream. On the day before her execution, Perpetua dreamt that she had to fight against an ugly Egyptian. During this fight she was encouraged by God in the shape of the agonothetes. In the end she managed to defeat her opponent and realized that this fight foreshadowed her own final victory (*Passio Perpetuae* 10). Now we know that Carthaginian women had read the *AP* and Perpetua also seems to have either read or heard of these *Acts*[28]. In the light of the resemblance between Marcellus' dream and that of Perpetua, I would now suggest that Perpetua had also read the *APt*. Considering the date of the *Actus Vercellenses* (§3), she will have read the *APt* not in Latin, but in the Greek original[29].

2. *Demons and magic*

In the *APt* we are at various times confronted with demons and magic. In principle, these are of course very different categories, but in the ancient world they were often associated through the employment of magic in exorcising demons. The mingling of these two categories appears clearly in the contest between Peter and Simon Magus, who is still called only Simon in the canonical *Acts* (8) and, presumably, received his epithet from the Christians.

Before Simon entered Rome he stayed in Aricia, a small town outside Rome with an important cult of Diana/Artemis and Hekate and

---

malvagio nel mondo classico', in M. Sordi (ed), *Conoscenze etniche e rapporti di convivenza nell'antichità* (Milano, 1979) 108-35; L.A. Thompson, *Romans and Blacks* (London, 1989) 110-3.

[27] M. Pion. 2.3, cf. L. Robert, *Le martyre de Pionios, prêtre de Smyrne* (Washington DC, 1994) 51.

[28] Cf. Bremmer, *AAP*, 44.

[29] For her knowledge of Greek see *Passio Perpetua* 13.4 *coepit Perpetua Graece cum illis loqui*; for bilingualism in Africa in general, Hunink, *Apuleius* II, 22f.

so, presumably, the appropriate place for Simon to stay. Apparently, he had already made a great impact in Rome, since he had been acclaimed as *in Italia deus* and *tu Romanorum salvator* (4). The latter acclamation clearly reflects the Greek *soter*, a common acclamation which need not reflect a divine status, but the earlier undeniably acclaimed him as a god. In this absolute sense, though, *deus* used for a human only occurs very rarely in Latin and the combination of *theos* and *soter* almost certainly is more Greek than Roman.

The divinization of Simon recurs later, when Marcellus confesses to Peter that he has erected a statue for Simon with the inscription *Simoni juveni deo*, undoubtedly a mistranslation of the Greek *Simoni neooi theooi* (10). Simon's statue is mentioned first by Justin (1 *Apol*. 26) who gives as the inscription *Simoni deooi sanktooi*, an adaptation, as has long been seen, of a dedication to the presumably Sabine god *Semoni Sanco Deo Fidio sacrum*. The dedication *neooi theooi*, which further adapts the Latin inscription for a Greek audience, is not very frequently found but not wholly unusual either: both Gaius Caesar and Germanicus had received this title (*IGRom* 4.1094, 74-5). Once again, we seem to be in the Greek world rather than in Italy.

If ruler cult is often stimulated from the top down, there remained the tendency from the bottom up to divinize people who had performed impressive deeds. We can still observe this tendency in the New Testament where the Maltese said of Paul 'that he was a god', after he had survived the bite of a viper (Acts 28.6). Even more interesting is the visit of Paul and Barnabas to Lystra in Lykaonia. After the apostles had healed a lame man, the inhabitants started to call Paul Hermes and Barnabas Zeus, a divine pair which was popular in that very region, as epigraphy and archaeology amply attest[30]. Philostratus provides another example, closer to the time of the *APt*, in his biography of Apollonius of Tyana. After the pagan sage had told his Assyrian host that he spoke all languages and even understood all human secrets, 'the Assyrian prayed to him... and considered him to be a god (*daimona*)' (1.19). It is in line with this tendency that people instantly worshipped Simon (*adorantes*) after he had flown through the sky (4)[31].

---

[30] *Acts* 14, cf. L. Robert, *Hellenica* 13 (1965) 29; C.P. Jones, 'A geographical setting for the Baucis and Philemon legend', *Harvard St. Class. Phil.* 96 (1994) 203-23.
[31] This tendency also occurs elsewhere in the *AAA* and the pagan novel

Having been depicted as received with divine honours, Simon immediately promised to perform perhaps the most impressive deed a magician can do other than a resurrection, that is flying. The theme was not uncommon and occurs in a fragment of a novel[32], Lucian's *Philopseudes* (13), and in Philostratus' biography of Apollonius (3.15, 17 and 6.10-1), that means, works closely contemporary with our *Acts*.

Peter, on the other hand, also could demonstrate his own powers. When Marcellus had stepped outside his house and confessed his sins, Peter noticed somebody, who was possessed by a demon, laughing in secret. His laughter may have been a mocking of the apostle, but the passage may also show the ambivalent attitude of the early Christians towards laughter, which was condemned by many a Church Father[33]. Peter exorcised the demon *in nomine domini nostri Jesu Christi*, thus following Jesus' command in the gospels to perform miracles in his own name[34], and ordered the demon to show himself to the bystanders. What follows is truly remarkable.

The demon left the young man and caught hold of a great marble statue of the emperor in the courtyard of Marcellus' house and kicked it to pieces. Both in Rome and the Greek world images of emperors have been found in private houses, if not very frequently; thus its presence in the house of a senator can not have been something uncommon to the contemporary reader. These statues were very important and any sign of disrespect or damage to them wrought with danger. Even urinating near such a statue could already be cause for execution[35]. It is therefore not surprising that Marcellus immediately

---

cf. R. Söder, *Die apokryphen Apostelgeschichten und die romanhafte Literatur der Antike* (Stuttgart, 1932) 95-100; add Achilles Tatius 3.23; *AA* 3; *ATh* 106.

[32] S. Stephens and J. Winkler, *Ancient Greek Novels: the fragments* (Princeton, 1995) 173-8.

[33] Bremmer, 'Jokes, Jokers and Jokebooks in Ancient Greek Culture', in J. Bremmer and H. Roodenburg (eds), *A Cultural History of Humour* (Cambridge, 1997) 11-28, esp. 21-3; note also L. Moulinier, 'Quand le Malin fait de l'esprit. Le rire au Moyen Age vu depuis l'hagiographie', *Annales ESC* 52 (1997) 457-75.

[34] M. Smith, *Jesus the Magician* (London, 1978) 114.

[35] S.R. Price, *Rituals and Power. The Roman imperial cult in Asia Minor* (Cambridge, 1984) 119-20 (houses; add our example), 192-5 (where he wrongly speaks of accidental damage in our case); Th. Pekáry, *Das römische*

feared for his life. After Peter had removed his fear by letting him repair the statue with water, Marcellus naturally 'believed with his whole heart in the name of Jesus Christ the Son of God, through whom all things impossible are (made) possible' (11)[36].

Having witnessed this not unimpressive miracle, the crowd requested more signs of Peter's power, since 'Simon too did many signs in our presence, and therefore we followed him' (12). It is somewhat surprising that the author of *APt* did not notice new converts after the exorcism of the young man, since in our sources conversion is often connected with exorcism[37]. However, Peter did convert many people by making a dead fish swim (13) – a rather curious reason to believe, one would have thought[38]. Subsequently, he made a young child speak to Simon and tell him that he would have to meet Peter on the next sabbath and, once again in the name of Jesus, make him dumb and leave Rome. Spells for speechlessness frequently occur in the magical papyri and often concern opponents in legal disputes[39]. Peter's use here of the same device shows the small difference between his behaviour and that of his opponent. Interestingly, Simon left immediately and stayed in a *stabulum*, an inn with a stable (15)[40], the kind of place where Jesus was born.

In these cases we can see the importance of using the name of Christ in performing miracles, just as magicians call out the name(s) of their gods. Peter, though, did something more. He resurrected the

---

Kaiserbildnis im Staat, Kult und Gesellschaft (Berlin, 1985) 139; D. Fishwick, *The Imperial Cult in the Latin West* II.1 (London, 1991) 532-40; R. Turcan, 'La promotion du sujet par le culte du souverain', in A. Small (ed), *Subject and Ruler: the cult of the ruling power in classical antiquity* = *J. Roman Arch. Suppl.* 17 (Ann Arbor, 1996) 51-62.

[36] R. Reitzenstein, *Hellenistische Wundererzählungen* (Leipzig, 1906) 54 rather fancifully suggests an Egyptian model behind this story.

[37] R. MacMullen, *Paganism in the Roman Empire* (New Haven and London, 1981) 50.

[38] Unless, as Ton Hilhorst suggests to me, there is here a reference to Christians as *pisciculi* (Tertullian, *De baptismo* 1). Or does the scene refer to Peter as 'fisher of man', as Kathleen Coleman suggests to me?

[39] Daniel and Maltomini, *Magical Papyri* II, no. 55, 58.8-9.

[40] T. Kleberg, *Hôtels, restaurants et cabarets dans l'antiquité romaine* (Uppsala, 1957) 18f.

widow's son by touching his side and let the prefect Agrippa resurrect one of his slaves by taking his hand (28). Touching and the use of the hand were very common in magical practice. We can see this already in the gospels where Jesus frequently used his hand, but the practise also occurs in magical papyri and is mentioned in Philostratus' biography of Apollonius of Tyana. A girl had died 'in the hour of her marriage', but Apollonius resurrected her by touching her and whispering something (*V. Apoll.* 4.45)[41].

Finally, I would like to stress a detail in the reaction of the crowd towards the loser in the contest between Peter and Simon. After Simon had called out: 'Men of Rome, if you see the dead man restored to life, will you throw Peter out of the city?' And they answer: '... that self-same hour we will burn him with fire'. This threat was clearly not meant as hyperbole, since as soon as Simon caused the dead man to raise his head, 'they began to look for wood and kindling, in order to burn Peter'. Moreover, after Peter had demonstrated his powers, they called out 'let Simon be burnt instead of Peter' (28). Is this reaction of the crowd just part of the author's dramatization of the situation or is it a credible reflection of contemporary behaviour? I fear that the latter is nearer to the truth, as a similar accident may illustrate, which is also very interesting in the light of the breaking of the imperial statue in Marcellus' house. After Apollonius of Tyana had arrived in Pamphylian Aspendus, he found out, according to Philostratus' biography, that at that very moment the population had become so angered by the corn hoarding of the rich that 'a crowd of all ages had set upon the governor, and were lighting a fire to burn him alive, although he was clinging to the statues of the Emperor, which were more dreaded at that time and more inviolable than the Zeus in Olympia'[42].

In these cases the potential victims escaped unhurt, but others were less lucky. The Thessalian Petraeus was burnt alive during riots under the rule of Augustus. And after the Asiarch Philip had refused to let loose a lion on Polycarp, the mob decided 'that Polycarp should

---

[41] S. Eitrem, *Some Notes on the Demonology of the New Testament* (Oslo, 1966²) 41-6.
[42] Philostratus, *V. Apoll.* 1.15, tr. F.C. Conybeare, cf. J.-J. Flinterman, *Power*, Paideia & *Pythagoreanism* (Amsterdam, 1995) 111f who overlooked the Christian examples.

be burnt alive' and 'immediately collected logs and brushwood from the workshops and baths'[43]. Lynching, then, was not just an invention of the American South.

3. *Place of origin and date of the APt*

According to Schneemelcher, the place of origin of the *APt* 'cannot be certainly determined'. Rome or Asia Minor have been suggested... But for the present we cannot get beyond conjecture' (*NTA* II, 283). This conclusion is perhaps too pessimistic. As Peter Lampe recently observed, the many Greek names in the *APt*, the ignorance of the 'trophy' of Peter on the Vatican and the place of Peter's funeral (40), all point to Asia Minor rather than Rome[44]. In addition to these more negative arguments, there are also more positive indications for an origin of the *APt* in Asia Minor. I have already stressed the significance of the expression 'the friend of the Emperor' and the adaptation of the inscription on Simon's statue, but we may have one more important indication.

After the apostle had raised a widow's son from the dead (§1) during his contest with Simon Magus, he was approached by another mother (§1), who had evidently heard about this resurrection. She requested him to resurrect her own son too, who was a senator. Peter consented and the mother had her son carried towards him in great style. Her slaves put their caps on their heads and walked in front of the bier together with everything that was normally offered for a deceased person, whereas the mother followed her son in the company of many senators and their wives, for 'Nicostratus was noble and much liked among the senate' (28).

The scene is well written and through the interest of the senatorial community the reader is impressed by the standing of the son and is made to share the mother's grief. It is interesting to see that the deceased son receives a typically Roman funeral, as the use of the *pillei* and the bier demonstrate. It was normal Roman custom that the bier was carried by freed slaves, who wore a felt cap as the sign of

---

[43] Plutarch, *Mor.* 815D, cf. C.P. Jones, *Plutarch and Rome* (Oxford, 1972[2]) 40f; *Mart. Polycarpi* 12-3.
[44] P. Lampe, *Die stadtrömischen Christen in den ersten beiden Jahrhunderten* (Tübingen, 1989[2]) 99 n. 299.

their recent freedom[45], whereas in Greece the corpse was transported on a chariot or sometimes carried by the local ephebes, as in the case of Chariton's *Callirhoe* (1.5). The somewhat vague description 'all that was to be used for the body' probably refers to the expensive unguents and perfumes to be used for the funeral.

How old, though, was the senator? The text is very explicit at this point. Three times he is called a *puer*. This is very surprising. How can a Roman senator be so young that he is still called a boy? Vouaux rightly seems to speak of the 'naïveté, un peu maladroite' of our author at this point[46]. And indeed, in imperial Rome it was only after having been quaestor that a man could become senator – hardly an age at which still to be called *puer*. It is true that during the Principate since Augustus sons of senators could attend the senate, but that does not make Nicostratus a senator. On the other hand, in the Roman East it became normal in the course of the second century that sons of urban elite families became associated with the activities of the *boule* at an early age and performed all kinds of offices[47]. The young senator, therefore, fits an origin in Asia Minor much better than in Rome where such a young politician would be hardly credible.

Can we go even further? Ficker has persuasively argued that the author of the *APt* came from Bithynia. His main arguments are the mention of a *hospitium Bithynorum* (4) and the name of the senator Marcellus, whom Ficker has connected with Granius Marcellus, a proconsul of Bithynia under Augustus[48]. One could add the name Balbus (3) and connect him with Q. Iulius Balbus, the proconsul of Asia of £100/1 or 101/2[49]. The proposed identifications may look improbable at first sight, but the mention of the historical figures of Tryphaena and Falconilla (below) in the *AP* demonstrate that the authors of the

---

[45] The Latin translation uses *iuvenes* but the Greek original most likely had *paides*. For freed slaves at a Roman funeral see J. Marquardt, *Das Privatleben der Römer*, ed. A. Mau (Leipzig, 1886²) 355; for an illustration see H. Flower, *Ancestor Masks and Aristocratic Power in Roman Culture* (Oxford, 1996) Plate 5 (cf. p. 94).

[46] L. Vouaux, *Les Actes de Pierre* (Paris, 1922) 385.

[47] Cf. M. Kleijwegt, *Ancient Youth. The ambiguity of youth and the absence of adolescence in Greco-Roman society* (Diss. Leiden, 1991) 221-72.

[48] A. Stein and L. Petersen, *Prosopographia Imperii Romani* IV² (Berlin, 1952-56) 40 no. 211 (AD 14/5 proconsul in Bithynia).

[49] *Prosopographia* IV², 152 no. 199.

AAA occasionally used names of historical persons[50]. Christians within the province are already mentioned in the preface to 1 Peter and in the famous letter of Pliny to Trajan about the Christians. Considering the rich social variety within the *APt*, one might perhaps think of Nicomedia. Around 170 this important city already had a Christian congregation, witness a letter of Dionysius of Corinth with a warning against Marcion (Eusebius, *HE* 4.23). Nicomedia would also have been the residence of Granius Marcellus. This specific location is of course no more than speculation, but the variety of classes and the strong Roman presence and familiarity with Rome certainly seem to point to one of the larger cities of Asia Minor. In any case, the identification would fit the fact that the *APt* lack the social terminology of 'a first of the city' which is so typical of the smaller cities in Southern Asia Minor and which helps to locate the place of origin of the *AJ*, *AP* and the *Acts of Andrew*[51].

Regarding the date of the *APt* we are still very much in the dark. It would help if we could at least provide a relative date by establishing the priority of the various *AAA*. Junod and Kaestli have argued that the *AJ* was the oldest of the *AAA* and probably written in Alexandria[52]. The latter proposition can hardly be correct because of the social terminology of the *AJ*[53]. Andronicus (31) is called 'a first of the Ephesians'. This social terminology is absent from Alexandria or Ephesus and therefore makes an origin in Alexandria most improbable. Unless we assume that the author had copied this terminology from the *AP*, it seems more natural to think that the author of the *AJ* knew this terminology from his own experience and thus came from the South-West part of Asia Minor, like the author of the *AP*[54].

---

[50] For Tryphaena see Bremmer, *AAP*, 52. Regarding the name of Tertullus in the *AJ* (59), we may perhaps also think of C. Iulius Cornutus Tertullus, the consul suffectus of 100 and husband of the famous Plancia Magna of Perge, cf. H. Halfmann, *Die Senatoren aus dem östlichen Teil des Imperium Romanum bis zum Ende des 2. Jahrhunderts n. Chr* (Göttingen, 1979) 117 no. 22; *Tituli Asiae Minoris* II, 642.

[51] Cf. Bremmer, *AAP*, 41 and 'Correspondences between the Apocryphal Acts and the Ancient Novel', in H. Hofmann and M. Zimmerman (eds), *Groningen Colloquia on the Novel*, IX (Groningen, 1998).

[52] E. Junod and J.D. Kaestli, *Acta Iohannis* II (Turnhout, 1983) 694-700.

[53] Hopefully, I am improving here on what I wrote earlier in Bremmer, *AAJ*, 55; but see also P.J. Lalleman, *ibidem*, 118.

[54] For the terminology see Bremmer, *AAP*, 41.

Regarding the date of the *AJ*, both Stanley Jones and Dennis MacDonald have recently argued that the *AJ* are dependent on the *AP*. And indeed, several of their adduced instances from the *AJ* seem to elaborate on or to copy passages of the *AP*. However, certainty in this matter is very hard to attain and in his forthcoming Groningen dissertation on the *AJ* Pieter Lalleman will again argue the case for the priority of *AJ*[55].

For the *AP* we have no certain chronological indications, but there is one interesting, hitherto neglected pointer. The deceased daughter of Tryphaena carries a most unusual name, Falconilla. However, the name is not unique. Various inscriptions mention a Pompeia Sosia Falconilla, the granddaughter of the consul suffectus of 108, Q. Pompeius Falco, and daughter of the consul in 149, Q. Pompeius Sosius Priscus, whose own husband M. Pontius Laelianus was consul in AD 163[56]. There can be little doubt that Tryphaena's daughter's name was taken from this lady. Although her 'origin' does not contribute towards a very precise *terminus post quem* of the *AP*, it does mean that they cannot have been that early.

If the *AP* dates from between about 150 and the beginning of March 203, the date of Perpetua's execution, what about the *APt*? Independent of the mutual relationship of *AP* and *APt*[57], which need not have large chronological implications, one cannot but be struck by the large variety of upper-class Romans described as being Christians or interested in the new faith. It is this aspect of the *APt* which led Carl Schmidt to date them to the last decades of the second century[58]. In principle, this suggestion still seems to be correct, although we have now a much more precise idea of the extent of Christian influence in

---

[55] F.S. Jones, 'Principal Orientations on the Relations between the Apocryphal Acts (*Acts of Paul* and *Acts of John*, *Acts of Peter* and *Acts of John*)' and D.R. MacDonald, '*The Acts of Paul* and *The Acts of John*: Which Came First?', in E.H. Lovering (ed), *SBL 1993 Seminar Papers* (Atlanta, 1993), 485-505 and 506-10.
[56] Falconilla: *CIL* VIII.7066; *Année Epigr.* 1935.25; *SEG* 26.261, cf. W.C. McDermott, *Ancient Society* 7 (1976) 238f; W. Eck, 'Senatorische Familien der Kaiserzeit in der Provinz Sizilien', *ZPE* 113 (1996) 109-28, whose analysis of Falconilla's family replaces earlier studies. Werner Eck also kindly put at my disposal the forthcoming lemma of Pompeia Sosia Falconilla in *PIR*.
[57] See now Rordorf, this volume, Ch. XIV.
[58] C. Schmidt, 'Zur Datierung der alten Petrusakten', *ZNW* 29 (1930) 150-5.

the highest Roman circles. Considering the enormous number of senators in those years – we must think of about 6000 – the number of known Christian senators in the second century is amazingly small. Werner Eck, to whom we owe the best study of this subject, is unable to mention a single Christian senator by name, but he does mention some senatorial women[59]. Both the general and individual mention of Christian senators occur in the reign of Septimius Severus – probably the influence of the persecution free time of Commodus. Of course, we can attribute a fanciful imagination to the author of *APt*, but it seems more credible that he wanted to show off the success of the new faith by mentioning its senators and senatorial women.

On the other hand, these senators could hardly demonstrate public allegiance to Christianity without losing their official functions. It seems that the author took this aspect of their allegiance into account: Marcellus has no ecclesiastical function and it is the resurrected son of a poor widow, not the resurrected young senator, who is said to become deacon and bishop in due time (27)[60]. I would therefore date the *APt* to the last two or the final decade(s) of the second century and, given the markedly conservative character of its *regula fidei*[61], preferably earlier than later.

The dream of Perpetua (§1) seems to show that the *APt* virtually immediately became known in Africa. But when and where were they translated into Latin? After the studies of Westra (Ch. XI) and Poupon (Ch. XV) in this volume, there can be no doubt left that the Latin translation originated in Africa. C.H. Turner dated it to the 'third or fourth' century[62], and he is followed by Poupon in this volume (Ch. XV), who thinks it not 'improbable' that the first Manichaean missionaries had brought the text along from Egypt and translated it

---

[59] W. Eck, 'Das Eindringen des Christentums in den Senatorenstand bis zu Konstantin d. Gr.', *Chiron* 1 (1971) 381-406; for some possible additions see now T. Barnes, 'Statistics and the Conversion of the Roman Aristocracy', *J. Rom. Stud.* 85 (1995) 135-47, esp. 135f.

[60] According to Stoops, Jr, 'Christ as Patron', the author of *APt* 'wanted to obligate the wealthy to fulfil their duties as benefactors, without granting them the honor and loyalty which are the normal responses to such patronage' (154). Both explanations are perhaps valid.

[61] Westra, this volume, Ch. XI.

[62] C.H. Turner, 'The Latin Acts of Peter', *JTS* 32 (1931) 119-33, esp. 119.

upon their arrival in Africa. However, there is a passage in the translation which prevents us from dating it too early.

The best evidence for determining the date of a text is often an institutional detail[63]. In this case, too, there is a passage in the translation which has not yet received the interest it deserves. When the demon had kicked the marble statue to pieces (§2), Marcellus called out: *Magnum flagitium factum est: si enim hoc innotuerit Caesari per aliquem de curiosis, magnis poenis nos adfliget* (11), which Schneemelcher translates as follows: 'A great crime has been committed; if Caesar hears of this through some busybody, he will punish us severely'[64]. However, his translation overlooks the fact that the *curiosi* were not 'busybodies', but a nickname for the *agentes in rebus*, a kind of imperial secret police[65]. It is only from AD 359 onwards that they reported directly to the emperor and, therefore, became feared as spies[66]. Consequently, the *APt* were translated into Latin in the second half of the fourth century[67]. It fits such a date that knowledge of the Latin translation is not attested before Augustine (*Contra Adimanti calumnias* 17). Although Schneemelcher states that 'the Latin translator has obviously followed the Greek text practically word for word'[68], it is now equally obvious that he also 'updated' his translation in order to make it more interesting.

[63] For another example from Late Antiquity see my 'An Imperial Palace Guard in Heaven: The Date of the *Vision of Dorotheüs*', ZPE 75 (1978) 82-8.
[64] Schneelmelcher, in *NTA* II, 297.
[65] As was pointed out by Pekáry, *Das römische Kaiserbildnis*, 139 n. 66.
[66] Cod. Theod. VI.29.1,4; VIII.5.50, cf. A.H.M. Jones, *The Later Roman Empire: a social, economic and administrative survey* (Oxford, 1964) II, 578-80; J. Triantaphylopoulos, '*Kouríosos* (P. Vindob. Sijpesteijn 22ᵛ', in *Atti dell' XI Congresso Internazionale di Papirologia* (Milano, 1966) 249-259 and '*Kouríosos*', *Ephemeris Hellen. Nomikoon* 32 (1968) 711-2; W. Blum, *Curiosi und Regendarii: Untersuchungen zur Geheimen Staatspolizei der Spätantike* (Munich, 1969); G. Purpura, 'I *curiosi* e la *schola agentum in rebus*', *Annali del Seminario Giuridico di Palermo* 34 (1973) 165-273; C. Vogler, *Constance II et l'administration impériale* (Strasbourg, 1979) 201-9; P.J. Sijpesteijn, 'Another curiosus', ZPE 70 (1987) 143-6; *SEG* 35.1523.
[67] I will come back to the problem of the date of the Latin translations of the *AAA* in my 'Man, Magic and Martyrdom in the *Acts of Andrew*', in Bremmer (ed), *The Apocryphal Acts of Andrew* (Louvain, 1998).
[68] Schneemelcher, in *NTA* II, 276.

Admittedly, the precise date and place of origin of the *APt* and their Latin translation still remain problematic, but we may have come somewhat closer to the truth[69].

---

[69] For information and comments I would like to thank Kathleen Coleman, Ken Dowden, Ton Hilhorst, Peter van Minnen and Rolf Schneider. Stephen Harrison kindly corrected my English.

II. Agrippa, King and Prefect

ISTVÁN KARASSZON

Competition before the public must have been something crucial to the author of the *Acts of Peter* (*APt*), since the apostle many times challenges his enemy, Simon, to demonstrate his magic power, and the issue at stake is to demonstrate the opposite: that Peter's God and Saviour is the only one. Even the way of challenging is miraculous. Once, e.g., a dog ran and rushed into the midst of Simon's company and calls out with a loud voice: 'I (tell) you Simon, Peter the servant of Christ is standing at the door, and says to you, "Come out in public; for on your account I have come to Rome, you most wicked deceiver of simple souls"' (9). Simon's denunciation then becomes public and the Christians, Simon's adepts and impartial outsiders alike must testify to the subjection of Simon to humiliation. In *cc*.23-9 this competition takes place in the Forum; a large crowd, including senators and prefects, surrounds the opponents – obviously the author is interested in demonstrating that the whole population of Rome could be persuaded. Simon first curses Jesus Christ, allowing no other role for him than that of a simple carpenter. Peter's reply to this calumny is filled with biblical quotations which prove the divine descent of Christ (23-4).

The competitors then switch over to testifying to their special message: Simon offers a miracle and challenges Peter to reverse it, if he can. The miracle consists of putting a young man to death – Peter has to raise the same person. In this context it happens for the first time that Simon refers to the prefect: 'If the prefect permits' (24).

1. A dual role

It seems that the role of the prefect in this contest is to play the impartial arbiter. Indeed, the text explicitly states that the prefect wishes to display impartial behaviour. Nevertheless, at this point we can also be convinced that the prefect himself was not neutral toward the events: he offers one of his *alumni*, whom Simon must put to death and Peter must raise. Later on, when it turns out that the person concerned may remain dead, he complains to Peter: 'But I trusted in you, and in your Lord whom you preach' – this is almost a confession (26).

Only at this moment is the name of the prefect uttered: he is Agrippa. Further on he tries to remain impartial, but several times he seems to lose patience: at the failed attempt of Simon to resuscitate the dead person, he gets up and pushes Simon away with his own hand. He is the first to suggest that Simon should be burnt instead of Peter. This is high time for Peter to reply: 'we have not learnt to repay evil with evil; but we have learnt to love our enemies and pray for our persecutors'. This is one of the crucial messages of Christians in a Roman society hostile to the Gospel (28).

All in all, we may state that the figure of Agrippa is positive in this episode, even if it is not free from contradictions. The prefect as representative of the Roman authorities is in the first place impartial. As such, he can testify to the excellent character of Christianity over against its enemies. At the same time, he is favourable toward Christianity and gives a free rein to Christian confession. Both characteristics are definitely positive; both characteristics are needed in the logic of the narrative. But beyond any doubt, they are contradictory: an impartial arbiter may not take sides with Christianity, and if the prefect takes sides with Christianity, he is no longer impartial. Apparently, this contradiction did not prevent the author from describing the prefect in this two-faced way. His intention was nothing other than to display the superior quality of Christianity and the friendly attitude of Roman authorities toward Christianity.

In the *Martyrdom of Peter* the picture changes considerably. This is not surprising in view of the course of the events. The author had to explain the martyrdom of the apostle despite the fact that he defeated the enemy and enjoyed much regard among the Romans. In order to move forward smoothly, the author needed a real expedient in the order of history – and he found it in one of the widespread ideas of ancient Christianity, the motive of chastity. Agrippa's four concubines, Agrippina, Nicaria, Euphemia and Doris become Christians and on hearing the preaching of purity renounced love with the prefect; even when being molested, they resisted (33). Of course, the prefect bursts with rage, and in his fury the fate of the apostle is sealed. The use of this motive underscores that the enmity of the heathen world is not directed toward the Christian message as a whole, only to one of its characteristics. All the same, the author stresses that purity and chastity were irritating for traditional pagans.

Remarkably enough, Agrippa, though filled with fury, does not decide to put Peter to death. The author introduces another person, the friend of Caesar, Albinus, whose beloved wife, Xanthippe, converts to Christianity and, impressed by the message of purity, separates from her husband. The text states that this Albinus rages like a wild beast and wishes to do away with Peter; indeed, it is his suggestion to Agrippa to execute Peter: 'either you must get me satisfaction from Peter, who caused my wife's separation, or I shall do so myself'. The prefect agrees (34). All kinds of intervention, that of Xanthippe as well as that of the people of Rome (rich and poor, orphans and widows, capable and helpless) were in vain. This was the direct cause of Peter's death, a death in the image of the Lord: crucifixion (35).

The inconsistencies within this story are clearly evident. First, if the prefect was inclined toward Christianity, why did he stop halfway? His reaction to the concubines' behaviour was by no means different from that of any tyrant. Second, if the prefect was ill-minded toward Christianity, why did he hesitate to act? What are the reasons for the insertion of the person of Albinus? The role of Albinus and Xanthippe does not contribute anything to the course of events; they only repeat what has been said above. All in all, one does not have the impression that the persons are real characters – they rather seem to be personified characters of the age and of the society in which the story takes place.

2. The historical Agrippa

My suggestion is that it is no use looking for an historical person behind the story. We rather have to uncover the different motives which contributed toward shaping the characters of Agrippa and Albinus. The name of the prefect might blaze the trail for us. Although Agrippa is a common Roman name, there were several persons with this name in the first century AD who played important roles in history. Among the persons bearing the name Agrippa, we may consider the outstanding representation of King Agrippa I in Jewish and Christian traditions. As is well-known, King Agrippa I (10 BC – 44 AD) was the last king of Judaea; his contradictory figure was recorded in several important documents. Philo of Alexandria in his *Legatio ad Gaium* reports on his visit to Alexandria in 38 AD; both in his *Antiquities* and in the *Jewish War* Flavius Josephus gives plenty of evidence about his activities, even if full of contradictions.

Christian literature documents the faithfulness of King Agrippa to Jewish traditions. When Acts 12 reports the violent death of James, Luke ascribes the main role to King Agrippa. It is intriguing to note that both Acts 12 and Josephus report on the death of the king – surely, they both used an ancient tradition which had formerly been handed down orally. This entitles us to suppose that the historical figure of King Agrippa I was susceptible to the accretion of traditions[1], and it is not impossible that traditions about him were still current in the second century.

Of course, we do not claim to resolve all the problems emerging from the historical questions concerning Philo's, Josephus' and Luke's portraits of King Agrippa[2]. Our study is limited to tracing motives which, possibly, became parts of the oral tradition in the first century and as such might have influenced authors in the second century. To begin with, we have to pay attention to the title of Agrippa in Acts 12.1: he is called king and bears the name Herod (!) – indeed, he was the grandson of Herod the Great. In a different context I argued that Luke perhaps confused the successors to Herod's throne[3]. However, in the present context I feel justified in looking for a tradition behind Luke's text because the rule of Agrippa I reveals that he wished to allude to his grandfather's kingship. Indeed, he inherited the whole territory over which Herod the Great had once ruled. But his intention to continue the tradition became evident from his policy in appointing the High Priests: until his rule the High Priest came from the Ananide dynasty but he removed the last representative of the family (whom we know to have been on good terms with the Roman

---

[1] I mean: 'traditionsbildend.'
[2] I draw much upon the brilliant work of Daniel R. Schwartz, *Agrippa I, The Last King of Judaea* (Tübingen, 1990).
[3] See my *History of Israel* (in Hungarian), concerning the place and the date of Jesus' birth.

administration), Theophilus by name, and appointed one of the representatives of the dynasty of Boethus, Simon Cantheras.

This was a significant act displaying his intentions: he wished to appear as Herod's heir. Nor was it merely an ambitious desire, for in 37 he was able to annex Philip's tetrarchy to his kingdom and after the quarrel with Antipas in 39, he ruled over the territories of the latter, i.e., Galilee and Perea. To be sure, Antipas was also proud enough to use the title king, but this was only out of jealousy (fuelled mainly by his wife, Herodias). Real king was Agrippa alone.

This state of affairs can be corroborated by an important *argumentum e silentio*: under Gaius Caligula there was no governor of Judaea. Josephus only mentions the 'chief of cavalry'[4]. Apparently, Roman authorities did not seek any tight control over the country. And Agrippa was bold enough to begin to lay the foundations of the so-called 'third wall' of the capital, Jerusalem, another fact that testifies to his royal plans and aspirations. Much of the details of this third wall remain enigmatic to us, but it is clear that he felt free to act as a real king. All this was possible only because of his extraordinary good relations with the court of Rome.

It is remarkable that Agrippa managed to maintain good relations with the emperors despite turbulent events in their accessions to the throne. In 33/34 he gained the favour of Tiberius who desired a close relationship between Agrippa and his grandson, Tiberius Gemellus. The reasons for this favour cannot be seen today, but Schwartz is perhaps right when assuming that 'Agrippa's trip to Rome in 33 or 34 put him in the right place at the right time. Just when Tiberius was faced with the question of what to do with a third of Herod's kingdom, a member of the royal family, who had grown up in Rome, was back in view[5].' At any rate, Agrippa was clever enough to conspire – not with Tiberius Gemellus, but with Gaius Caligula! Philo thinks that Agrippa did so in view of the future principate of Caligula[6], and, indeed, for a time he also got into trouble because of this friendship (he was imprisoned). In the long run, however, this friendship secured his rule over Judaea. Similar things happened, *mutatis mutandis*, to Claudius' accession to the throne. Josephus may exaggerate when he states that

---

[4] ἱππάρχης = *magister equitum*.
[5] Schwartz, *Agrippa I*, 53.
[6] Philo, *Legatio ad Gaium*, 32.

Agrippa advised Claudius how to behave before the Senate (*Antiquities* 19) – the decision was rather made by the army. But his intimate relationship with the Emperor secured Agrippa further promotion and, once again, he may have been the right man in the right place and at the right time: his kingdom was beyond any doubt and was even enlarged. By virtue of his personal relationship with the emperors, Agrippa was bearer of different honorific titles: under Gaius Caligula he was awarded the *ornamenta praetoria*, under Claudius the *ornamenta consularia*. He also could use the title *philos tou Kaisaros* ('friend of Caesar')[7]. Our historical records testify to an international career which helped Agrippa take power in Judaea and maintain it.

It goes without saying that this career may have evoked mixed feelings among Jews. First, they may have been proud of the kingdom and of the continuation of the Hasmonaean tradition. Indeed, Agrippa seemed to prefer Pharisaic traditions, and in doing so he attached to the politics of Salome Alexandra. But at the same time, Jews must have been mistrustful about the unclarified relationship of their king with the Roman emperors – with the enemy. As to the Christians, they rather felt hostility toward a king who strengthened the traditions which rejected the Christian message. This twofaced reception of Agrippa's person and rule is widely attested in our records. Acts 12.23 reports that Agrippa went to a festival in Caesarea and appeared before the people in royal vestments. At that moment, an angel of the Lord struck him down so that he was eaten by worms and died.

This report is surely negative in its intention: the story wishes to state that the king received divine punishment because 'he did not give praise to God'. The term 'eaten by worms' cannot be explained medically, it is rather a way of expressing damnation. Remarkably enough, the text does not openly reproach the king on account of his persecution of the Christian church; instead, it was in common with Josephus' report that the reason for Agrippa's punishment was his *hybris*, i.e., he did not give praise to God. We might be right in drawing the consequences: there was a tradition behind Luke's and Josephus' report on Agrippa's death; contents of this tradition might have been resistance to Agrippa's rule (perhaps with the charge of self-deification). Nevertheless, it was not Agrippa who declared himself to

---

[7] On this title as applied to Albinus in the *APt*, see Bremmer, this volume, Ch. I.1.

be God; Acts 12.22 declares that it was the crowd which shouted 'This is the voice of a god, not of a man'. Agrippa was not in need of Jewish supporters, so it seems very unlikely that he would have organised this scene. Luke and Josephus report on the flattery which was given to him as to the great king. This might entitle us to formulate our hypothesis: the tradition concerning Agrippa I was contradictory, moving in two opposite directions and reaching the extremities. All that could be seen in one's eyes, was surely bad in the other's.

3. Conclusion

Our study stops here. Its aim was to demonstrate how the contradictions in a historical figure's behaviour infiltrated the tradition of first century Jewish thought and resulted in contradictory elements in literary documents. The above mentioned first-century documents amalgamated the different motives and moulded them into the respective works – so did Philo, Josephus and Luke as well. The historical role and importance of King Agrippa I are beyond any doubt in this respect; unfortunately, the ensuing Jewish War put his oeuvre and his importance into the background – no doubt because of the historical experience: the political coquetry with the Romans proved to be a *cul de sac* and had to be discarded as a political option. Nevertheless, it is by no means necessary that all this applied to literature as well. I suggest that we should seriously consider the possibility that contradictory elements in religious traditions were regarded as appropriate literary tools in drawing characters in second-century novels. In this way, contradictions regarding the figure of the prefect can be explained much better than by means of source analysis. The prefect as an impartial arbiter on the one side and as bitter enemy of Peter on the other, as a hesitating Roman citizen on the one hand and as the acting Roman office-holder on the other, showing sympathy toward Christianity one time and persecuting the apostle later, cannot be explained by looking for an historical person behind the figure, but rather by presuming roles and models which had previously been formed in the history of literature.

By stating this, we may affirm previous insights concerning the literary aim and purpose of the *APt*. Recently, Peter Lampe used the term 'volkstümliche Unterhaltungsliteratur'[8]. I cannot decide the debate between Lampe and Vielhauer as to whether the author belonged to the middle class or was a man with literary ambitions[9]. In both cases, however, we may reckon with a set of motives and characters which the author used according to his taste. In this set the contradictory person of a Roman office-bearer, nurtured by the historical figure of King Agrippa I, might have had its proper place.

---

[8] P. Lampe, *Die stadtrömischen Christen in den ersten beiden Jahrhunderten* (Tübingen, 1989²) 102. Later on he adds that the Christian readers of Rome had 'ein Faible für romanhafte Literatur.'
[9] Ph. Vielhauer, *Geschichte der urchristlichen Literatur* (Berlin, 1975) 714-5.

III. *Theios aner* Traits in the Apocryphal *Acts of Peter*

PÁL HERCZEG

Researching traditions and transmitted texts is far from straightforward. Beside the bulk of known, systematized, and tangible information there is a multitude of unanswered questions. Let me consider briefly just two of them. One group of difficulties concerns the tension between experience and tradition. It is always problematic to express in speech or writing the events and occurrences that we have lived through, since this requires us to give a verbal mould to what was originally a series of acts. The problem escalates when we encounter something extraordinary, something that is beyond rationality: when we meet transcendent, divine revelation and events, and try to give verbal expression to our experience. What kind of vocabulary should we use? With what concepts should we express that which has no analogy? How should one render in human categories that which is so ultimately non-human?

We encounter similar problems when transmitting the recorded tradition. P.-G. Müller writes about the difficulties of the process of tradition within and outside the New Testament. He describes the lengthy procedure between the 'sender' and the 'receiver' as well as the modifications and interpretations which ineluctably present themselves during this process[1]. One of the major questions is how far the words, vocabulary, set of concepts, historical and cultural context of the 'sender' at the starting point of the chain of tradition are identical with, or different from 'those of the receiver'. And if they are considerably different, by which ways, transpositions, and modifications does the transmitted piece of tradition reach its goal and meet reception?

---

[1] P.-G. Müller, *Der Traditionsprozess im NT* (Freiburg, 1982).

Now let us shift the focus closer to our subject. It is generally considered that the Old Testament stands firmly behind the New. So events and passages of the latter generally call up countless analogies from the former, the two Testaments are held to utilize identical or cognate concepts, and moreover the New Testament is thought knowingly to use Old Testament figures and events as prototypes. Not only is this meaningful for the literary nature of the text but it also has its theological relevance. The names of many Old Testament personalities appear lending their names to later (mostly apocryphal) writings, which indicates that these traditions were consciously accepted and continued. Thus the names of Enoch, Moses, Elijah and others reappear in later writings. But even earlier, Jesus was made to 'imitate' Elijah, or expected to act in terms of contemporary theology and piety. That is, we may well be aware of the presence of such conditions when considering and characterizing Biblical agents. Let us quote just the best-known example. When Jesus asks who people say he is, analogies, that is, expectations are put forth: the prophet, one of the prophets, Elijah, and so on.

If we move beyond the New Testament period, from the second century AD we witness the emergence of a new domain of tradition and literature, namely, the bulk of New Testament apocrypha, which fall within the field of our recent investigation. On the one hand, the tradition and influence of the events and persons of the New Testament continues in them. They contain a number of analogies: the names, miracles, speeches, and sermons support evidence of imitation of types, and the survival and utilization of analogies. On the other hand, contemporary literature, especially the genre of the ancient Greek novel, exerted considerable influence on this corpus by lending its own vocabulary, concepts, types, and analogies. We can no longer even speak of two equally important sources: the New Testament canon serves less and less as the source of this literature, while the style and form of the novel becomes its primary basis.

In the case of the *Acts of Peter* (*APt*) we have the opportunity of making an interesting comparison. In the New Testament passages concerning the apostle Peter the influence of the Old Testament is well perceptible. However, even in this picture there are detectable Greek traits. These are then reinforced in the portrait of Peter as transmitted into the apocrypha, and are even more apparent in the characterization of Simon Magus. These traits, which will stay in the foreground of our investigation, can be encapsulated in the concept of the *theios aner*.

The dictionary defines *theios* (or *daimonios*) as a person who displays divine charateristics, who is superhuman in his origin. Later the usage of the word changed and deepened. Bieler enumerates the stages by which heroes, sages, and kings acquired this adjective. At the end of the development these people not only acquire the adjective, but also arrogate it to themselves, and their contemporaries and posterity invent myths about their persons and deeds[2]. Leipoldt and Grundmann give the following summary of the meaning of the term: 'Antiquity ascribed qualities and faculties surpassing the human dimension not only to deities or deified heroes, but also to individual outstanding personalities who displayed miraculous gifts during their lifetime. The concept of the *theios aner* ensued very early in connection with these persons[3].' Among others Pythagoras and Empedocles were already granted this adjective, but Apollonius of Tyana or Simon Magus from the New Testament period show the perfect type. The *theios aner* thus developed into a type or category that designates persons who possess θεῖα φύσις or θεῖα δύναμις, that is, persons whose existence carries the following attributes.

Their birth is usually foretold by a divine messenger, and neither its time nor its place are customary. Immediately after their birth miracles occur to them. Their abilities, as well as their birth and upbringing are extraordinary. Their lives are full of dangers, and they work miracles, even after their death. Bieler makes an interesting observation: obvious abilities and 'talent' are accompanied by the 'religious element', and thus divine men emerge as charismatic persons. Sometimes they can be called even more than that: they are part of the divine sphere. Their miraculous abilities include knowledge and revelation of hidden things, walking on water, and levitation. Their contemporaries attribute not only σοφία, but also δύναμις and ἐξουσία to them, though sometimes it turns out to be mere illusion: magic and fraud, μαγεία and γοητεία. They usually work miracles to provoke faith from the spectators, but many times it is an *ultima ratio* supposed to convince non-believers. The latter holds true especially for the punishing miracles.

---

[2] L. Bieler, *Theios aner* (Darmstadt, 1967²).
[3] G. Haufe, 'Hellenistische Volksfrömmigkeit', in J. Leipoldt and W. Grundmann (eds), *Umwelt des Urchristentums* I (Berlin, 1965) 68-100, esp. 74.

Let us quote one more idea from Bieler's summary. Though the persons designated *theios aner* are sometimes close to magic and fraud, they represent more than that: their deeds belong to the category of *theurgy*. Their contemporaries denote them as *theioi andres* but in the eyes of their followers they are divine epiphanies.

1. *Canonical Peter*

I will apply this distinction to the persons of Peter and Simon, in order to draw theological and theoretical conclusions. First, I will deal with Peter's realistic characterization in the canonical passages, then with his divine man characteristics.

a) In the synoptic passages Peter does not show superhuman traits in any way. He is a disciple in the traditional sense, whose task is to be a witness following Jesus. The only event that can be called supernatural is his walking on the sea (Mt 14.22). However, this is not connected with his abilities, since the text clearly states the acting subject of this phenomenon is Jesus: notably it is Jesus who invites Peter to step out of the boat. There is nothing extraordinary in the accounts: Peter is just a human being, and like all humans, he is fallible.

b) In canonical Acts the situation is somewhat different. Most of the time, Peter obviously bears the traits of the Old Testament יהוה מלאך and especially its realistic features. He is God's messenger, God's commissioner for carrying out a specific task. The task usually consists in delivering some message, though it is sometimes accomplished by certain deeds[4]. Accordingly, this deed may be extraordinary, perhaps a deliverance from some danger or misery (Gen 19; Ex 14; Judg 13). Nonetheless, the commissioner is just a deputy, and the real acting subject is obviously God.

Ficker, however, makes an interesting remark about the relation of the commissioning and commissioned persons, noting that in the Old Testament it is often difficult to differentiate exactly between the two of them[5]. He offers three solutions: *Repräsentationstheorie, Identitätstheorie*, and *Hypostasentheorie*. This is a step towards our subject.

---

[4] R. Ficker, 'Mal'ak', in E. Jenni and C. Westermann (eds), *Theologisches Handwörterbuch zum Alten Testament* I (Munich, 1971) 900-8.
[5] Ficker, *ibidem*, 906.

Peter's Pentecost address, the healing of the crippled man, and Peter and John's appearance before the council (Acts 2-4) realize traditional roles of the מלאך יהוה. Even if Peter does something extraordinary, it serves only to authenticate his message and testimony, while his personality does not play a particularly important role.

Acts 5 presents a somewhat different case. While the testimony of Ananias and Sapphira still fits the preceding events, Acts 5.12 shows interesting new traits. Here nobody dares to join the apostles, but people hold them in high esteem (from far away?), and even Peter's shadow heals the sick. The story of the apostles' deliverance (5.17-26) is again more reserved regarding their personalities. In Cornelius' house (Acts 10) Peter is a preacher, as well as in Acts 12 and 15. In *c*.12 once more Peter plays a passive role in his own miraculous deliverance.

In sum, only Acts 5 contains traits which go beyond the conceptual basis of the Old Testament and endows Peter with *more* than the office of God's messenger or commissioner.

While surveying the canonical passages, it is worth referring briefly to the presentation of Simon Magus. In Acts 8.9-13 he requests the charisma of distributing the Spirit, and offers money, for which Peter curses him. In the New Testament Simon is obviously a magician and an impostor. He is *only called* the Great Power (δύναμις μεγάλη).

2. *Apocryphal Peter*

The *APt* give a substantially different picture of Peter. We mention only the most characteristic elements:

a) On the ship to Rome the captain approaches Peter (5): 'I hardly know you, whether you are God or man; but in my opinion, I take you for a servant of God.' The captain then receives a revelation in the night about Peter being worthy of the highest esteem among the passengers of the ship. When the captain is baptized in a boat a young man appears greeting them with 'peace'. Before the baptism the ship was becalmed. However, while they are celebrating the eucharist a wind comes that does not slacken until they reach Puteoli. Nothing is said about proclaiming Jesus.

b) In *c*.9 Peter is not admitted into Simon's house; moreover, Simon's personnel are commanded to say Simon is not in. When the doorkeeper (on Peter's request) lets loose the big dog watching the house, it goes up to Peter and addresses him in a human voice, asking for his orders. On Peter's order the dog goes into Simon's house, and summons the magician – in front of his guests – to go out to Peter. As a consequence, Marcellus, who has earlier erected a statue to 'Simon the young God', joins Peter (10). Then the dog quarrels with Simon (11) for not obeying Peter's order. In the same chapter we read that a young man (while rescued from a demon) breaks the emperor's statue, which is supposed to bring about punishment. But Peter, in order to overrule Marcellus' unbelief, commands him to sprinkle the broken pieces with water, and the statue becomes intact again.

c) The speaking dog is reintroduced in *c*.12, where it calls Peter God's true messenger and apostle. Some people in the crowd are ready to throw themselves at Peter's feet, and others request further miracles from Peter, because Simon also did numerous miracles.

d) The resuscitation of the smoked tunny comes in the next chapter (13), authenticating Peter's proclamation.

e) Before *c*.15 Simon claims that Peter believes only in a carpenter's son. Peter sends a woman to Simon, whose seven-month-old infant miraculously speaks to him, thus humiliating Simon.

f) In *c*.17, Peter unmasks Simon and his two helpers stealing two golden satyrs weighing two pounds each[6].

g) Though *c*.20 has already related the curing of a blind person, it is amplified in the next one. The blind women not only receive back their sights, but they also see various visions – in fact, only human figures. Actually, they all see the Lord in particular forms.

h) Visions are continued in *c*.22, where Marcellus sees a dancing woman who looks like an Ethiopian. The whole power of Simon is present in the woman, and Peter commands Marcellus to decapitate her. Since he is not willing to do that, Peter calls upon the real sword, Jesus Christ, who 'not only cuts off the head of this demon, but cuts all her limbs in pieces'.

i) In *cc*.25-8 there are three resuscitations one after the other. The first person is put to death through Simon's scheming at the prefect's request, in order to test Peter's power. Then comes the raising of the widow's son, who is carried in on a stretcher: the story has traits in common with Jesus' raising the widow's son at Nain (Lk 7.11-17).

---

[6] Cf. Bremmer, this volume, Ch. I.1.

Finally, Peter resuscitates a senator at his mother's request. Each episode includes a confession. In the first case: 'There is but one God, the one God of Peter!' In the second: 'Thou art God the Saviour, thou, the God of Peter, the invisible God, the Saviour!' In the third Peter says: 'Do not look at me, as though by my own power I were doing what I do!' The third resuscitation is narrated in the greatest length and with the most details. First, Simon Magus performs an imitated resuscitation on the corpse, but it turns out to be mere illusion. Then Peter raises the body. At the beginning of $c.29$ it is stated that from that time on 'they venerated him as a god, and laid at his feet such sick people as they had at home, so that he might heal them'.

j) Simon wants to deceive the people by ascending into the air. When he is actually carried up Peter prays that his proclamation shall not be disbelieved, and asks the Lord to show his grace by causing Simon fall down and break his leg in three places – much like an answer to Simon's earlier mockery. And Simon, indeed, falls down and dies miserably not long later.

k) Following his execution, Peter once more appears to Marcellus (40), quoting rather enigmatically Jesus' words of Mt 8.22.

In sum, we can discern that Peter's deeds are only exceptionally accompanied by any explanation or proclamation. His miraculous deeds are usually intended to verify Peter's person and power, as opposed to Simon's falsity. Neither Simon's false claims, nor Peter's 'abilities' are described in detail, but rather they show the contrast of darkness and light, falsity and truth. The faith of the eyewitnesses is summarized in one sentence, as the prerequisite or consequence of the miraculous experiences. The *content* and *effect* of faith are not articulated in the account.

3. *Simon Magus*

The figure of Simon Magus is obviously a negative copy of Peter, or even worse than that. Even before arriving in Rome his activity is mere fraudulence (4). *C*.8 tells a rather discrediting story about Simon's impact on Marcellus. Simon also applies magic to steal Eubola's pearls and golden image so that the reader has no doubt about his identity (17). *C*.23 interestingly gives Simon's apology: 'You presume to talk of Jesus the Nazarene, the son of a carpenter and a carpenter himself... You men of Rome, is God born? Is he crucified?

He who owns a Lord is no God!' In c.28 he manoeuvres so that the dead man raises his head and moves, opens his eyes, and so on.

When Simon sets out for the final trial he is called an impostor (31), and later he makes a promise to the people: 'For I by ascending will show to all this crowd what manner of being I am' (32). And lo and behold, he was carried up into the air, and everyone saw him in Rome, passing over its temples and its hills; while the faithful looked towards Peter...'.

What stands out clearly from the apocryphal writing is that Simon was successful in deceiving and swindling the crowd. But after Peter's arrival, Simon's chances are restricted to constant defence and furious resistance. He does not seem a match for Peter for a minute. The *theios aner* traits are carried by an impostor this time. When compared with Acts 8, Simon's spectacular deceptions and his fall in the apocryphal writing surpass the account of the canonical book.

What are the results of this comparison? As I have mentioned at the beginning, the first problem shows itself by the transmission of experiences, or events, that is, by the verbal or scribal recording of the story. At this stage, the mediator of the tradition has to use a given set of concepts and analogies. In the New Testament, these concepts and analogies were supplied by the Old Testament. It was made possible, because their stories were interconnected, and the message of the Old Testament had not become obsolete (though it was in need of a christological reinterpretation, as it were.) The concept of the מלאך יהוה thus continued to supply the analogy of witnesses, preachers, and messengers.

The case was different when the Hellenistic world developed its myths, stories of divine heroes, and its own set of concepts and vocabulary. When gentile Christianity began to dominate the Church, this vocabulary irresistibly presented itself in the language of the tradition. Interestingly enough, theoretical sections of the New Testament (Eph, Col, and the Pastoral Letters) show the influence of Hellenistic expressions and ideas well before the historical parts. The missionary activity of the Church and the need to communicate its ideas necessitated such improvements. However, even in the canonical Acts the 'wonder-worker apostles' mostly fit the framework supported by the Old Testament. When the tradition lets in more freely the 'narrative energies'[7], the door is open also for the style of the pagan novel. Thus

---

[7] See my 'Sermons of the Book of Acts and the Apocryphal Acts', in Bremmer, *AAJ*, 152-70, esp. 170.

Peter becomes similar to the divine men of the Hellenistic world. In the apocrypha the stories about him and his peers already show traits of this category.

So, on the one hand, the 'traditional' vocabulary and set of concepts still survive and exert an influence on the accounts even when these already follow other literary patterns (we will come back to this problem later); on the other hand, 'divine man' traits radiate through the figures of the canonical writings, and modify their events and characters. As a result, it becomes very difficult to trace back the historical core of the apocryphal texts, because they bear traditional, as well as new literary traits. This is especially problematic with Simon Magus, who is a rather simple character in the canonical passages, an impostor and (partly) a *theios aner* in the apocrypha, and finally with the church fathers becomes a gigantic figure, the head of all heresy. Was his figure transformed so much only during the literary development, or was he originally more than indicated in the canonical text? Further research may give an answer to this question.

Let us briefly consider two more problems. One of these problems concerns the existence and deeds of 'pagan charismatic' figures. Though the expression may sound rather awkward, we have to take them seriously (perhaps not only in the antiquity but in every age). Their existence presents a theoretical problem, which cannot be handled in detail now, but should at least be kept in view. Their deeds and stories utilized the vocabulary and style of the Old Testament and biblical literature, and present a counterpart of our subject. (It seems to me interesting that many divine men validate themselves by raising dead people. But what did raising the dead mean for pagans? Was its meaning identical with the biblical sense? For a Greek pagan, life and death, body and soul, and Hades carried totally different meanings than for a Jew or a Christian.) This question is worth further consideration from the theoretical and theological points of view.

Another question regards the essence and function of the pagan charisma and charismatic persons (i.e., divine men). We usually identify the role and function of biblical charismatic persons and messengers as the service of God, and of God's revelation. Thus acts and words are inseparable in the accounts and also in the tradition, and the words and acts have a promptly detectable message or revealing effect, which is often *expressis verbis* stated in the texts. This is the revelation and presentation of God's power, person, and current will. The messenger-commissioner-agent is himself aware of this 'status', and takes it obediently upon himself. Pagan charismatic persons are, however, more 'independent' beings. Their charisma serves not to reveal but to legitimate, to authenticate, their personalities and 'abilities'. When they get into rivalry with each other, their charisma and abilities are the means by which they overcome their adversaries. These are the crucial questions: Which one has more powerful charisma than the other? Which is the more authentic? Though Bieler writes about the meekness and helpfulness of divine men, we never find this in later passages. What we find is rather Simon Magus as a counterfeit of the apostle Peter (in my opinion also of a real *theios aner*), i.e., just a magician and an impostor. His abilities and possibilities are only virtual. Interestingly, Peter is also 'assimilated' to the divine man category. His claims about Jesus Christ are mainly restricted to the (almost magical) use of Jesus' name. Peter's main concern is to destroy Simon Magus' authority and work. Due to the given framework, the biblical figure of the flesh-and-blood Peter has undergone considerable transformation.

IV. Simon Magus as a Narrative Figure in the Acts of Peter

GERARD LUTTIKHUIZEN

This chapter is focused on the *Acts of Peter* (*APt*) as a story text, more particularly on the role and character of Simon the Magician within the context of the narrative[1]. The *APt* do not yield much if we just approach the text as a source of information about the ideas of the historical Simon, but it will appear that this work has some conspicuous qualities as a narrative fiction.

1. Are encratite ideas involved in the battle between Peter and Simon?

Léon Vouaux, Gérard Poupon and others have found reasons to assume that the *Actus Vercellenses* may not represent the original text of the *APt* but rather a more or less orthodox revision[2]. They argue that in the lost earlier text, the mission of Peter in Rome was not yet linked with the activity of the apostle Paul in that city. The opening chapters of the *Actus Vercellenses* speaking about Paul's stay in Rome simultaneously as a prisoner and a free teacher, and about his travel to Spain might have been prefixed to the Petrine stories in order to bring the text more into agreement with New Testament information about Paul's connections with the Roman church[3]. The result of this alleged addition to the text and of the other mentions of Paul (*e.g.* in the last chapter, *c.* 41) is that Paul and Peter together are now presented as the apostolic founders of the Roman church. So far the argument is highly plausible.

---

[1] For Simon Magus see also Adamik, this volume, Ch. V.
[2] L. Vouaux, *Les Actes de Pierre* (Paris, 1922) 23-42; G. Poupon, 'Les "Actes de Pierre" et leur remaniement', *ANRW* II.25.6 (1988) 4357-83.
[3] Cf. the NT Book of Acts 28.30-1 and Rom 15.23-4.

But Poupon makes a further suggestion. In his opinion, the purpose of the revision was not only to present Peter and Paul as the two founders of the Roman church: it was also the aim of the revision to depict the apostle Peter as defender of the possibility of remission of sins for apostates and other grave Christian sinners, the so-called *lapsi*.

Poupon points to the clear contradictions in the *Actus Vercellenses* between the fierce encratite attitude of Peter and passages that lay stress on God's mercy and willingness to forgive sins. On the one hand, he argues, the *APt* tell how Peter was prepared even to be crucified because of his teaching of sexual continence, on the other hand, he accepts 10.000 pieces of gold from a wealthy woman, called Chryse, who was notorious for her adulterous behaviour. Peter even laughs when brothers bring the woman's antecedents to his attention and says: 'I do not know what this woman is as regards her usual way of life; but in taking this money I do not take it without reason, for she was bringing it as a debtor to Christ...'[4]

Indeed, on several occasions we hear that God can forgive the sins of a believer (*e.g* 2 and 10) and that Jesus Christ is able to restore the minds of Christians (6). But I doubt that the idea expressed in these passages was introduced into a later edition of the *APt*, and that the introduction of this issue was connected with early third century discussions about the position of Christian sinners and the possibility of a second penance.

What militates against the solution proposed by Poupon is the fact that we do not find a specifically encratite tendency in those parts of the *Actus Vercellenses* that deal with the confrontations between Peter and Simon. On the contrary, this central story of the *APt* is based on the narrative fact (quite probably a wholly fictitious fact) that the great majority of early Roman Christianity was affected by the misleading and treacherous actions of Simon the Magician. The story about the activities of Peter and Simon in Rome could never have been told without the supposition that remission of sins is possible for Christians who committed grave sins, notably for those who had fallen into apostasy.

In my opinion, the uncompromisingly encratite message of the story fragments about Peter's daughter[5] and the gardener's

---

[4] *APt* 30 (the first chapter in the Greek MS Patmos 48).

[5] Preserved in a Coptic translation, cf. J. Brashler and D.M. Parrott, *Nag Hammadi Codices V 2-5 and VI with Papyrus Berolinensis 8502, 1 and 4* (Leiden, 1979), 473-93 ('The Acts of Peter, BG 4: 128,1-141,7').

daughter[6] is instead a reason to call into question the broad consensus that there is a literary connection between these stories and the stories about Peter's battle with Simon in the *Actus Vercellenses*. In fact, I doubt, too, whether the connection between the Peter and Simon episodes and the Martyrdom of Peter is original[7].

2. *Actus Petri cum Simone*

The interest of the surviving text of the *APt* is clearly in Peter's fight against Simon[8]. The heading provided by Lipsius to his edition of the Vercelli text, *Actus Petri cum Simone*, is therefore well chosen. (In the Vercelli manuscript the *APt* lack a title.) It may be the case that about one-third of the text has been lost[9], but whatever may have been reported in the lost text, the fact remains that the greater part of the surviving text is concerned with Peter's struggle with Simon.

It is obvious that the *APt* do not have the character of a refutation of heretical ideas (the ideas of Simon or of later forms of Simonian Gnosis). In fact, the text does not include any fresh information either about the historical Simon or about Simonian teachings[10]. Indeed, Simon the Magician seems to be nothing more than a rather arbitrary embodiment of evil. His words are anti-Christian in a quite unspecified way, and his battle against Peter and the Roman Christians is described as just a battle between good and evil (seen from a particular early Christian point of view).

---

[6] This story is part of the apocryphal Epistle of Titus, *De dispositione sanctimonii*, cf. Schneemelcher, in *NTA* II, 57, 279, 287.

[7] In his survey of agreements between the *Actus Vercellenses* and the Coptic fragment about Peter's daughter, C. Schmidt, 'Studien zu den alten Petrusakten', *ZKG* 43 (1924) 326f mentions the alleged encratite tendency of both texts. But as far as the *Act. Verc.* are concerned he only points to *c.*34, a passage of the introduction to Peter's martyrdom.

[8] The storyteller does not seem to realize that 'Simon' was also the former name of Peter.

[9] This is indicated by the stichometry of Nicephorus.

[10] The information about Simon's activities as a magician and his claim to be the great power of God goes back to the New Testament (Acts 8.9-11) and possibly to a tradition about the worship of Simon as a god and the erection in Rome of a statue for 'the god Simon' (preserved in Justin, *Apol.* I,26). How the author was informed about Simon's self-identification as 'He that Standeth (ὁ Ἑστώς)' is not clear. See further T. Adamik, this volume, ch. V.

3. *The ironical introduction of Simon in c.4*

The figure of Simon the Magician is introduced in *c*.4. It is reported that a great commotion arose in the church of Rome for some said that they had seen strange things (*mirabilia*) done by a man named Simon who at that moment was in Aricia (a small place on the Via Appia some 16 miles to the south of Rome). Those spreading the news about Simon added[11] that he claimed to be the great power of God (*magna virtus dei*) and that he did nothing without God. The Christian speakers even wondered if he was the Christ (cf. John 4.29).

At this point the author or a later editor inserts some flashback information about the preaching and the miracle-working of the apostle Paul. Unfortunately, the subsequent statement about Simon is badly preserved. Lipsius reads: *haec autem quaerit dimicationes; scimus*. This reading is at the basis of Elliott's English translation: 'This power (*haec*) seeks conflict, we know.' In his apparatus, Lipsius mentions a correction proposed by Bonnet: *haec autem quae sit dimicatio nescimus*. This emendation is followed by Schneemelcher-Wilson: 'What this contention is, we do not know.' Poupon suggests reading *dei vocatio* for *dimicatio*: *haec autem quae sit dei vocatio nescimus*. Poupon does not translate this interesting emendation but I assume that it must be understood as: 'What this appeal to God means, we do not know', in other words, the Christian people in Rome say that they had never heard this designation *magna virtus dei* before, it had never been mentioned to them[12].

It should be observed that in these passages the story-teller avoids unequivocally negative statements about Simon. Obviously he wishes to create tension in the introductory scene of his story about the contests between Peter and Simon: There is commotion (*turbatio magna*) in the church because some people had witnessed the miraculous deeds of a man who pretended to be or to represent the great power of God. To the Christians in Rome, a man who calls

---

[11] Lipsius reads *adiecerunt* for *adiecit*.
[12] The continuation of the statement is corrected by Bonnet and Poupon in the same sense. Instead of *non enim minima motio nobis facta est* ('no small excitement has come upon us') they read: *non enim minima notio* (Bonnet) or *monitio* (Poupon) *nobis facta est*, which may be rendered as: 'this has never been mentioned to us'.

himself God's power, who does not do anything without God, and who performs miraculous deeds, can hardly be anyone other than Christ himself. The Christian readers or listeners, for their part, will wonder how in the course of the story this serious problem will be solved.

A feature of the story which deserves our special attention is the ironical style. We shall see that this narrative technique is highly characteristic of the author, notably in his stories about Simon the Magician. For the first time the ironical treatment of Simon becomes manifest in the comments of the ones who spread the news about Simon. When they have reported that Simon called himself the great power of God etc., they add (if, that is, the emendations by Bonnet and Poupon are basically correct) that it is obscure to them what his claim means. The irony will become more prominent in the continuation of the introductory account.

The reporters of the rumours about Simon reckon with the possibility that the magician has already come to Rome[13], for they know that the day before he had been invited with great acclamations to do so. They cite the acclamations: 'You are God in Italy, you are the saviour of the Romans, hasten to Rome quickly'. While these divine and imperial acclamations are still in the background of the story scene, Simon himself comes on stage[14]: The first thing we hear is: 'he spoke to the people *voce gracili dicens*'. I assume that the storyteller wished to say that Simon spoke with a 'shrill' (thus James and Elliott) or with a 'soft' or a 'weak' voice[15]. The contrast between the reported great acclamations and the shrill or weak voice of Simon has an ironical effect.

The words of Simon are quoted in direct speech: 'Tomorrow about the seventh hour you shall see me fly over the gate of the city in the form in which you now see me speaking with you'. The reporters of the news about Simon conclude their words with an appeal to their Roman audience: 'So, brethren, let us go and carefully await the outcome of the matter.'

Thereupon the narrator tells how the audience reacted to this appeal and how Simon realized his act. Once again his tone is

[13] Lipsius proposes reading *iam introivit* for *iam introibit*.
[14] The narrator still reports what Roman Christians have seen and heard.
[15] Cf. *c*.12 where the speaking dog mentions Simon's 'weak and useless voice (*vocem tuam infirmem et inutilem*)'.

ironical: 'They all ran together and came to the gate. And when the seventh hour had come, behold (*ecce*) suddenly in the distance a dust-cloud was seen in the sky looking like smoke and shining with rays from far away. And when it reached the gate, it suddenly vanished. Then he appeared standing in the midst of the people.'

Quite wittily the narrator refers to the allegedly flying Simon as a cloud of dust. The short duration of the appearance is stressed, probably with a view to underlining that some kind of magic was at issue. Later on, in *c.*13, we are told that the people saw that Peter had made a dead fish swim in a pond[16]. The author adds: 'and he made it swim not only for that hour but, lest they said it was a deception, he made it swim longer...' In *c.*31 we hear that Simon spoke at length about his magical art and that he made the lame and the blind appear to be cured for a short time. In the view of the author, magical tricks are recognizable by their short life[17].

The listeners or readers are aware that Simon used some trick to delude the Romans. But, as usual, they know more than the persons figuring within the story do. When Simon appears among the multitude, the author goes on to tell how they all worshipped him since they realized that it was the same man they had seen the day before. That is hardly a great wonder, the reader will probably think, but happily the people within the story react quite differently: their faith was seriously shaken[18]. While Simon's reputation grew more and more, all those who were established in the Christian faith were led astray except seven persons[19]. They devoted themselves to prayer day and night and entreated the Lord that someone might

---

[16] See also Bremmer, this volume, Ch. I.2.

[17] This sheds some light on the curious story about Simon's unsuccessful attempt to resuscitate a dead man (*c.*28): 'Simon came to the head of the dead man, bowed three times, and he showed the people how the dead man raised his head and moved it, opening his eyes and lightly bowing to Simon.' See further Vouaux, *Les Actes*, 386f, n. 3, and Thomas, this volume, Ch. VI.

[18] If the narrative figures had reacted in the same way, this would probably have been the end of the story.

[19] The presbyter Narcissus is mentioned, together with two women in a hospice and four other persons who could not leave their houses (and therefore were not deluded by Simon?).

come to care for his servants whom the devil in his wickedness had caused to fall[20].

4. *The debasement of Simon*

In the next chapter (5) Simon's opponent, the apostle Peter, is introduced. From now onwards the reports about Simon are not only ironical but also utterly negative. This is especially clear in statements which the storyteller has put into the mouths of Peter and several other narrative characters, notably Christ or God himself. Christ is the first to utter a negative judgment of Simon. He appears to Peter in a vision reminding the apostle of his (Peter's) former contest with the magician: 'Peter, Simon, the one you expelled from Judaea[21] after having exposed him as a magician, has forestalled you (plur.!) at Rome[22]. In short you must know that all who believed in me he has perverted by the cunning and the power of Satan, whose agent he proves to be...'

It may be noted that Christ informs Peter that all (!) Romans who believed in him were perverted by Simon. Simon is qualified by Christ as an agent of Satan. This information is given to Peter but of course it is destined for the listeners or readers. From now on they can have no doubt whatsoever about the true character of Simon and about the source of his magical skills. Still – in spite of the fact that all the cards are now on the table – the listeners are kept in suspense, for they are anxious to know how Peter will proceed against Simon, how his sorcery will be unveiled, and how the Roman Christian will react.[23]

---

[20] It is difficult to believe that the report of the apostasy of the Roman Christians does not belong to the original story, as Poupon proposes (see above).

[21] Cf. *c.*17: Simon stayed in Judaea in the house of a woman called Eubola. In the *Actus Vercellenses* Simon is not a Samaritan but a Jew, cf. *c.*6: *Judaeum quendam inrupisse in urbem, nomine Simonem*; and 22: 'Tomorrow at dawn two Jews (viz. Peter and Simon the Magician) will contend in this place about the worship of God'.

[22] The plural does not fit within the present story for Simon did not forestall the apostle Paul in Rome, cf. Poupon, 4270, who argues that this detail indicates that the connection with Paul's stay in Rome is secondary.

[23] The author suggests that Simon will not easily give in. Cf. *c.*12 where the speaking dog says to Peter: 'Peter, you shall have a hard fight with Simon,

Indeed the first clearly negative statement about Simon comes from Christ in his visionary address to Peter: Simon is an agent of the Satan; he has perverted all Roman Christians. This turns out to be the beginning of a whole series of rejections of Simon. The narrator achieves a complete humiliation of Simon not only through explicit condemnations by Christ, Peter and several other narrative figures but also – indirectly – by the way Simon is approached and addressed and by reports about Simon's immoral attitude and about his contemptible behaviour. A few examples may suffice.

Ariston, the innkeeper, says to Theon, the captain: 'a certain Jew, named Simon, has invaded the city. By incantation and by his wickedness he has completely perverted the entire brotherhood...' (6)[24]. In his address to Peter in the same chapter, Ariston refers to Simon's proclamations as 'the teachings of a very wicked man (*scelestissimi hominis doctrina*)' and in his answer Peter speaks about the deceits of 'the one who tempts the whole world by his angels'. In this and in other statements Simon almost disappears behind the powerful presence of Satan. When in *c*.8 Peter is informed about the total change in the behaviour of Marcellus, who used to be a model believer, he exclaims; 'Oh, the manifold arts and temptations of the devil! Oh, the cunnings and devices of the evil one, treasuring up to himself the great fire in the day of wrath[25], destruction of simple men, the ravening wolf[26] devouring and destroying eternal life', etc.

As a result of Peter's speech more believers were added to the congregation (9). They entreat Peter to fight with Simon. This provokes Peter's first miracle (*magnum et mirabile monstrum*). Peter endows a big dog with a human voice and charges it to say to Simon – who tried to hide himself from Peter –: 'Come out in public... you wicked man and destroyer of simple souls.' A comparable miracle is reported in *c*.15. Here Peter orders a seven-month-old baby to address Simon with the voice of an adult man in the following way: 'You

the enemy of Christ, and with his adherents...' At the end of this chapter, some of the witnesses of the miracle of the speaking dog say to Peter: 'Show us another sign that we may believe in you as a servant of the living God, for Simon too did many signs in our presence, and therefore we followed him.'

[24] Again it is stressed that the whole of Roman Christianity was affected (*omnem fraternitatem dissolvit*).
[25] Cf. Rom. 2.5.
[26] Cf. Mt. 7.15 and Acts 20.29.

abomination of God and men, destroyer of truth and most wicked seed of corruption...' These actions by Peter are presented as great miracles but it is obvious that the report of Simon being addressed condescendingly first by a dog and then by a very young child is meant to humiliate and degrade the magician. Of course, we have to bear in mind here that in the ancient world honour and shame were very important social concepts.

We have noted already that in the story about Marcellus and the speaking dog Simon tries to hide himself from Peter. There can be no doubt that this narrative ingredient serves to depict him as a coward. In addition, the speaking dog unveils Simon's stupidity when it questions quite ironically: 'Have you thought for all these hours only to say, "Say that I am not here"?' (12).

The report about the treatment of Simon by Marcellus' slaves has the same purpose (14): 'The slaves overmastered him and treated him in the most shameful way; some struck him in the face, some beat him with a rod, some threw stones at him, while others emptied pots full of filth over his head.' Marcellus says to Peter that when he had thrown Simon out, he had cleansed his house completely and removed all traces of Simon's shameful dust. He had sprinkled his whole house, all the dining-rooms and all the colonnades as far as the door.

In the Eubola story Simon is exposed as a thief (17), and in a dream Marcellus sees Simon as a dark dancing woman, clothed in filthy rags, with an iron collar around her neck and chains on her hands and feet (22)[27]. The chains around the neck and on the hands and feet must be understood as a symbol of humiliation for this was the usual punishment of slaves who had run away[28]. In his dream Marcellus also saw how a man who looked like Peter came with a sword in his hand and cut the woman into pieces.

Also, in the account of the final contest between Peter and Simon in the Julian forum we find several hints at Simon's inferiority. Peter comes first and takes his place in the centre. Thereupon Simon appears: 'Simon also came in, and standing in confusion at Peter's side he gazed at him closely (*supervenit et Simon. conturbatus stans ad latus Petri inprimis respiciebat eum*)'. Peter reproaches Simon that he does not dare to open his mouth but later on (end of *c*.24) the

---

[27] For this episode see also Bremmer, this volume, Ch. I.1.
[28] Vouaux, *Les Actes*, 359, n.6.

narrator mentions Simon's impertinent address to Agrippa, the prefect (or did the shy man just take courage? *Simon audacia sumpta dixit*). In *c*.31 Simon is laughed at by perseverant Christian believers as well as by the Roman crowds. Then he complains that people pay more attention to Peter than to himself.

Simon's second attempt to fly is described as a caricature of the ascension of Christ (32). As Peter shows compassion for the magician, he prays that Simon may not die when he falls down but merely become crippled. When he came down he was stoned once again. Even his faithful friend, Gemellus, seeing that 'God's power' was literally broken, turns away from Simon. A few days later, after unsuccesful medical treatment from another sorcerer, he dies in Aricia, rather unheroically and lonely.

5. *The final contest?*

At the beginning of *c*.7 the narrator tells how the rumour was spread among the scattered brothers of the city that Peter had come to Rome because of Simon, in order to expose him as a fraud and a seducer of good people. The baby speaking with an adult voice predicts that the contest between Peter and Simon will take place the next Sabbath in the forum of Julius. In the name of Jesus Christ, the child orders Simon to leave the city till the Sabbath. The information about the battle on the coming Sabbath is repeated in the subsequent chapters, which suggests that this contest will be the final and decisive one.

In *c*.23 it is reported that on the Sabbath the brethren and all those that were in Rome gathered together, and that on payment of a piece of gold each took a place. Senators, prefects, and officers were also present. Then Peter comes on stage and, after him, Simon (see above). Upon the entry of Simon there was a long silence. Obviously the storyteller is trying to add further tension to his account.

As we might expect, Peter is the first to raise his voice. It would seem that initially he intends to persuade the audience by a judicial type of speech[29]. He summons the Romans to be 'our true judges'.

---

[29] For the distinction of species of ancient rhetoric and the characteristics of the judicial speech see G.A. Kennedy, *New Testament Interpretation through Rhetorical Criticism* (Chapel Hill and London, 1984) 19f and 86ff.

What he plans to defend is that it is he who believes in the living and true God. In the central part of his speech he gives an overview of his earlier fights with Simon in Judaea[30]. This part of his speech is meant to ridicule and defame his opponent. Peter concludes with his thesis: he believes in the living God through whom he shall destroy the magical arts of Simon. He challenges Simon to perform one of his *mirabilia* in the presence of the Roman audience.

As yet Simon has not had many occasions to present his teaching[31]. His reaction to Peter's public speech is again relatively short. Basically, he rejects Peter's thesis on the grounds that believing in Jesus means believing in a mere man, a Jewish carpenter[32]. He appeals to the common sense of the audience: 'You men of Rome, is a God born? Is he crucified? Whoever has a Lord is no God!' His words provoke a murmur of approval.

Now the story takes a somewhat curious turn. Peter accepts Simon's challenge and parries his attack with quotations from Scripture and from other sacred sources. But it is difficult to imagine ourselves back in the supposed historical situation: how could he believe in persuading his pagan audience in Rome in this way? Apparently this part of the story meets the needs of Christian readers. Of course, *they* were reassured by these references to their sacred texts from the lips of Peter.

The Roman public, however, is not likely to have gathered just to listen to speeches[33]. They expect to find out who is the greatest wonderworker. Therefore Peter, at the conclusion of his defense, once again challenges Simon to do one of the signs whereby he deceived the Romans before. Thereupon Peter shall undo Simon's action through his Lord Jesus Christ.

Now the author allows the prefect to speak. He complies with Peter's proposal. But he interprets Peter's words in a macabre and at the same time quite comical way. Peter meant an example of Simon's magical art, but the prefect proposes that Simon kill a boy and that

---

[30] Cf. above, n. 21.
[31] The narrator allows Peter to speak many more words than Simon (approximately ten times more).
[32] Cf. the conclusion of *c*.14.
[33] Although the Julian forum was the right place to attend legal speeches. Cf. Vouaux, *Les Actes*, 316f, n. 4.

Peter try to resuscitate this person. This seems to be unequal fight. It is evidently easier to kill a man than to revive him. On the other hand, Peter is given an opportunity that is withheld from Simon. From now on the account of the contest becomes slightly chaotic.

When Simon, in his own peculiar way, has killed the boy, a widow out of the public calls upon Peter. She asks him to resuscitate her son, who is her sole help and stay. This action at least is not anticipated by the prefect. Apart from that, Simon is sidetracked. But Peter raises the first boy and then the second. He even receives a third request, this time from the mother of a senator. She asks him to raise her son too.

At the conclusion of this last episode something happens that could have been expected much earlier. While the third dead man is being brought to Peter, he calls on the Romans to judge who believes in the living God, he himself or Simon. He challenges Simon to raise the third dead man. If he is not able to do so, it will be his own turn. In this way he will expose Simon as a sorcerer and a deceiver. At first Simon is speechless. But then a curious trick is reported[34]. He shows the public the dead man raising his head and moving it, etc. Of course Peter unmasks Simon and then proceeds to resuscitate the man. This induces the Romans to worship Peter as a god.

I suspect that in the course of the history of the text, one or two resuscitations were added. That the text has undergone some kind of reworking is also clear from the continuation. At the conclusion of *c*.29 mention is made of a meeting on the day of the Lord in the house of Marcellus. But *c*.30 reports another meeting apparently on the same day[35].

It is remarkable to find that Simon was not defeated decisively during his contest with Peter in the Julian forum. A few days later he is present again (31). It is as if the story is repeating itself. Again Simon performs his tricks and again Peter refutes Simon. Simon intends to prove that not he but rather Peter is a deceiver. He will leave the godless people in Rome and fly up to God 'whose power I am'. By ascending to God he will demonstrate who he actually is. The storyteller does not leave room to doubt that again we are dealing with a magical trick.

---

[34] See above, n. 17.
[35] Cf. Poupon (note 2), 4377f.

6. *Peter's contest with Simon and his martyrdom*

I will now come back to a literary-critical observation made at the beginning of this chapter. The account of the final contest in the forum of Julius is not only incoherent, if not chaotic, it is also a rather unsatisfying story since we do not get the impression that Simon was defeated once and for all. Simon just continues his magical practices.

Actually, the *martyrium* of Peter may well have had a different tenor or purpose than the story about the confrontations between Peter and Simon. The original purpose of the *martyrium* was quite likely to contrast the miserable and insignificant death of Simon with Peter's heroic martyrdom. At some time the two texts were interconnected. Indeed, in the *martyrium* mention is also made of Simon's activity as a sorcerer and an imposter. The uncertainty about the character of the contest in the Julian forum seems to be the result of the combination of two different texts (a story of Peter's confrontations with Simon ending with their final contest on the forum of Julius and a story about the martyrdom of Peter which was introduced by other episodes with Simon).

In the present text, the contest does not end with the final exposure of Simon as a dangerous deceiver and with his complete elimination, as the readers would expect. It only produces a halfway score. The final elimination of Simon is only realized by his unheroic death which is viewed as a result of the unsuccessful attempt of this bold imposter to imitate the ascension of Jesus Christ.

V. The Image of Simon Magus in the Christian Tradition

TAMÁS ADAMIK

In present-day political life it is very important for a statesman to shape his image in the general public's mind. An image, however, is a two-edged sword. What seems to be of crucial importance to an individual person, may be distorted by the public opinion of a party or a community. This happened – in my opinion – to Simon's image[1]. He arrogated to himself to be 'the great power of God' (Acts 8.10), and he wanted to stress with this self-revelation that he had a share in the secret knowledge of God. In other words, he was a gnostic philosopher and possessed a spark of the divine spiritual substance. The Christians, on the contrary, concluded from the same revelation of Simon that he was a magus, who used sorcery and bewitched the people, and as an enemy of Christianity he destroyed the Christian communities founded by the apostles.

This double-edged interpretation of Simon Magus' image is found in the canonical Acts:

> But there was a certain man, called Simon, which beforetime in the same city used sorcery, and bewitched the people of Samaria, giving out that himself was some great one: To whom they all gave heed, from the least to the greatest, saying, This man is the great power of God. And to him they had regard, because that of long time he had bewitched them with sorceries. But when they believed Philip preaching the things concerning the Kingdom of God, and the name of Jesus Christ, they were baptized, both men and women. Then Simon himself believed also: and when he was baptized, he continued with Philip, and wondered, beholding the miracles and signs which were done (8.9-13).

---

[1] For Simon Magus see also Luttikhuizen, this volume, Ch. IV.

This image of Simon Magus is typical. As a pagan he had been a magus, then under the influence of Philip's miracles he was converted to Christianity. According to the same pattern other great pagans were also converted and became famous Fathers of the Church, e. g. Tertullian, Lactantius, Augustine. But Simon went another way. Already Acts indicates the possibility of Simon's estrangement from Christian ideals. For in the same chapter of Acts we read:

> Now when the apostles which were at Jerusalem heard that Samaria had received the word of God, they sent unto them Peter and John: Who, when they were come down, prayed for them, that they might receive the Holy Ghost.... Then laid they their hands on them, and they received the Holy Ghost. And when Simon saw that through laying on of the apostles' hands the Holy Ghost was given, he offered them money, Saying, Give me also this power, that on whomsoever I lay hands, he may receive the Holy Ghost (8.14-9).

In this description by Luke there is a meaningful fact. Simon wanted to buy spiritual power from Peter. That is why simony was named after Simon: 'the buying or selling of ecclesiastical pardons, offices, or emoluments'.

But why did Simon want to buy, not to merit spiritual power? Because Luke wanted to emphasize that Simon was unfit to receive divine grace by his way of life. This interpretation can be supported by the third part of the story of Simon Magus in Acts:

> But Peter said unto him, Thy money perish with thee, because thou hast thought that the gift of God may be purchased with money. Thou hast neither part nor lot in this matter: for thy heart is not right in the sight of God. Repent therefore of this thy wickedness, and pray God, if perhaps the thought of thine heart may be forgiven thee. For I perceive that thou art in the gall of bitterness, and in the bond of iniquity. Then answered Simon, and said, Pray ye to the Lord for me, that none of these things which ye have spoken come upon me (8.20-4).

As this quotation shows, Peter was very angry with Simon, and he expressed clearly that Simon was unsuitable for salvation, because he was 'in the bond of iniquity'. But the answer of Simon is interesting, too. He asks Peter to pray for him, 'that none of these things which ye have spoken come upon me'. As later Christian tradition about Simon shows, his request was not fulfilled.

On the basis of Luke's description I believe that Simon was more than a magus. It is true that according to Luke he used sorcery and bewitched the people of Samaria, as magi do, but he arrogated himself to be 'the great power of god', that is, he stressed a quality which became later a central concept in gnosticism[2]. According to Jürgen Roloff, Luke even describes Simon as a *theios aner*[3].

However, Philip was convinced that Jesus Christ was the true Redeemer, so he could not call Simon the Redeemer, although Simon called himself 'the great power of God'. He would not describe him as a Redeemer, only as a magus. Thus from the characterization of Simon given by Philip we cannot conclude that Simon was not a gnostic philosopher. Pesch (note 2) himself admits that Simon was a representative of a syncretistic religiosity. If this is so, Simon had to have some teaching on this topic which was his own. What could be his teaching?

1. *Simon's teaching*

Perhaps we can receive an answer from B. A. Pearson, according to whom 'this tractate [the *Testimony of Truth*] is clearly a most important document of Christian Gnosticism'[4]. In the text there are passages which contain haggadic discussions of texts from the Old Testament. The first passage consists of a midrash on the serpent of Genesis 3. In this midrash the serpent is 'wiser than all the animals that were in Paradise'. The serpent's role is that of a teacher: 'Eve instructed Adam, and the serpent had instructed Eve'. Another gnostic document, 'The Nature of the Archons' interprets the Paradise narrative of Gen. 2-3, wherein the 'Spiritual Woman' (the heavenly Eve, Sophia) comes into

---

[2] This is denied by G. Schille, *Die Apostelgeschichte des Lukas* (Berlin, 1984) 208: 'dieser selbst aber wirklich nur ein berühmter Magier, nicht ein gnostischer Sektenstifter'; similarly, but with a greater subtlety, R. Pesch, *Die Apostelgeschichte* (Zürich, 1986) 274: 'Simon ist also Vertreter einer synkretischer Religiosität.... aber dass der Magier Simon kein gnostischer Sektenstifter war, dürfte heute geklärt sein'.

[3] On Simon as *theios aner* see Herczeg, this volume, Ch. III.

[4] B.A. Pearson, 'Jewish Haggadic Traditions in the Testimony of Truth from Nag Hammadi (CG IX, 3)', in *Ex orbe religionum. Studia Geo Widengren oblata* I (Leiden, 1972, 457-70) 458.

the serpent, the 'Instructor', and gives instruction to the fleshly Adam and Eve'. Similar speculations occur in 'On the Origin of the World', in which there is a discussion of the origin of the 'Instructor' whose mother 'the Hebrews' call Eve-Zoe, which is the Instructor of Life. It can hardly be doubted that the gnostic interpretations are derived from Jewish sources'[5].

According to Pearson this midrash is the only text which identifies the tree of knowledge in Genesis as a fig tree. 'Adam hides, and in reply to God's query, "Where are you?", Adam says, "I have come to the fig tree". Then God knows that he has eaten from the forbidden tree.'[6] The identification of the tree of knowledge as a fig is a widespread tradition in early Jewish, apocryphal, rabbinic, and (derivatively) early patristic sources. The gnostic version does not regard the eating of the forbidden fig tree as a sin. In this midrash, too, Adam has sinned against a God who envies him both knowledge and life.

Finally, Pearson states that there are clear lineaments of the monstrous figure of the gnostic Demiurge: he is blind and a fool. In this text the foolishness or ignorance of the Creator is tied to the question in Genesis 3,9: 'Adam, where are you?'. The envy of the Creator here and elsewhere in gnostic literature is derived from the devil in Jewish haggada. Hans Jonas stressed the element of 'revolt' in Gnosticism. In Pearson's opinion 'the sources we now have tend to show that this revolt does indeed arise from within Judaism – though it is axiomatic that once Gnosticism is present "Judaism" has been abandoned'. The conclusion of Pearson is as follows:

> Historical existence in an age of historical crisis – for a people whose God after all had been the Lord of history and of the created order – can, and apparently did, bring about a new and "revolutionary" look at the old traditions and assumptions, a "new hermeneutic". This 'new hermeneutic' arriving in an age of historical crisis and religio-cultural syncretism is the primary element in the origin of Gnosticism. When and where? This is a vexing but important question, one that I am not competent to answer definitively. My guess is: Palestine and Syria in the first century B. C[7].

---

[5] Pearson, 'Jewish Haggadic Traditions', 464.
[6] Pearson, *ibidem*, 465.
[7] Pearson, *ibidem*, 470.

Pearson does not say it, but I think that this age of historical crisis arrived in 64 B. C. when Pompey had taken the temple of Jerusalem after a three-month siege. The Jews were properly shocked, but they were now at Pompey's mercy: their God did not defend them, although their priests continued to worship him. The Jewish historian Josephus writes: 'And now did many of the priests, even when they saw their enemies assailing them with swords in their hands, without any disturbance, go on with their divine worship, and were slain while they were offering their drink-offerings, and burning their incense, as preferring the duties about their worship to God before their own preservation' (*BJ* I. 7.4-5).

There is another important point in the account by Luke of Simon Magus. He spread his religious ideas among the people of Samaria. And when Philip arrived in Samaria and began to diffuse the teaching of Jesus Christ, they became rivals, and out of this competition Philip came out as winner[8].

All this means that Simon not only used sorcery, but he taught his religious ideas as well to the people of Samaria. Luke does not reveal the content of his teaching, but from the comments of modern researchers it is evident that Simon taught some kind of syncretistic religion. Pearson mentions 'religio-cultural syncretism'[9]. Roloff highlights the same in a more concrete way. He refers to the dualism in Simon's teaching[10], in which the idea of two Gods is of crucial importance: the first God is good, the second God, the creator, is inferior[11].

---

[8] As is admitted by Schille, *Apostelgeschichte*, 216: 'Hierin könnte sich ein Nachhall davon verbergen, dass die simonianische Bewegung mit der Christenheit zusammenstiess, als erste Wanderapostel in Samarien auftauchten'; similarly, Pesch, *Apostelgeschichte*, 217; Roloff, *Apostelgeschichte*, 134: 'Philippus hat seinen Erfolg gegen einen gefährlichen Konkurrenten errungen, der bereits vor ihm in der Stadt das Feld beherrschte und dessen Wirken in den Augen der Öffentlichkeit auf der gleichen Ebene wie das seine zu liegen scheint'.

[9] Pearson, 'Jewish Haggadic Traditions', 470.

[10] Roloff, *Apostelgeschichte*, 138: 'Den Anlass dazu können allerdings neben der Selbstbezeichnung als "grosse Kraft" die in der Lehre des historischen Simon aller Wahrscheinlichkeit nach bereits vorhandenen Elemente eines synkretisches Dualismus gebildet haben'.

[11] As H.-Ch. Puech, *En quête de la Gnose* (Paris, 1978) 50 defines it.

It is possible that there was some kind of gnosticism in pre-Christian times which is defined by *The Oxford Classical Dictionary* in such a way: 'A wider, imprecise use of the term describes a syncretistic religiosity diffused in the near east, contemporaneous with and independent of Christianity... Many ingredients of 2nd-cent. Gnosticism are pre-Christian'[12].

This pre-Christian gnosticism, too, was based on a myth of redemption, and it can be regarded as certain that Simon, too, preached a redemption (or messianism) in Samaria, just as Philip did. This is important information, since Samaria had been occupied by the Macedonians in the 4th century BC and thus became hellenised. Due to the influence of hellenism there was everywhere a growing interest in mystery religions involving initiation ceremonies and promises of individual salvation. W.K.C. Guthrie, e. g., supposes the influence of Orphism: 'The adoption of Orpheus by the Christians was only a continuation of previous adoption by Jews. It was easy to see in the characteristic picture of Orpheus not only a symbol of the Good Shepherd of the Christians... but also parallels to the lore of the Old Testament'[13]. Prophecy and redemption are also important elements of Virgil's *Fourth Eclogue*, and the influence of Orphism on the Old Testament cannot be excluded. There are terms such as *mysteria* and *mystikos* in Gnostic and Hermetic texts, and much of their ideas and language derives from Plato. So Simon could know Platonism, the hellenistic form of Orphism, and the Jewish elements listed by Pearson, when he formed his doctrine which provided a rival religion of redemption with a Redeemer replacing Jesus. Which were the most important ingredients of his doctrine?

This question can perhaps be answered after having examined the earliest and most reliable reports on his teaching, those of Justin, Irenaeus and Hippolytus of Rome. Justin Martyr (*ca.* 100-65) was born in ancient Shechem in Samaria, of pagan parents. For some years he led a peripatetic life searching for truth successively in Stoicism, Aristotelianism, Pythagoreanism, and finally Platonism. Evidently, he well knew both the Samarian traditions about Simon Magus and hellenistic philosophy, and as a Christian he believed that Christianity was the true philosophy.

---

[12] J.M. Dillon, 'Gnosticism', in S. Hornblower and A. Spawforth (eds), *The Oxford Classical Dictionary*³ (Oxford, 1996) 641.
[13] W.K.C. Guthrie, *Orpheus and Greek Religion* (London, 1952) 264.

Justin informs us that Simon Magus first lived in Samaria, but under Claudius he went to Rome, where he performed miracles. The Romans regarded him as a god, put up a statue to him, and worshipped it as that of a god. Indeed, all Samaritans, and other people as well, worshipped him as a god. His statue contained the inscription *Simoni deo sancto*[14]. His partner, Helen, a prostitute, was worshipped by the people as *ennoia*, the first conception which originated from him (1 *Apol.* 26). In his *Dialogue with the Jew Trypho* he notices that Simon was taken for the Supreme Being (120).

Justin's information can be regarded as authentic, because he knew pagan and Jewish philosophy and theology well. He confirms the assertion of Acts, on the one hand, and on the other, he supplies new data on Simon. It is true, that he confused his statue with that of *Semo Sancus Dius Fidius*, a deity of puzzling origin and function, said to be Sabine, who in historical times was connected with oaths and treaties – hence the common oath *medius fidius*. Tertullian makes the same mistake (*Apologeticum* 13.9). But from this mistake we cannot conclude, that Simon did not receive a statue in Rome. But it is more important that Justin mentions Helen, the *ennoia* of Simon. This emphasis on woman as principle of knowledge is in harmony with the midrash on Eve mentioned by Pearson, and with Greek mythology concerning Metis, the counsel personified, the consort of Zeus, and wisest of gods and men (Hesiod, *Theog.* 886 ff.). It is also in harmony with the figure of Diotima, the legendary priestess from Mantinea and teacher of Socrates (Plato, *Sympos.* 201d), who is the mouthpiece for his metaphysics of love, and finally with the love lyric of Sappho, to which Socrates, too, refers, when he explains the divine love in Plato's *Phaedrus* (235c).

Irenaeus (*ca.* 130-202), who is called the first systematic Christian theologian, was born in Asia Minor and thus knew both eastern and western thought well. His important work, the anti-Gnostic *Adversus haereses*, which survived mainly in a Latin translation, contains precious information on Simon's teaching. He describes the activity and the doctrine of Simon in detail. First he quotes and interprets the text of Acts on Simon. According to him, Simon converted to Christianity in order to acquire the knowledge of Christians, that is he feigned to become Christian because he wanted to obtain the spiritual power of the apostles in order to be yet a greater magus (1.23.1).

---

[14] See also Bremmer, this volume, Ch. I.2.

He did not believe in God and Jesus Christ, but he pursued magic with big success, therefore everybody admired him. Because of his magical practices he received a statue in Rome from the Emperor Claudius. Among the Jews he pretended to be Son (*Filius*), in Samaria Father (*Pater*) and to other people to be the Holy Ghost (*Spiritus Sanctus*). That is, he pretended to be the Supreme Power (*sublimissima Virtus*) (1.23.1).

Before he describes the doctrine of Simon, Irenaeus makes a statement: all heresies originated from him (*ex quo universae haereses substituerunt*: 1.23.2). He bought Helen, a prostitute from a brothel in Tyrus, and took her with him as a companion, calling her the first conception of his mind (*primam mentis Conceptionem*: 1.23.2). Helen is the mother of everything because by her Simon conceived the idea of creating angels and archangels. Helen, his *ennoia*, got to know everything which her father wanted her to know. She descended to the netherworld and generated the Angels and Powers who created this world. After having created them, she was detained by them because they envied her, and they ignored him, that is Simon, the Supreme God. She suffered from them because they did not permit her to return to her father, and they closed her in a human body. So from century to century she transmigrated into women's bodies as from vase to vase (*de vase in vas*). This same *ennoia* resided in that Helen who caused the Trojan War. Transmigrating from body to body, she was always offended. In order to stop her suffering, finally she prostituted herself in a brothel: she is the lost lamb (*hanc esse perditam ovem*). From this statement I conclude that Simon was the good shepherd.

Simon became incarnate, assumed a bodily form to find her, the first Helen, in order to release her and to bring salvation to the people by recognition (knowledge) of himself (*hominibus autem salutem praestaret per suam agnitionem*: 1.23.3). For the Angels govern the world badly because each of them wants to become the leader. That is the reason why he, Simon, came in a body to improve the world. He descended transfigured, resembling the Potences, Powers and Angels, in order to appear to men as a man, although he was not a man, and he seemed to suffer in Judaea, without suffering really.

Here we seem to observe the roots of docetism in gnosticism. The prophets prophesied under the influence of the Angels who created this world. The people, therefore, should not heed them, but be free of their teaching, since Simon brings salvation, not their prophecies.

There are no just deeds and acts by nature, therefore there are only conventions by which the Angels want to subdue the people. Therefore Simon promised to destroy the world and to liberate the people from the power of those who had created this world (*Quapropter et solvi mundum et liberari eos qui sunt eius ab imperio eorum qui mundum fecerunt repromisit*: 1.23.3). This teaching could be dangerous in the political climate of the Roman Empire, and that is perhaps why Simon laid stress on his magic in the Rome of Claudius.

Having expounded this doctrine of Simon, Irenaeus lists the various sorts of his magic: philtres, charms, assistance of divine powers, sending dreams. Finally, Irenaeus notices that Simon and Helen have images which represent the face of Zeus and that of Athena. They have a name, too, derived from Simon: *Simoniani, a quibus falsi nominis scientia accepit initia* ('Simonians from whom the science of the false name [*gnosis*] began': 1.23.4). This was the doctrine of Simon in general outlines, according to Irenaeus.

Adelin Rousseau and Louis Doutreleau correctly emphasize that all important features of gnosticism are to be found in the exposition of Irenaeus: the opposition of the supreme God and the demiurgical angels, the depreciation of the physical world, salvation by *gnosis*, and the indifferent character of human acts concerning morality[15]. This doctrine of Simon was connected with magical practices. But in contrast to Luke, who focused on the magic of Simon, Irenaeus was interested in his teaching. He therefore only alluded to his magical activity and success, but he did not describe it. It follows from the foregoing that I regard Irenaeus' report on Simon's doctrine as authentic.

Later Christian authors, such as Hippolytus (*ca.* 170-236) and Epiphanius (*ca.* 315-403) ascribe to Simon the more complex doctrine of later Simonians and gnostics; I therefore do not deal with them in detail. I select only one passage from Hippolytus' *Refutatio*: 'there are two offshoots of all the aeons... One of these appears on high which is the great power (*megalé dynamis*), the mind of the universe (*nous tóu holóu*), governing all things, which is male; and the other below, the great conception (*epinoia megalé*), which is female, which generates all things. Within is the Father who upholds all things.... This is

---

[15] Irénée de Lyon, *Contre les Hérésies* I, ed. A. Rousseau and L. Doutreleau (Paris, 1979) 151-2.

who stands, took his stand and will stand, being a male-and-female power (*hestos, stas, stésomenos, ón arsenothélys*) (6.18.2-4)[16].

Hippolytus cites this passage from the *Megalé Apophasis* ('Great Revelation') which is an important witness of the later Simonian movement[17]. Giovanni Filoramo comments on it as follows:

> The pre-existent principle produces as an image of itself an entity that is also androgynous. According to its male dimension, it is Nous or Intellect, which governs everything; according to the female dimension, it is the Thought whose responsibility it is to give birth. Thus we find a duplication of the functions attributed by the Simonians of Irenaeus to Ennoia: cognitive power within the Father of his own mystery and generative power towards the world. Together these functions reconstitute the perfect image of the Father, whose direct intention is to save the created world and Man. This entity, which is, was and will be upright, offers the ideal model for the perfect Gnostic[18].

In this phase of development, which is mirrored in the *Megalé Apophasis*, the doctrine is detached from the figure of Simon. Filoramo is correct when he writes as follows: 'Having abandoned the symbolism hidden behind the Ennoia-Helen myth, the Simonian of this generation appears to reflect more optimistically and rather more universally on the very essence of the Gnostic myth: the meeting with the self as an attempt to reconstruct the original androgynous unity'[19].

Hippolytus refers to the Greek sources of Simon's ideas as well, for example to Empedocles (6.11-2) and to his allegorical interpretation of the Old Testament and of Homer's epics (6.15-6), meaning that Simon knew and adopted the allegorical method of the Stoics. So Hans Leisegang emphasizes rightly that the teaching of Simon is older than that of the Gospels, and that Greek myth and philosophy have a great part in it[20].

[16] P. Wendland, *Hippolytus Werke III: Refutatio omnium haeresium* (Leipzig, 1916) 144.
[17] J. Fickel, *Die 'Apophasis megale' in Hippolyts Refutatio* (Rome, 1968).
[18] G. Filoramo, *A History of Gnosticism*, tr. A. Alcock (Cambridge, Mass., 1994) 150.
[19] Filoramo, *History of Gnosticism*, 151.
[20] H. Leisegang, *Die Gnosis* (Stuttgart, 1985) 88-93. K. Rudolph, *Die Gnosis* (Göttingen, 1990³) 319 admits it, too, but in less detail.

John Ferguson writes as follows: 'For Bousset argued that Gnosticism was really the cult of the Great Mother under another name, and in many of the sects, the Collyridians, Montanists, Naassenes and Nicolaitans, the Holy Ghost was seen as the Female Principle.'[21] It is not accidental that the Roman poet Catullus wrote a poem (63) on Cybele, the great mother-goddess of Phrygia, which is connected by Britt-Mari Näsström with gnosticism[22].

2. *Simon's magic*

Irenaeus and Hippolytus only enumerate the various sorts of Simon's teaching. The *Pseudo-Clementines* and *APt*, on the contrary, focus on the magic of Simon. The Pseudo-Clementine romance about Peter's travels and conflicts with Simon Magus was originally written *ca*. 200. It survived in two divergent fourth-century recensions, viz. *Homilies* (Greek) and *Recognitions* (Syriac and Rufinus' Latin). They treat the magic of Simon romantically, but they expound his doctrine on the basis of later gnostics, and they are very controversial; I therefore omit them. The Latin translation of *APt* (*Actus Vercellenses*) concentrates totally on the magical practices of Simon, and in an artistic form that is worth analysing.The translator expounds the story of Simon's and Peter's competition in the form of a perfect drama which consists of six parts.

In *part 1*, there is the preparation or the antecedents of Simon's and Peter's competition. Paul leaves Rome, but Simon comes to Rome in order to ruin the results of Paul's missionary activities. The danger is great because Simon wins over many Christians to himself, and the remaining Christians are driven to despair (1-4).

In *part 2*, God sends Peter to Rome in order to prevent the ruin of Christianity in the city. Peter embarks at Caesarea, then arrives at Puteoli, from where without any rest he sails for Rome. Meanwhile he converts the captain, and receives bad news about the magical activity of Simon; he therefore hurries to Rome (5-6).

In *part 3*, Peter arrives in Rome, and the Christian congregation asks him to get square with Simon, who dwells in the house of Marcellus. This Marcellus, a Roman senator, deserted his Christian faith

---

[21] J. Ferguson, *The Religions of the Roman Empire* (Ithaca NY, 1985) 31.
[22] B.-M. Näsström, *The Abhorrence of Love* (Göteborg, 1989) 88-92.

under the influence of Simon. Peter goes to Marcellus' house, but Simon does not receive him. Then Peter sends into the house a big dog that speaks the message of Peter with a human voice. Simon is terrified by the talking dog, and Marcellus is converted by this miracle, and he throws out Simon of his house. In order to confirm Marcellus in his Christian faith, Peter works some miracles. Simon comes to the house where Peter lives, and he begins to vilify Jesus, saying that Jesus was only a petty Jew, the son of a carpenter. At this point Peter sends to Simon a mother with her suckling baby. This informs Simon, with the voice of a grown man, that Peter will challenge him at the Forum of Julius Caesar. Then in the name of Jesus Christ the baby orders Simon to become dumb and to leave Rome till the next Saturday. And so it happens (7-15).

In *part 4*, Peter prays to God to receive power for the competition with Simon and then delivers a speech to the Christians. In his speech he explains how they have to read and interpret the Gospel, as well as the divinity of Jesus Christ, which Simon denies again and again. Then he cures some blind women in the name of Jesus Christ[23]. After having received back their sight, they behold Jesus Christ in a bright light in different figures (16-21).

Part 5 begins with the dream of Marcellus: an ugly black woman danced in front of him. She was the demon of Simon and Peter killed her[24]. Finally they realize that the dream was a good sign sent by God. Then they go to the Forum and meet Simon. Simon again abuses Jesus Christ saying: he was a carpenter, nothing else. At this point Peter proves from the Holy Scripture that Jesus is God. At that moment the competition begins. The prefect, Agrippa, gives them a young man and orders them to kill him with magical practice, then to raise him from the dead. Simon kills him with magic, but he cannot actually raise him from the dead. Peter prays to God, and first he raises the son of a widow, and then the young man, with the power of Jesus Christ. With this miracle he proves that Jesus Christ is the true God, and Simon is a skilful magus, nothing else (22-9).

But Simon does not acquiesce in his defeat. In *part 6* he declares that he will prove that Peter believes not in the true God, but in an

---

[23] For the women see Bremmer, this volume, Ch. I.1.
[24] For the black woman see Bremmer, this volume Ch. I.1; Luttikhuizen, this volume, Ch. IV.4.

invented god. Then he promises to fly up to god, whose power he is. And he does so. He flies up, but Peter prays to Jesus Christ and asks him to let Simon fall down and to break his leg. Jesus fulfils Peter's request: Simon falls down, and breaks his leg. He is brought to Kastor magus, who wants to perform an operation on him, but Simon dies on the operating table (30-2).

This analysis shows clearly that the translator of the *APt* aimed not only at entertaining simple Christian people, but also wanted to prove the divinity of Jesus Christ against the charges of Simon Magus, who repeatedly denied Jesus' divinity. So I think that Wilhelm Schneemelcher is mistaken when he asserts that the author of the *APt* wanted only to stress that Simon was a magus, nothing else[25]. This is important, too, but the point is the divinity of Jesus Christ and 'his benevolent and inexhaustible mercy'[26].

The conclusion of my investigation is that the main elements of Simon's teaching were to be found in the syncretistic religions of the 1st century BC, on the one hand; on the other, the image of Simon, both that of magus and that of gnostic philosopher, was discredited by Christian apologists[27].

---

[25] W. Schneemelcher, in *NTA II*, 281.
[26] J.B. Perkins, 'The *Acts of Peter* as Intertext: Response to Dennis MacDonald', in E.H. Lovering (ed), *SBL 1993 Seminar Papers* (Atlanta, 1993, 627-33) 627.
[27] For the process of discrediting see also Czachesz, this volume, Ch. VII.

VI. ... Revivifying Resurrection Accounts: techniques of composition and rewriting in the *Acts of Peter* cc.25-28

CHRISTINE M. THOMAS

This study examines a constellation of three accounts describing resuscitations of the dead performed by Peter, which are found in the *Acts of Peter (APt)*, as known from the sixth or seventh-century manuscript Codex Vercelli (*Actus Vercellenses*)[1]. The *APt* have been reworked in numerous later texts that date from the fourth century onward. Most of them, however, do not contain the contest between Simon Magus and Peter that forms the setting of these resurrection accounts, since their concern is the preservation of the martyrdom, significant for the developing liturgical calendar[2]. Two later texts, however, contain versions of a resurrection story as an element of the contest between Simon Magus and Peter: that found in the late

---

[1] This manuscript presents a third or fourth-century Latin translation of a third-century Greek text; on the date of the translation, see C.H. Turner, 'The Latin *Acts of Peter*', *JTS* 32 (1931) 119-33; Bremmer, this volume, Ch. I.3. See G. Poupon, this volume, Ch. XV, on the date of the Greek redaction it translates.

[2] The fourth-century version attributed to Linus, bishop of Rome, begins only at the arrest ('*Martyrium beati Petri apostoli a Lino episcopo conscriptum*,' in R.A. Lipsius and M. Bonnet [eds], *Acta Apostolorum Apocrypha* [Leipzig, 1891] 1.1-22). The text attributed to Marcellus, the sixth-century version that enjoyed greatest circulation of all the versions of the tale of Peter, replaces the miracle contest in the forum with a verbal disputation between Peter, Paul, and Simon Magus before the emperor (Μαρτύριον τῶν ἁγίων ἀποστόλων Πέτρου καὶ Παύλου, in Lipsius, 1.118-77, with an alternate version, Πράξεις τῶν ἁγίων ἀποστόλων Πέτρου καὶ Παύλου, in Lipsius, 1.178-222).

fourth-century history of Pseudo-Hegesippus[3], and that found in the *Acts of Nereus and Achilles*, which dates to the fifth century[4].

Pseudo-Hegesippus and the *Acts of Nereus and Achilles* are generally characterized as literarily dependent upon the *Actus Vercellenses*[5]. In addition to the resurrection, Pseudo-Hegesippus also presents other episodes known from the *Actus Vercellenses* (but also appearing in the mid-fourth century Linus text): Simon's disastrous attempt to fly over the city of Rome, Peter's arrest, his quick departure from Rome, the *Quo Vadis* episode, and his execution upside down. *Nereus and Achilles*, in addition to reworking the resurrection accounts, also reformulates the account of Peter's daughter, who becomes paralyzed on her wedding night to safeguard her body from the uncleanness of sexual congress (15). It is the purpose of this paper, however, to call into question an unnuanced notion of literary dependence, not so much to attack its possibility as to plead for a more exact description of the relationships among texts that may show knowledge of one another. 'Literary dependence' can mean many things. In much recent work on the *Apocryphal Acts of the Apostles* (*AAA*), consensus has emerged that an unnuanced concept of literary dependence is insufficient for describing the numerous possible relationships between two texts; clearly use of written texts in antiquity encompasses a number of possible procedures. Most scholars, with few exceptions, no longer understand even 'literary dependence' as slavish imitation of one text by another, involving word-for-word correspondences between the two – a phenomenon uncommon in antiquity even in cases of explicit citation. Still under discussion, however, is the nature of the new model of intertextual relations and the appropriate terminology[6].

---

[3] V. Ussani, *Hegesippi qui dicitur historiae libri V* (Vienna and Leipzig, 1932) 1.183-7.

[4] Text and comments on the dating in H. Achelis, *Acta SS. Nerei et Achillei* (Leipzig, 1893).

[5] Summarized in Schneemelcher, in *NTA* II, 277.

[6] In the work of the Seminar on Intertextuality in Christian Apocrypha of the Society of Biblical Literature (SBL), theoretical approaches have ranged from very oralist to very fixed-textual models, with many waystations in between. See for a representative sample, D.R. Cartlidge, 'Combien d'unités avez-vous de trois à quatre? What Do We Mean by Intertextuality in Early Church Studies?', in D.J. Lull (ed), *SBL 1990 Seminar Papers* (Atlanta,

Two general cautions are voiced here: first, the mere designation of literary dependence often obscures, or at least stops the search for, authorial creativity, aesthetic merit, and historical value in the presumed 'dependent' texts. Second, particularly in the case of the *AAA*, the tendency to rewrite these documents was so prevalent that one often faces a constellation of several closely related, but not identical texts, appearing over the relatively short span of a century or two; it therefore is in question exactly which earlier text provided the literary model for the later text, especially, as is likely, if texts such as the *Actus Vercellenses* themselves had earlier, but no longer extant, written versions[7].

In the present example, even the presumed close narrative correspondence that one would expect of dependent texts evaporates upon closer inspection. The two later texts do not present three resurrections, but only one, so that even a genuine *imitatio* of the supposed source text is not apparent. Moreover, the two later versions unite in the single account the various narrative motifs that are separated into

1990) 400-11; D.R. MacDonald, 'The *Acts of Paul* and the *Acts of Peter*: Which Came First?', and R. Valantasis, 'Narrative Strategies and Synoptic Quandaries: A Response to Dennis MacDonald's Reading of *Acts of Paul* and *Acts of Peter*', in E.H. Lovering (ed), *SBL 1992 Seminar Papers* (Atlanta, 1992) 214-24 and 234-9; J. Perkins, 'The *Acts of Peter* as Intertext: Response to Dennis MacDonald', in E.H. Lovering (ed), *SBL 1993 Seminar Papers* (Atlanta, 1993) 627-31; R.F. Stoops, 'Departing to Another Place: The *Acts of Peter* and the Canonical Acts of the Apostles', in E.H. Lovering (ed), *SBL 1994 Seminar Papers* (Atlanta, 1994) 390-404; J.V. Hills, 'The Acts of the Apostles in the *Acts of Paul*', in E.H. Lovering (ed), *SBL 1994 Seminar Papers* (Atlanta, 1994) 24-54; F.S. Jones, 'A Jewish Christian Reads Luke's Acts of the Apostles: The Use of the Canonical Acts in the Ancient Jewish Christian Source behind Pseudo-Clementine *Recognitions* 1.12-71', in E.H. Lovering (ed), *SBL 1995 Seminar Papers* (Atlanta, 1995) 617-35; C.R. Matthews, 'Peter and Philip Upside Down: Perspectives on the Relation of the *Acts of Philip* to the *Acts of Peter*', in *SBL 1996 Seminar Papers* (Atlanta, 1996) 23-34.

[7] On the sources and redactions of the *Actus Vercellenses*, see G. Poupon, 'Les "Actes de Pierre" et leur remaniement', *ANRW* II.25.6 (1988) 4363-83; C.M. Thomas, 'Word and Deed: The *Acts of Peter* and Orality', *Apocrypha* 3 (1992) 125-64 and 'The Prehistory of the *Acts of Peter*', in F. Bovon (ed), *Harvard Studies in the Apocryphal Acts of the Apostles* (Cambridge, MA, forthcoming).

three independent narrative units in the *Actus Vercellenses*. In short, even if the *Actus Vercellenses* was known by the two later texts – a possibility that is quite likely – the use of the source text is not *textual* in that the later versions do not even preserve its most basic features, such as the number of resurrections, or any of its redactional concerns. Such an inexact use of a source could just as well be based on memory, or on the knowledge of one of the sources of the *Actus Vercellenses*; there is no way of demonstrating which of these possibilities was the case. Instead of arguing for an elusive, no longer extant independent source for all the accounts, however, it is more interesting to explore the possibility that Pseudo-Hegesippus and *Nereus and Achilles* did know a text of the *APt*. For then, in this case of literary dependence, one would have to recognize that the written text is not privileged, but is used as a basis, along with other Christian texts, for an elastic, creative, and elusive reworking of the source. Other principles beside imitation are at work.

Once freed from the tyranny of the earliest source, the later texts appear not as mere different *later* versions of the tale, dependent texts devoid of historical or creative merit, but as *different* later versions of the tale. The early *Actus Vercellenses* have by far the most literarily complex rendition of the resurrection account; comparison with the later versions can help unlock its compositional techniques. Because of the close similarity in the compositional development between the *AAA* and other narrative Christian literature, particularly the gospels[8], the investigation of compositional technique in this example offers a window into early Christian literature in general.

The *Actus Vercellenses* comprise several distinct narrative components. The story begins when Peter comes to Rome in response to God's call. Already, the overwhelming majority of Christian believers in the capital city have fallen away into apostasy because of the powerful works of Simon Magus, who claims, successfully in their view, to be the 'power of God.' Peter initially counters these asseverations through a combination of preaching and miracle-working, all of which are done under the shadow of a brewing confrontation with Simon. The conflict finally comes to direct encounter in a contest in the

---

[8] See the comments in F. Bovon, 'La vie des apôtres: Traditions bibliques et narrations apocryphes', in idem (ed), *Les Actes apocryphes des apôtres* (Geneva, 1981) 141-58, and Thomas, 'Prehistory'.

Forum Iulium, before the crowds of the great city. Although Peter emerges from this successful, the narrative concludes with his arrest and execution at the hands of Roman officials.

Cc.25-28 present the three resurrection stories as the main fabric of the contest in the forum between Peter and Simon. The prefect Agrippa places a young man, a favorite of the emperor, still alive, before the two contestants. Simon slays him with a word. As the young man lies dead, before Peter can respond, a poor Christian widow cries out to Peter from the crowd that, likewise, her only son is dead; Peter instructs her to bring the body to the forum. Agrippa complains that his candidate for resurrection is still lying unattended; Peter commands Agrippa to raise up the boy by the hand, and the boy lives again, to the acclamation of the crowd. The widow's son now arrives, and Peter raises him, too. After this, jumping on the resurrection bandwagon, a senator's mother requests that Peter raise her son, Nikostratos. Peter lets Simon have the first attempt at this, but Simon succeeds only in making the man's head nod and open its eyes. Peter angrily denounces this as mere sham. Annoyed at this attempt to beguile the crowd, Agrippa pushes Simon away, and the man lies dead as before. After securing from the mother a promise that all the slaves who had been freed upon the man's death would retain their freedom, and that the money that would have been spent on his funeral would be given instead to the Christian widows, Peter raises Nikostratos.

Similarly to the main resurrection in the *Actus Vercellenses*, in Pseudo-Hegesippus, the young man who is resuscitated is a 'friend of Caesar's' (*adulescens nobilis propinquus Caesaris*)[9]. He already lies newly dead when the contest begins, not yet buried, and the subject of mourning throughout the city. The text makes much of Simon's ability to deceive the crowds by making the dead man's head move:

> *(Simon) accessit ad lectum defuncti, incantare atque immurmurare dira carmina coepit. uisus est agitare caput qui mortuus erat. Clamor ingens gentilium quod iam uiueret, quod loqueretur cum Simone.*
> Simon approached the dead man's bed and began to chant and murmur horrifying spells. The fellow who had been dead was seen to move his head. The crowd screamed wildly that he was already alive and that he was talking to Simon[10].

---

[9] On 'friends' of Caesar, see Bremmer, this volume, Ch. I.1.
[10] Ussani, *Hegesippi historiae*, 184.26-9. Translations mine unless otherwise noted.

In this account, Peter himself takes over the role of Agrippa in debunking the ruse:

> *Tunc sanctus apostolus poposcit silentium et ait: 'si uiuit defunctus, loquatur; si resuscitatus est, surgat, ambulet, fabuletur'.*
> Then the holy apostle called for silence and said, 'If the dead man is alive, let him speak; if he has been revived, let him rise up, walk, talk to us'[11].

The corpse, of course, is unable to do these things, and Peter proves the superiority of the power of his God by raising the man completely. At the end of the account, he returns the young man to his mother:

> *Et dedit eum Petrus matri suae. Ait: 'Secura esto, mater, de filio, non uerearis, habet custodem suum'.*
> And Peter gave him to his mother. He said: 'Be free from care, mother, about your son, do not fear, he has his guardian'[12].

In the *Actus Vercellenses*, these various narrative details are distributed among the three resuscitation episodes. The main resurrection, as in Pseudo-Hegesippus, is that of the young man (*puer*) who is dear to the emperor (*quem et imperator libenter habet*); the other two resurrections are interruptions of this action, and occur as a response to a personal request made to Peter. The *Actus Vercellenses* provide the detail of Simon magically moving the dead man's head for the third of the resurrections, that of the son of the senatorial mother (*ostendit populo elevasse caput et agitare*). The conclusion of the story of Pseudo-Hegesippus is similarly well-represented in the *Actus Vercellenses*: in the cases of the second and third resurrections, Peter restores the resuscitated young men to their mothers.

The *Acts of Nereus and Achilles* unite slightly different details in their account of the resurrection. Here, the contest happens, not in the forum, but in the streets of Rome, as Peter and Simon see a funeral procession passing by. Similarly to the second resurrection accounts in the *Actus Vercellenses*, the young man is a widow's only son. As with the third resurrection account in that source, the one concerning the

---

[11] *Ibid*, 184.30-185.2.
[12] *Ibid*, 185.10-4.

young senator, Simon is able only to make the corpse's body jerk about in his attempt to resuscitate it (12):

Τότε ὁ Σίμων τοὺς δαίμονας ἐπικαλεσάμενος τῇ μαγικῇ αὐτοῦ τέχνῃ ἤρξατο ποιεῖσθαι σαλεύεσθαι τοῦ τεθνεῶτος τὸ σῶμα, ὅπερ οἱ ὄχλοι θεασάμενοι ἤρξαντο κράζειν ἐπαίνους τῷ Σίμωνι προσάγοντες, τῷ δὲ Πέτρῳ ἀπώλειαν καταψηφιζόμενοι.
Then, by invoking the *daimones* with his magical procedures, Simon began to make the body of the dead man jerk about. When the crowd saw this, they began to shout in praise of Simon, and to cry out in favor of Peter's execution[13].

In a manner exactly parallel to the account of Pseudo-Hegesippus, Peter saves himself from the wrath of the crowd by exposing Simon's trickery:

Τότε Πέτρος μετὰ βίας ποιήσας αὐτοὺς σιγῆσαι εἶπεν πρὸς τὸν λαόν· Ἐὰν ζῇ, λαλησάτω, περιπατησάτω, μεταλάβῃ τροφῆς καὶ ἀποστραφήτω εἰς τὸν οἶκον αὐτοῦ·
Then Peter, barely managing to silence them, said to the crowd, 'If he is alive, let him speak, let him walk about, let him take food, and go back to his home.'[14]

Similarly to the account in Pseudo-Hegesippus, and to the second and third resurrection accounts in the *Actus Vercellenses*, the story ends with the happy restitution of the living son to his mother:

ἀποδοθήτω ὁ ὀρφανὸς καὶ μονογενὴς τῇ χήρᾳ τῇ μητρὶ αὐτοῦ.
Let the orphan and only child be restored to his mother, the widow[15].

These three texts stand in a web of intertextual connections, not only among themselves – for *Nereus and Achilles* may well know Pseudo-Hegesippus – but with other Christian literature. All three sources for the resuscitation account of the *APt* owe a significant intertextual debt to the account of Jesus' resurrection of the widow's son at Nain, found in Luke 7.11-7. Both the *Actus Vercellenses*, second resuscitation, and the *Acts of Nereus and Achilles* explicitly describe the young man as

[13] Achelis, *Acta*, 11.27-31.
[14] Achelis, *Acta*, 11.31-12.1.
[15] Achelis, *Acta*, 12.18-9.

the only son of a widow, which, in the context of early Christian literature, is best read as an allusion to the miracle of Jesus (μονογενὴς υἱὸς τῇ μητρὶ αὐτοῦ καὶ αὐτὴ ἦν χήρα, 'he was his mother's only son, and she was a widow,' Lk 7.12). All three texts, even the account of Pseudo-Hegesippus that does not contain the motif of the widow, remain true to this general story pattern by closing their accounts with the restitution of son to mother. The *Acts of Nereus and Achilles* sharpen the Biblical allusion by placing the story in the streets of Rome, in which the apostle encounters the funeral procession, with the bereft widow mourning loudly, as they wind along:

υἱὸς μονογενὴς χήρας τινὸς ἐπὶ κλίνης ἐξεκομίζετο, ἡ δὲ τούτου μήτηρ μετὰ πλείστου ὄχλου ἀκολουθοῦσα θρηνώδεις καὶ ὀδυνηρὰς φωνὰς προσέφερεν.
The only son of a certain widow, dead, was being carried out on a bier, and his mother was following with a large crowd, crying out dirges and mournful wails[16].

The similarity to the Biblical account is unmistakable:

καὶ ἰδοὺ ἐξεκομίζετο τεθνηκὼς μονογενὴς υἱὸς τῇ μητρὶ αὐτοῦ καὶ αὐτὴ ἦν χήρα, καὶ ὄχλος τῆς πόλεως ἱκανὸς ἦν σὺν αὐτῇ·
A man who had died was being carried out. He was his mother's only son, and she was a widow; and with her was a large crowd from the town (Lk 7.12; ET NRSV).

Not only are there the typical details of the widow's only son, and the sizable crowd of mourners; the verb for carrying the corpse is also ἐκκομίζω in both cases. All three Petrine texts, however, indicate their debt to Luke. Although *Nereus and Achilles* distinctively structure their narrative after Luke's account, they do not preserve the main Biblical allusion, the command that resuscitates the son; this is, however, present in both the *Actus Vercellenses* and Pseudo-Hegesippus: νεανίσκε, ἐγέρθητι ('young man, arise,' Lk 7.14)[17].

The ductus of the Biblical model within the three texts cautions us that source relations, however they be construed, are not linear

---

[16] Achelis, *Acta*, 11.18-21.
[17] Albeit in slightly different translations. Pseudo-Hegesippus has *adulescens, surge*, the *Actus Vercellenses*, *iuvenis, surge*.

genealogical relationships between two texts alone. Source relationships take place in an intertextual context, within the world of early Christian texts in general. In this case, all three of the texts are influenced by the gospel accounts, but in varying degrees. The picture becomes yet more nuanced when one takes into account that even the story of the widow of Nain does not have its sole source as an event in the life of Jesus, but itself owes an intertextual debt, at least in the manner of its narration, to the story of Elijah and the widow of Zarephath in 1 Kings 17.17-24 (see esp. vs. 23).

The Biblical allusion, however rich in associations it might be for early Christians, is at odds with the location of the resurrection story in the contest between Simon and Peter. In the two accounts which portray the conflict as a set event, Pseudo-Hegesippus and the Actus Vercellenses, the resurrection (or, in the case of the *Actus Vercellenses*, the main resurrection) is performed upon a favorite of the emperor's, which is incompatible with the motif of the widow's only son. The *Actus Vercellenses* bases its two additional resurrection accounts on these varying details[18]. Pseudo-Hegesippus solves the inconsistency by merely retaining the motif of the restitution of the son to his mother, without stressing her widowhood. In *Nereus and Achilles*, the setting itself is more consonant with the Biblical allusion, for the resurrection does not take place as part of a set contest between Peter and Simon.

The *AAA*, with their sometimes extremely complex textual connections and interlacings, have provided a touchstone for the explanatory utility of alternate concepts of intertextual relationships, running the gamut from a fairly static view of literary appropriation to fluid, oralist descriptions that eschew any written contact at all. The truth most likely lies somewhere in between. Rather than reject the notion of literary dependence, it would represent progress to characterize the various possible types of such dependence with more specificity and nuance. In an important study, François Bovon distinguished between citations, imitations, and adaptations of one text by another, thus providing three possible levels of dependence[19]. Citations are attributed

---

[18] As R.F. Stoops, *Miracle Stories and Vision Reports in the Acts of Peter* (Diss. Harvard, 1983) 62, 177 notes in his detailed commentary on this passage, the narrative of the poor widow's only son does not suit the context of the contest, for neither Simon nor Agrippa has any role in it.

[19] F. Bovon, 'The Synoptic Gospels and the Noncanonical Acts of the Apostles', *HTR* 81 (1988) 19-36.

quotations, such as the words of Jesus found in nearly all the *AAA*. Imitation is the application of a saying or action typical of a character in one text to another; Peter's raising of the widow's only son is an imitation of the account of Jesus and the widow of Nain. An adaptation is a rewriting of the text of one document by another; in our case, Pseudo-Hegesippus and *Nereus and Achilles* are adaptations of the *Actus Vercellenses*.

In describing the overall relationship of these three texts in generative terms, however, I would follow Richard Valantasis's suggestion and apply the distinction between 'fabula' and 'sjuzhet' developed by the Russian Formalists[20]. The fabula is the most generic form of a narrative trajectory: it denotes the events in their logical and chronological sequence, and includes the basic elements of the narrative, such as situation, location, and characters. In the case of the various versions of the *APt*, the fabula would be the sum of individual narratives about Peter, arranged according to the external dictates of his life. For example, the events in Jerusalem precede those in Rome; the contest with Simon takes place before Peter's trial and execution, and the *Quo Vadis* story as he attempts to flee Rome just before his arrest. A 'sjuzhet', or, as I will call it, 'storyline', is a particular rhetorical organization of a fabula by an author or compiler that may readjust standard temporal or logical sequences[21]. The materials of the fabula may be restructured, for example, by the technique of flashback; similarly, the motivations of the characters may not be presented in logical fashion. A good example of this would be the relationship between the *Actus Vercellenses* and the text of Linus. This text tells the same story as the *Actus Vercellenses*, although there is no verbal overlap, and the text begins at a later point in the story. To these two categories, narratologists have added that of 'text,' the storyline told on one occasion by a particular narrative agent, for example, an oral performance, or a manuscript[22].

[20] Valantasis, 'Quandaries'.
[21] This is the general usage in literary-critical handbooks and dictionaries, cf. G. Prince, *A Dictionary of Narratology* (Lincoln, Nebraska and London, 1987), *s.v.* 'fabula' and 'sjuzhet,' 30, 87.
[22] Mieke Bal, *Narratology: Introduction to the Theory of Narrative* (Toronto, 1985) adds this third category of 'text' to the two already described by the Russian Formalists. See 5-8 for basic distinctions between the three categories, 119-50 on the topic of 'text.' In this translation, 'sjuzhet' is translated as 'story.'

These distinctions have explanatory power for the *AAA* because the overlap between these texts is often not at the *textual* level, but at the level of storyline, or even fabula. In sheerly narratological terms and apart from considerations of literary dependence, the three sources for the resurrection accounts of the *APt* adhere, not on the level of text or storyline, but on the level of fabula. The three accounts disagree fundamentally on the number of resurrections, their settings, and other salient details, while maintaining a sort of family resemblance; thus each attests a different storyline, although they should clearly be assigned to the same fabula.

If one were to reconstruct a resurrection account on the basis of the elements shared among the three sources, at its center would be the detail that Simon was able to move the corpse's head, but not to resurrect the body. Peter's exposure of the ruse is also crucial, as well as his verbal response, so markedly similar in the accounts of Pseudo-Hegesippus and the *Acts of Nereus and Achilles*, cited above, and also present in the *Actus Vercellenses*:

> *Si ergo hoc uisum est uobis, loquatur mortuus, surgat, si uiuit, solu<a>t[23] sibi mentum ligatum manibus suis, clamet matrem suam.*
> So, if this is agreeable to you, let the dead man speak, let him rise up, if he is alive, let him loose his jawbone from its binding with his own hands, let him call to his mother[24]!

In all three, likewise, the resurrected individual is a youth. Last, all three sources present the feat as an element in a contest, in which Simon's magic fails, but Peter is at last able to resurrect the youth by the power of the one true God. Although the exact spatial location varies, the dramatic location of the story in the macro-fabula of Peter and Simon is the same: it is a public event that occurs at a crucial turning point in the narrative, the point at which the crowd's allegiance shifts from Simon to Peter. It is the underlying purpose of the entire narrative to describe the causative event of this transformation.

Thus, the unchanging elements of the story among the various sources are the named characters, the basic action, the setting within the larger narrative of the conflict between Peter and Simon, and the

---

[23] Ms. reads *soluit*.
[24] Lipsius, *Acta apostolorum* 1, 76.12-4.

memorable details of Simon moving the man's head, and Peter's denunciation of this. It is worth noting that the versions of the story that come closest to the simplest form of the story, the base narrative, are not in the earliest account, but in the two accounts that offer an epitomization of the story. Pseudo-Hegesippus's account is a very brief epitome of the entire *APt*. In *Nereus and Achilles*, the contest is retold as an aside in a narrative that is essentially about something else.

It is the earliest account of the resurrections performed by Peter in his contest against Simon that is the most literarily complex and filled out with redactional details. In the *Actus Vercellenses*, the two initial resurrection accounts are intercalated[25]. The raising of the emperor's favorite must wait while Peter responds to the widow who cries out from the crowd. Her only son is resuscitated only after the emperor's favorite is brought back to life. Though these first two resurrections are juxtaposed in a rather baroque fashion, one that is difficult to visualize in cinematographic terms, the intent of the literary activity is sophisticated: the interruption heightens the suspense of the account by delaying the conclusion of the first resurrection[26].

The third resurrection story (28) stands on its own, but is closely linked to the second of the stories in that it, too, recounts the plight of a woman bereft of her son. Identifying the woman as the mother of a senator significantly undercuts the pathos in the 'situation of need' that opens the story. Such a mother is clearly not as vulnerable as a poorer woman, since she would likely have means of sustenance in addition to the earnings of her son, if he in fact worked at all with his hands; moreover, this account neither specifies the woman as a widow, nor her son as the only son. The introduction of members of the senatorial class, however, allows the expression of the central redactional concerns of the *Actus Vercellenses*. Other parts of the narrative stress the conversion of the senatorial elite, and their duty to

---

[25] The early Greek vellum fragment of the *APt* (*P.Oxy* 849) spans the transition from the first resurrection to the second, so the two stories were intercalated in the Greek text, even before the Latin translation.

[26] Stoops, *Miracle Stories*, 61 and n., understands the dramatic purpose similarly, noting that the treatment of the seams here is akin to what one finds elsewhere in the *APt*: they are placed at points where characters are speaking, and introduced by a temporal phrase.

provide for the less fortunate in the Christian congregation[27]. The leading figure of the community in Rome is one Marcellus, a senator who is led astray by the ruses of Simon Magus, but later restored to the faith by Peter's miracles and teachings. Characteristically, he progresses from being the patron of Simon Magus to offering his hospitality and material support to Peter and the Christian community. Other episodes underscore the importance of financial support to the fledgling church, and encourage acceptance of donations from any repentant individual, no matter how questionable their previous way of life. *C*.30 contains a discussion of the generous gift to the community by the wealthy but promiscuous Chryse. Against opposition, the apostle Peter argues that the community should accept it without further ado. True to these redactional concerns, in the resurrection account, the mother of the deceased senator is asked to promise a significant donation to the church, as well as continued freedom for the slaves manumitted upon the death of her son[28], before Peter will perform his compassionate act of resuscitation.

Because of its strong coherence with the interests of the rest of the *Actus Vercellenses*, the third resurrection in the *Actus Vercellenses* is the most likely candidate for a relatively independent literary elaboration: it expresses the redactional concerns of this text transparently, and provides a structural counterpart to the story of the poor widow and her only son by presenting a rich senatorial mother[29]. Doubtless this narrative doubling also represents sociological realities in the audience of the *APt*: one story appeals to the poor, the other to the rich benefactors. Yet the story of the senator's mother is not a complete literary invention; it occurs as part of a brace of resurrection stories, and shares crucial details with the base narrative as found in other texts: Simon's ability to move the head of the dead man, without actually resurrecting him, Peter's denunciation of this sham miracle, and

---

[27] See R.F. Stoops, 'Patronage in the *Acts of Peter*', *Semeia* 38 (1986) 91-100 and 'Christ as Patron in the *Acts of Peter*', *Semeia* 56 (1991) 143-57.
[28] See Bremmer, this volume, Ch. I.3.
[29] Stoops, *Miracle Stories*, 65, notes that this account is also form-critically composite, suggesting that it is a secondary elaboration; he similarly believes that motifs from a single traditional story may have been used to create two episodes, because of the interest of the author in the relations of the rich and poor in his community (217-9).

his subsequent success. In addition, as in *Nereus and Achilles*, the crowd threatens, before the contest, to burn Peter alive if he does not perform the miracle successfully.

Pseudo-Hegesippus and *Nereus and Achilles*, though later reworkings of the *APt*, are thus also evidence of a simpler base form of the story common to all three texts. Their knowledge of the *Actus Vercellenses* can neither be asserted nor denied. The later two texts at least show no knowledge of the peculiar redactional features of the *Actus Vercellenses*. Most tellingly, there is no senator's mother, and no description of her promise to give a donation to the community and preserve the liberty of the son's slaves. In addition, it is characteristic of the *Actus Vercellenses* to show the senatorial elite assisting Peter in his miraculous works. In c.11, Marcellus himself miraculously restores a shattered imperial statue. In c.26, it is the prefect Agrippa who takes the deceased favorite of the emperor by the hand and raises him. Agrippa also pushes Simon away from the senatorial son after Peter exposes Simon's trickery. These details are likewise missing in both of the later versions. It is striking that the two later texts not only independently preserve the same few motifs in common and reduce the three resurrection accounts to one, but also successfully strip their accounts of those peculiar details most characteristic of the redaction of the *Actus Vercellenses*. One could argue, however, that it is precisely these sorts of details that would be left out of a condensation of the narrative; the most that can be said is that the typical smoking gun of the literary appropriation of a written text, the preservation of its distinctive redactional concerns, is not present in these two later texts. The issue of dependence among these three documents is a *non liquet* situation. If not dependent on the *Actus Vercellenses*, the later versions might just as well know its sources, for the earliest version did have these as well. One must correspondingly discard the notion of the 'zero point' of an earliest source, and instead attempt to describe with greater specificity the peculiar freedom and creativity with which the putative sources are employed.

In contrast, the sixth act of the recently discovered manuscript of the *Acts of Philip*, Xenophontos 32, provides a counter example that represents a more textual use of the *Actus Vercellenses*[30]. It is an

---

[30] See the complete French translation in F. Amsler, F. Bovon and B. Bouvier, *Actes de l'apôtre Philippe* (Turnhout, 1996). The Greek text, edited

adaptation of the resurrection account in *c*.28 that attributes the feat to Philip, as the final proof in his contest against the Jew Aristarchus, a contest roughly parallel to Peter's against Simon Magus. Their verbal disputation of scriptural texts is interrupted by a funeral procession involving an only son, similar to Luke's account of Jesus. Thereafter, however, appear several details that are specific to the *Actus Vercellenses* and not found in Pseudo-Hegesippus or *Nereus and Achilles*: the parents are very wealthy; Philip forces them, as a condition for performing the resurrection, to free the servants who are carrying the bier; the parents promise also to donate further riches to the Christians; and, when the father wishes to attack Aristarchus and the Jews, Philip tells him that his son will not be resurrected unless he renounces his hateful purpose. The story also contains the detail, shared among the Petrine accounts, of the opponent's failure to raise the dead man by magical means; Aristarchus not only touches its face and takes it in his arms, but also spits upon it several times ineffectually. The relationship between the *Acts of Philip* and the *Actus Vercellenses* at this point is much more specific than that among the three Petrine texts: the *Acts of Philip* is clearly using only one of the three resurrection narratives in the *Actus Vercellenses*, instead of creating a composite narrative such as those in Pseudo-Hegesippus and *Nereus and Achilles*, in which the details from all three resurrections in the *Actus Vercellenses* are compressed into a single resurrection account. One may grant that the use of the *APt* by the *Acts of Philip*, both at this point and elsewhere, is nevertheless not very textual[31]. Yet, under the general umbrella of intertextual relationships, this is a more exact case of overlap than that adhering among the Petrine accounts.

The most striking feature of the narrative of the *Actus Vercellenses* is its presentation of three, rather than one, resurrection storie. For it is characteristic of this narrative to present distinct versions of the same story, variant versions of a base narrative, or multiforms, side by side in the text as separate events. Peter's arrest is doubly motivated: not only is the prefect Agrippa deprived of sexual congress with his four concubines because of their conversion to Peter's sexually continent version of Christianity, the wife of the senator Albinus

---

by the same, will appear soon as part of the Corpus Christianorum, Series Apocryphorum.
[31] See Matthews, 'Upside Down.'

also withholds her connubial companionship from him. Both of them act jointly to arrest Peter (33-4). There are also twin stories concerning Peter's daughter (Coptic fragment) and a gardener's daughter (*Epistle of Pseudo-Titus*), in which death or paralysis in response to Peter's prayers on her behalf is considered beneficial to the young girl, because they keep her from the pollution of sexual intercourse. Last, Simon Magus astounds the crowds by flying over the city of Rome, first upon his entrance into the city (4), and then again, as his last volley against Peter at the end of the narrative (31). The last flight results eventually in his death, since he falls to the ground when Peter prays against him. In all of these cases, the two versions of the story are similar enough to be understood as variants of the same narrative unit. The author, however, who seems to have at his or her disposal more than one version of each of them, presents them as separate historical events.

I would suggest that similar processes are at work in the case of the resurrection accounts. The author may have heard or read different versions of a single resurrection story that remained distinct in his or her mind: a version concerning the favorite of the emperor, in which Simon slays the boy, and Peter raises him; a version in which Peter raises the son of a poor widow, as Jesus did at Nain; and a version in which Simon demonstrates his insufficiency by moving only the head of the corpse, and Peter challenges him angrily before performing the act correctly[32]. The author filled out these materials as well as could be done. The first two accounts were lengthened and given a spark of suspense by their intercalation. The third, which was only built around the spare central detail of Simon's magical procedure, was expanded by analogy to the second resurrection account, and dressed up with redactional concerns from the rest of the narrative.

It is pointless to engage in a disputation about what the 'original' form of the narrative was, and which of the three texts best portrays it. Such an original form never existed in the sense that it never appears in pure form in any of the five versions in these three texts. The 'base

---

[32] Some details in the individual stories suggest that they may be multiforms. The detail of Simon slaying the emperor's favorite by speaking in his ear (*ad aurum pueri locutus est*) overlaps somewhat with the magical practice he applies to the the dead senator, in which he bends over him (*inclinans se*) to say something to him (the rest of the text is corrupt here).

narrative,' as I have called it, is a scholarly reconstruction. In terms of the history of composition, it represents the narrative elements, details, and motifs that were available to the individual authors. Some of these elements are treated as fixed in the various texts, such as the identities of Simon and Peter, and the fact that the resurrected individual was a young man. Some of the elements remain fluid, such as the exact setting, or the exact identity of the young man.

The possibility also exists that the base narrative attracted motifs over time through intertextual contacts. One could not determine for certain, for example, if the young man in question was 'originally' the favorite of the emperor or the only son of a widow. These two identities do not cohere well, and both of them are 'dependent' on some larger narrative complex: the first on the setting of the resurrection in a public dispute arranged by Roman officials that forms part of one version of the *APt*, the second on the intertextual connection with the Gospel of Luke. It is clear from the later versions of the tale in Pseudo-Hegesippus and *Nereus and Achilles* that both possible identities, widow's son and emperor's favorite, enjoyed success, and sometimes coexisted in modified form.

From this analysis, there are a few general points that bear emphasis. The first is the recognition that the 'base narrative' that describes the family resemblance between various multiforms of a story, although by definition the simplest possible version, may be neither the earliest nor the most original[33]. This is an important modification of a common assumption, based on an unnuanced application of form criticism, that simple is both early and most original. The authors of the accounts in Pseudo-Hegesippus and *Nereus and Achilles* had at their disposal at least as much narrative information as the author of the *Actus Vercellenses*, for they present in one concise form all the scattered details of the longer account. Their accounts are shorter because of their respective narrative contexts. Pseudo-Hegesippus is a very brief epitome within a much larger historical work; the *Acts of Nereus and Achilles* tell of the conflict between Simon and Peter as part of a letter from Peter's follower Marcellus to provide background

---

[33] This is the same anomaly presented by Matthews, 'Upside Down', esp. 16-7: he estimates that a 'more primitive' form of an agraphon is found in a text, the *Acts of Philip*, which is later than other texts containing the same logion.

information on Simon Magus to two young Christians who have encountered his disciples. Even between the two, the length and amount of narrative detail differ: *Nereus and Achilles* tell a better tale, with more description of the dramatic context and more dialogue. In the *Actus Vercellenses*, the earlier account by two centuries, essentially the same narrative material is worked up in grand scale because it forms the centerpiece of one of the main narrative units of the text, the contest between Simon Magus and Peter. Thus, the 'most original' form of the base narrative is in evidence when, for reasons that dictate concision, the story is told in the simplest possible manner, free of creative elaborations that would lengthen and complicate the account. Temporal priority has nothing to do with it.

Nor is the base form of the narrative the most original, because motifs, such as the widow's son/emperor's favorite, enter into the narrative stream at later points through the continuing creativity of the individual authors or storytellers within an intertextual context. This pair of motifs may never have figured in the first story about the confrontation between Simon and Peter, but, once introduced, they were retained because they were successful elements, useful in dressing up the narrative and lending it dramatic flair.

In conclusion, I have argued for an understanding of compositional processes in the narratives of the *APt*, and, by extension, in similar narratives in early Christian literature, which is a more elastic and fluid conceptualization of intertextual relationships. The multiple versions in this example are not mechanical doublets from multiple written sources. Nor are they multiforms in the sense of statically transmitted oral units. Instead, an elastic 'base narrative' would represent a combination of fixed and fluid elements: within the limits of the fixed items that are necessary to the recounting of a narrative unit, necessary to assure its identity as one story and not another, exist a fluid number of accessory motifs and details. These can be used to expand or contract the rewriting of the unit to fit the exigencies of the context, whether of length, of thematic unity, or of polemical concern. Even the limits of expansion are strikingly elastic: the *Actus Vercellenses* create three complete narrative units on the basis of this single complex of structures and motifs. The 'base narrative' thus does not operate without conscious authorial creativity. A 'base narrative' is also not a monolith, but can expand over time as individual turns of creativity become favorite motifs in the repertory of an individual story.

In theoretical terms, this understanding of compositional processes is not entirely new. At heart, it is related to form criticism, but shares some critical structural commonalities with generative linguistics. Instead of asserting a fixed relationship between social matrix and base form, a *Sitz im Leben*, the focus here is instead on authorial creativity. Thus, the issue of social matrix is not unaddressed, but translated to another level. Individual authors of written texts worked along much the same lines as did oral tradents, mixing and matching from a larger fund of narrative elements, and they did this in the context of the differing social and theological concerns of their audiences. This took place, however, not in an oral performative context, but *in writing*. Oral and written also had a seamless co-existence: individual written versions contributed back into the elastic fund of narrative elements, and elements remembered from other Christian narratives entered the stream. The written stories that resulted were treated not as fixed and privileged, but as examples of individual performances, as creative actions within the context of numerous narrative possibilities[34].

---

[34] This paper was presented at the SBL Annual Meeting, 23 November 1996, in New Orleans. My thanks to those who participated in discussion or later made comments, and especially to Robert Stoops, whose response is the source of most of the improvements in the present text.

VII. Who is Deviant? Entering the Story-World of the *Acts of Peter*

ISTVÁN CZACHESZ

'Upside-down' has been duly considered by recent literary critics as the ruling metaphor in the *Acts of Peter* (*APt*). The symbolism of Peter's hanging from the cross downwards (and especially his own teaching about it) allows various literary, linguistic, sociological, and theological implications. In her study about the social world of the *APt*, Judith Perkins sets out to read the text as one 'projecting a social and political agenda'. In Perkins' view, the *APt* has a message that 'plainly contests the prevailing systems of power'. Challenging various aspects of Roman society, including the emperor, the traditional classes, the system of patronage, and finances, the *APt* is 'issued from a community interested in constructing an alternative social structure'. Thus Peter's quoting Jesus about the necessity of turning 'what is on the right hand as what is on the left...and what is above as what is below and what is behind as what is before' is – according to Perkins – 'a message with obvious radical social overtones'[1].

In this paper we will suggest a less radical meaning of the notable 'upside-down' metaphor as a description of the social world of the *APt*. In order to enter the (upside-down) narrative world of the book, we will examine conflict in the *APt*, employing a specific literary-critical scenario[2].

---

[1] J.B. Perkins, *The Suffering Self* (London, 1995) 141 (twice), 137, 132, respectively.
[2] For now, let us define 'narrative world' very simply as an experimental 'playground' of its own rules, created by the author and the reader. It is the rules of this game that move the plot of the story, and we will describe some of these rules in the *APt*.

1. *Understanding conflict*

'Conflict' has more than one meaning in literary theory. According to Aristotle's *Poetics* (18), δέσις (complication) extends from the beginning of the tragedy to the occurrence of the μετάβασις (climax), including the introduction (τὰ μὲν ἔξωθεν, 'the outer parts') as well as some of the action (ἔνια τῶν ἔσωθεν, 'the inner parts') of the story. Complication thus produces tension, the driving force of the plot of the tragedy. This basic idea has been further developed in several ways in the formalist-structuralist tradition. Vladimir Propp in his fundamental study, *Morphology of the Folktale*, expanded the complication into a series of functions, like reconnaissance, villainy, mediation, counteraction and departure[3]. Whereas Propp examined the chronological structure of the Russian folktale[4], conflict in the 'deep structure' appeared as bipolar oppositions in Lévi-Straus's and Greimas' hermeneutics[5].

In this study, literary theory proper will be supplemented by Bruce J. Malina and Jerome H. Neyrey's socio-psychological approach to Biblical texts. Basically, we will utilize two models of conflict: (1) the challenge-response game and (2) the labeling process. With the help of these methods we will pursue the ('paradigmatic' rather than 'syntagmatic', see notes 4 and 5) analysis of individual conflict situations in the *APt*. Regarding the fragmentary nature of the *AAA*, it seems inadequate to establish any rounded-off 'plot' of the narrative. An analysis of conflict situations, on the other hand, helps us to enter the 'story-world' and understand 'the rules of the game' (see note 2), which is precisely what we call 'plot motivation' in narrative-critical terms.

---

[3] V.J. Propp, *Morphology of the Folktale*, tr. L. Scott (Austin, 1968²).
[4] This aspect of the story is also called the 'syntagmatic' or 'surface' structure. Propp himself sets out to identify the variations of the *sjuzet* (plot) in order to classify folk tales. He concludes by establishing a single 'formula' which depicts any of the stories in his collection.
[5] Borrowing Saussure's terminology, this is called the 'paradigmatic' analysis, cf. E.V. McKnight, *The Bible and the Reader* (Philadelphia, 1985) 49-54. An application of Greimas' 'actantial' theory to the Gospel of John is found in M.W.G. Stibbe, '"Return to Sender": A Structuralist Approach to John's Gospel', *Biblical Interpretation* 1 (1993) 189-206.

The challenge-response game is a model for social interaction in first century Mediterranean society[6]. People challenged others in order to gain honour from them by depriving them of their own. According to the model of 'limited goods' based on the division of land[7], goods could be divided and redivided, but the total amount always remained the same. This understanding was extended also to non-material goods of life. Honour, the supreme value of this society, was also limited and could be increased only if someone else lost it. The challenge-response game was the channel of this 'transaction'.

A negative challenge occurred when somebody was insulted or threatened. If the challenged person did not respond, he lost honour immediately[8]. If the challenge was accepted, then a counter-challenge was made, and a contest followed. The challenge-response game was a contest for honour between two equals, normally between two males. It may be regarded as the basic model of public communication, inasmuch as any interaction outside the household was seen as challenging the honour of the male.

While the model of the challenge-response game aims at describing conflicts between two persons in front of a community, deviance labeling describes conflicts between the individual and the community[9]. The goal of the labeling process is to declare someone as deviant, and push this person outside the society. Now let us examine the components of the deviance labeling model. The first three elements concern the social network of labeling, while the other three deal with the deviance process proper.

---

[6] In the discussion of the challenge-response game we draw mainly on B.J. Malina, *The New Testament World* (Louisville, 1993) esp. 28-62. Though Jan Bremmer called our attention to the differences between Roman and Palestinian societies, for now we will follow Malina's model of challenge-response and honor and shame as more or less universal models of social interaction in the first century Mediterranean world.

[7] See e.g. J.E. Stambaugh and D.L. Balch, *The New Testament in Its Social Environment* (Philadelphia, 1986) 65, 68, 74.

[8] The masculine pronoun is used because only males were challenged in this way, cf. Malina, *New Testament World*, 35.

[9] In modeling the labeling process we draw basically on B.J. Malina and J.H. Neyrey, 'Conflict in Luke-Acts: Labeling and Deviance Theory', in J.H. Neyrey (ed), *The Social World of Luke-Acts* (Peabody, 1991) 97-122.

(1) The *agents of censure* include persons who create rules and apply these rules to the behaviour of people. By means of new moral interpretations, they label something or somebody as a threat or danger.

(2) For the labeling process to be successful, new moral interpretations have to be publicly supported. This is achieved by *dissemination* and gaining *broader respectability*. Views are propagated in public appearances, alliances are made with groups and persons, and endorsement is sought from prominent personalities.

(3) The labelers not only want to gain sympathizers, but also totally to convert others to their point of view, and thereby develop a counter ideology. This is called the *rule enhancement*. Rule enhancers must create a pessimistic attitude towards deviance, so that people think it an intolerable evil.

(4) The deviance process itself begins with *denunciation*. The perpetrator is identified with some negative feature of human existence, e.g., sedition, idolatry, or blasphemy. The perpetrator is shown to be in opposition with respected figures: you have to condemn the perpetrator, or else you reject these respected symbols.

(5) Once a person is declared as a deviant, data from the person's life are sought to underpin this judgment through *retrospective interpretation*, and compiling the deviant's case records. Retrospective interpretation points out injury or harm that resulted from the deviant's actions, names the victims, and condemns the deviant appealing to God's will, the good of the people, or the honour of the nation.

(6) Finally, deviance labeling must be completed by a *status degradation ritual*. Such rituals publicly stigmatize the deviant. Trials are typical status degradation rituals[10].

2. *Christians as deviants*[11]

In the Gospels, conflict theory can be used to analyze the attacks upon Jesus and his disciples by representatives of the Jerusalem elite, the

---

[10] The spatial limitations of this study prevent a more substantial analysis of authority and discourse. The classical delineation of these relations is found in M. Foucault, *The Archeology of Knowledge*, tr. A.M. Sheridan Smith (London and New York, 1972) esp. Part II, 'The Discursive Regularities', 20-76.
[11] For a sociological analysis of discrimination and criminalization vis-à-vis early Christianity see E.W. and W. Stegemann, *Urchristliche Sozialgeschichte*.

priests, and other political factions. Jesus' labeling as a deviant and his trial in Jerusalem also shaped Luke's presentation of the ministry of the apostles. The moves of Jesus' trial are imitated in the deviance labeling of Stephen and Paul[12]. Peter, John, Stephen, and Paul equally 'rejoiced that they were considered worthy to suffer dishonour for the sake of the name' (Acts 5.41).

Deviant labels attached to Jesus include 'possessed by Beelzebub' (Mk 3.22), 'a glutton and a drunkard, a friend of tax collectors and sinners' (Mt 11.19), 'perverting our nation, forbidding us to pay taxes to the emperor, and saying that he himself is the Messiah, a king' (Lk 23.2), 'stirring up the people' (Lk 23.5), 'destroying the temple, and changing the Mosaic law' (Acts 6.14).

The apostles were likewise labeled as 'speaking blasphemous words against Moses and God' (Acts 6.11), 'saying things against this holy place and the law' (Acts 6.13), 'turning the world upside down' (Acts 17.6), 'acting contrary to the decrees of the emperor, saying that there is another king' (Acts 17.7), 'persuading people to worship God in ways that are contrary to the law' (Acts 18.14).

In Paul's trial the deviant labels are 'teaching all the Jews among the Gentiles to forsake Moses', 'telling them not to circumcise their children or observe the custom' (Acts 21.21), 'teaching everyone everywhere against our people, our law, and this place', 'bringing Greeks to the temple and defiling the holy place' (Acts 21.28). A list of Paul's deviant labels is given by the orator Tertullus: λοιμός (plague, pestilence), κινῶν στάσεις (agitator), πρωτοστάτης τῆς τῶν Ναζοραίων αἱρέσεως (leader of the party of the Nazarenes), who 'even tried to profane the temple' (Acts 24.5-6).

Altogether this makes up a comprehensive list of social deviance: demonic possession, libertinism, (high) treason, agitation, blasphemy, idolatry, sacrilege, and public danger. If all these labels were applied to Jesus and his followers, why were not all the leading figures of the movement put to death in a short time? The answer is what Malina

---

Die Anfänge im Judentum und die Christusgemeinden in der mediterranen Welt (Stuttgart, 1995) 272-305.

[12] D.P. Moessner, *The Lord of the Banquet* (Minneapolis, 1989) esp. 294-307, and L.T. Johnson, *The Acts of the Apostles* (Collegeville, 1992) 142-3, 165.

and Neyrey describe as techniques of *interrupting the labeling process*[13]. In their opinion, the Christian narrative applied neutralization and alternative interpretation in order to interrupt negative labeling.

In the *APt*, Simon Magus appears as an agent of censure interpreting the activity of Christians in Rome as a public danger. In his farewell address Simon uses three expressions to *denunciate* the Christian movement in Rome: (1) *perseduxit enim vos* (he deceived you, or ἠπάτησθε you are deceived), (2) ἀθεοτάτοι (most profane), and (3) ἀσεβεστάτοι (most impious) (31). Thus he creates a new moral interpretation of Peter and the Christians in Rome as social deviants: Peter is a crook, and his followers are atheists[14].

Simon also offers *retrospective interpretation*. Already in Marcellus' house he promises to demonstrate that Christians worship 'a Jew and the son of a carpenter' (14). Then in the Forum he depicts their God as 'Jesus the Nazarene, the son of an artisan and an artisan himself, whose family comes from Judea', and recalling Jesus' life and death he asks: 'Is God born? Is he crucified? He who owns a Lord is no God!' (23) This retrospective interpretation must sound highly reasonable because many of the audience answer: 'Well said, Simon!' Later on the *Via Sacra* he claims that the Jews had destroyed the Christian's God, and stoned his elected ones (32).

According to the *APt*, Simon seeks *broader respectability* by referring to the traditional values of uprightness and piety, and through his claim to be the agent (power) of God. These are in full accord with the similarly traditional charges he made about his enemies' atheism[15]. The *APt* also relates how successfully he disseminates his views for a while: under his influence, people denounce Paul as a 'sorcerer' and 'deceiver' (4). Marcellus, while under his influence, readily endorses Simon's views that Christians are 'impostors' (8). If Simon is able to gain back the support of prominent persons

---

[13] Malina and Neyrey, 'Conflict in Luke-Acts', 108-10.
[14] How far denunciatory phrases mentioned here and later in this study are based on Greco-Roman commonplaces or anti-Christian and anti-heretical polemic is beyond the scope of our study. Charges of atheism put into Simon's mouth here, however, certainly belong to the basic vocabulary of denunciation of the time, cf. V. Schmidt, 'Reaktionen auf das Christentum in den *Metamorphosen* des Apuleius', *VigChris* 51 (1997, 51-71) 57f.
[15] See previous note.

like Marcellus, he succeeds in having Christians labeled as social deviants. His final public appearance ('before all these onlookers') almost reaches its goal, as Peter's cry shows: '...all who believed on thee shall now be overthrown' (32). But Simon falls down, with his legs and the labeling process broken.

In sum, the *APt* depicts Simon Magus as a prominent agent of censure in the labeling process against Christians. How much the historical experience of persecutions and the actual deviance labeling of Christians influenced this picture of Simon would be difficult to trace back. Simon's accusations certainly include denunciative commonplaces as well as more specific charges against Christians.

It is logical to assume that Peter's martyrdom was preceded by a more successful process of deviance labeling. Here the *agents of censure* are the prefect Agrippa, and Albinus, the friend of Caesar. They form an *interest group* together with other Roman people who want to recover their spouses (34).

Albinus *denounces* Peter as περίεργος (busybody, troublemaker, 34), and Agrippa later adds to this the deviance label of 'atheism' (αἰτία ἀθεότητος, 36), echoing and summarizing Simon's charges (31, see above).

In *disseminating their views*, however, they are not any more successful than Simon. Not only the Christian congregation but also the people of Rome summon Agrippa: 'Answer the Romans' (36).

Peter's crucifixion thus fails to be a real status degradation ritual. It is rightly seen by the spectators as the cruel revenge of a mentally ill person. Agrippa acted out of madness. Without the support of the people of Rome, his deed was a private vendetta, and not at all an act of defending the moral order.

If Simon has the role in the narrative of demonstrating the powerlessness of charges against Christians, Agrippa and his associates' activity is to prove that atrocities on behalf of the ruling classes against Christian protagonists lack any public support and are in fact stimulated by the personal resentment of sick people.

3. *Challenge and response*

Both conflict situations can also be appropriately examined as challenge-response games. Simon's fall was actually the final episode in a series of challenges. The negative challenge is obvious from his mocking words. While he is carried up into the air, the faithful are looking towards Peter: the public evaluates the challenge-response game. If Peter neglects the challenge, he loses honour to the challenger. This is expressed in his desperate prayer: '...the signs and wonders which thou gavest them *through me* shall be disbelieved' (32). Thus he accepts the challenge, and the contest continues: '...let him fall down from height, and be crippled...' (32) His prayer is answered, and Simon falls down. The spectators then deprive Simon of his honour ('they stoned him'), and give it to Peter ('they all believed in Peter', 32). Here the challenge-response game concludes.

The conflict of Peter with Agrippa and Albinus presents a more complicated case. Here the challenge comes from Peter. Affected by Peter's teaching, four concubines of the prefect Agrippa, the wife of Albinus, and other women 'fell in love with the doctrine of purity'. Some men also ceased to sleep with their wives, which is, however, quite a different case.

In the Mediterranean world, a female was always embedded within some male's honour[16]. Consequently, any assault on a woman was actually directed at her husband. A husband who had no control over his wife's behaviour, was an object of mere ridicule. We can see now, how serious a challenge Peter's teaching of chastity represented for husbands in this society. Again, if Agrippa fails to respond, he loses honour to Peter, who has taken control of his concubines' behaviour.

But Agrippa does not fail to give an answer. On Albinus' advice he decides to have Peter executed, and thereby the challenge-response game continues. As Albinus notes, Peter's execution would also satisfy other husbands, that is, their honour would be restored, too.

Xanthippe reports Agrippa's intention to Peter, and now it is Peter's turn to accept or refuse the challenge. Running away would be a passive refusal, resulting in his dishonour. Thus he accepts Agrippa's challenge, and lets himself be caught and escorted to Agrippa. His behaviour, as well as his interpretation of the cross and

---

[16] For a discussion of honour and shame as pivotal values in Mediterranean society see Malina, *New Testament World*, 28-62; also B.J. Malina and J.H. Neyrey, 'Honor and Shame in Luke-Acts: Pivotal Values of the Mediterranean Society', in Neyrey, *Social World*, 25-65.

his death, transform the execution into a sympathy demonstration for Christianity. Even the pagan crowd condemns Agrippa, and when Peter concludes his sermon, 'the crowd that stood by shouted Amen with a resounding cry' (40).

That Agrippa did not actually gain honour through executing Peter is also attested by the emperor Nero's rebuke, who 'censured the prefect Agrippa', 'was greatly incensed', and 'for some time would not speak to Agrippa' (40).

We have examined two conflict situations in the *APt*: one between Peter and Simon, and another between Peter and Agrippa. In both conflicts Peter's adversaries attempted to label Peter and his followers publicly as deviants. However, the labeling process was not carried out successfully in either case. The difference is striking when we compare the crowd scenes in Jesus' and Peter's trials. In the Gospel narrative the crowd cries to the *prefect Pontius Pilate:* 'Crucify him!' (Mk 15.13-14). In the *APt* in turn the crowd cries to the *prefect Agrippa:* 'What harm has Peter done, Agrippa?... Answer the Romans!' (36).

The model of the challenge-response game showed that neither adversaries succeeded in depriving Peter of his honour. According to the *APt*, Christians cannot be labeled as deviants, that is, they affirm the moral order of the universe. In addition to this, they cannot be deprived of their honour, that is, they are *honourable,* and therefore, *successful citizens* of the Roman empire.

4. *Christians as labelers*

In the New Testament tradition as well as in the *APt*, deviance labels are not attached exclusively to Jesus and his followers. To cite a few well-known examples from the Gospels, Pharisees and Sadducees are 'brood of vipers' (Mt 3.7); listeners, Pharisees, Herodians, and scribes are likewise 'hypocrites' (Mt 7.5, 15.7, 22.18 etc.); Herod Antipas is a 'fox' (Lk 13.32); Jerusalem 'kills the prophets' (Mt 13.37); Jesus' generation is 'adulterous and sinful' (Mk 8.38); Jesus' adversaries are 'from their father the devil' (Jn 8.44)[17].

---

[17] According to Luke, Christians used deviance labeling from the very beginning, but this is not the appropriate place to analyze the cases of Bar-Jesus (Acts 13.6-12, magician, false prophet, son of the devil, enemy of all

In Acts 5.1-11 we read a short but comprehensive deviance labeling process. Peter acts as the *agent of censure* in the narrative, and interprets Ananias and Sapphira's behaviour as deviant. Their withholding the proceeds of the land qualifies as 'lying' (vv. 3-4), consequently, Ananias and Sapphira are liars. *Broader respectability* is sought when Peter claims that they in fact lied to the deity, the Holy Spirit (v. 3), or God (v. 4). The same idea is expressed later in that they put the Spirit of the Lord to the test (v. 9). *Retrospective interpretation* is pursued through a legal process. Peter poses questions to the perpetrators such as: 'Why has Satan filled your heart? How is it that you have contrived this deed in your heart?' *Rule enhancement* is achieved when 'great fear seizes all who heard it' (v. 5), and 'the whole church and all who heard of these things' (v. 11). Finally, the *status degradation ritual* is very spectacular: both 'liars' die in the same hour.

In the *APt*, Ananias and Sapphira's case is paralleled by Paul's rebuking Rufina. Paul, filled with the Spirit, recognizes that Rufina has just committed adultery. She is labeled as 'not worthy (*non digna*) to come to the altar', and struck with paralysis.

It is important to note, that similar to Ananias and Sapphira, Simon in Acts 8 appears as a convert to Christianity. He believed and was baptized. As with Ananias and Sapphira, the conflict begins with money (they wanted to keep it, he wanted to give it). He too sins against the Holy Spirit, when he wants to 'obtain God's gift with money' (v. 20). He is denounced by Peter as 'having no part or share in this thing', 'his heart not being right before God', being in 'wickedness', 'gall of bitterness', and 'chains of injustice' (vv. 22-23). Some *retrospective interpretation* (case record) is also given: Simon previously practiced magic, amazed people, and called himself someone great (vv. 9-11). Yet he is not finally labeled as a deviant in Acts 8, and the story concludes with his humble request for Peter's intercession (v. 24).

Denunciations of Simon in the *APt* are innumerable: 'wicked' (*improbus*) or 'most wicked' (*improvissimus*), 'troubler (*sollicitator*) of simple souls', 'deceiver (*seductor*) of simple souls' (9), 'shameless' (*impuderatus*), 'arch-enemy (*inimicissimus*) of all that live', 'cheat'

righteousness, full of deceit and villainy, making crooked the straight paths of the Lord) and the magical practices in Ephesus (Acts 18.11-20).

(*planus*), 'deceiver' (*deceptor*), 'cursed', 'corrupter of the way to the truth of Christ' (12), 'most hateful and foulest of men' (*pestilentissimus*), 'corrupter of my soul and of my house' (14), 'abomination' (*horrendum*), 'destruction of the truth', 'most wicked seed of corruption', 'fruitless one of nature's fruits', 'son of a shameless father', 'unfaithful creature' (*incredibile genus*), 'devoid of any hope' (15), 'messenger of Satan' (18), 'magician' (31).

The above list could certainly be extended, but it gives a picture of the various insults hurled at Simon by men, dogs, and infants in the *APt*. It is obvious, however, that Simon is denounced here not as an adversary of Christians but as a public enemy.

Retrospective interpretation of Simon's life is given superfluously at several points in the *APt*: magical practices (5) and burglary (17) in Judea, arrival in Rome (4), contaminating the senator's household (8). We have a rich *case record* of Simon the deviant.

Dissemination of the Christian point of view is achieved through the involvement of the senator Marcellus, large crowd-scenes, and especially the contest before the public in the Forum (22-29). Here senators, prefects, and officers witness Peter's raising of the prefect's slave and the widow's son, who later becomes a bishop. Then Peter has to come back to the stage to resuscitate a senator, as well. A learned christological dispute (23-24) also takes place in this scene, during which Peter demonstrates his scribal skill by quoting Old Testament loci. And, in order to ensure the audience of his expertise, he concludes: 'If you were versed in the prophetic writings I would explain all this to you'. Simon obviously did not have the slightest chance from the beginning.

The success of *rule enhancement* is demonstrated when Simon's former followers are ready to burn him at the stake in the place of Peter (28).

After gaining the support of the Roman elite as well as of the mob, compiling Simon's case record, and labeling him as shown above, the only thing left for the deviance process to be complete is the *status degradation ritual*. This is achieved through hurling him out of Marcellus' house, emptying chamber pots over his head, and chasing him out of Rome to live in a stable (15). The final act of status degradation is, however, the unsuccessful aerial display over Rome, which concludes with a symbolic fall, stoning, and deadly wounds (33).

5. Conclusion

In our brief survey of conflict we have tried to enter the narrative world of the *APt*. This text as well as the Lukan Acts witness the early deviance labeling strategy of Christianity. The labeling process against Christians gradually loses its gravity in these writings, while Christians develop their own labeling technique against behaviour they regard as deviant. This is attested by Ananias and Sapphira's death, the punishing of Rufina, Paul's conflict with magicians, and most importantly, by the series of conflicts between Peter and Simon.

In the narrative world of the *APt* conflict practically becomes 'showtime' for Christian protagonists, while attempts to label Christians as deviants always fail in the end. Rather than contesting the prevailing systems of power, as Perkins suggested, Christianity interprets itself in these writings as a *vivid subculture*. Here the deviant labels that were applied to Jesus and his followers in the early days are reattached to rival charismatic persons and erratic members of the Christian community.

The deviance labeling strategies we have seen include (1) *denunciation* in a variety of ways (as opposed to the rather stereotyped vocabulary e.g. of Simon); (2) *retrospective interpretation* making up a 'case record' e.g. from Simon's past in Judea and Rome; (3) gaining wider *respectability* and disseminating the Christian point of view among higher class citizens as well as lower class crowds, convincing people that the enemies of Christianity are public enemies; (4) *rule enhancement*, demonstrated by people's readiness to burn Simon; (5) *status degradation rituals*, punishing people with lameness and different kinds of death.

There are also considerable shifts from the Lukan Acts to the *APt*. Instead of the 'domestic' milieu of Acts 5 or 8, ever larger crowds witness the defeat of Simon. While Luke is content with having Ananias and Sapphira fall dead in a minute (πίπτω), Simon falls (καταπίπτω) spectacularly in front of a large crowd, breaks his leg in three places, is stoned, and dies after miserable sufferings.

Indeed, the narrative world of the *APt* presents a utopia. This is, however, far from being the Kingdom of God realized on Earth. While Luke depicted Jesus eating in Simon's house and a prostitute anointing him (Lk 8.36-50), the *APt* presents its hero praying for Simon's death and taking a prostitute's money with a lofty smile. While they themselves still suffer constant persecutions, Christians begin to play with the idea of power. While their martyrs are burnt at the stake, they comfort themselves envisaging their adversaries (and erratic members?) about to be burnt. No doubt, the narrative world of the *APt* is a world about to turn upside down: Christians are becoming deviance labelers.

VIII. 'For the Lord always takes Care of His own'. The Purpose of the Wondrous Works and Deeds in the *Acts of Peter*

MAGDA MISSET-VAN DE WEG

In the *Acts of Peter* (*APt*) the Christian faith in the living God and his son Jesus Christ is presented as a matter of words and deeds, or even works and deeds: 'We must put no faith in words, but in actions and deeds' (*Non est in verbis habenda fides, sed in operibus et factis*, 17). These often wondrous works and deeds also provide the setting for and set the pace in the *APt*, which is moreover not devoid of a great deal of direct speech, so that it reads 'presque à la manière d'une pièce de théâtre'[1]. The plot hinges on the battle between good and evil, between the power of God and the power of Satan. The protagonists of the drama are the apostles Paul and Peter and their adversary Simon the Magician. The apostles represent and proclaim the power of the living God; they are his messengers who through him perform wonderful works and deeds (28). Simon also claims to be the great power of God (*se diceret magnam virtutem esse Dei*, 4 and 31) and is cast as a pseudo-messiah, himself a god[2], but is gradually exposed as the messenger of Satan, the enemy of Christ, as a wicked shameless deceiver, a cheat, a robber, a sorcerer, a *magus*, a perpetrator of frauds, a deceitful demon, who operates through the cunning and power of Satan[3].

---

[1] G. Poupon, 'L'accusation de magie dans les Actes Apocryphes', in F. Bovon (ed), *Les Actes apocryphes des apôtres. Christianisme et monde païen* (Geneva, 1981) 71-85, 77.
[2] Cf. *c.*4: '*Numquid ipse est Christus?*'; '*Hesterna autem die rogabatur cum magnis adclamationibus, dicentes ei: "Tu es in Italia deus, tu Romanorum salvator..."*', and see L. Vouaux, *Les Actes de Pierre* (Paris, 1922) 247 nn. 4, 5.
[3] Most eloquent on the subject are *cc.*17, 18 and 31.

The fundamental differences between the representatives of God and the representative of every wicked thing under the sun blend into their actions, but also determine their motivations and objectives. For example, in sharp contrast to the greed and idolatry surrounding Simon – a statue is erected to honour 'Simon the young god' (10, 17)[4] – it is hammered home that the apostles are not motivated by the achievement of personal gain or glory (23)[5]. The apostle is humble and will not take credit for his actions because all credit should go to God. This is eloquently phrased in c.28:

> You men of Rome, seeing that I too am one of you, wearing human flesh, and a sinner, but have obtained mercy, do not look at me, as though by my own power I were doing what I do; (the power) is my Lord Jesus Christ's, who is the judge of the living and of the dead. Believing in him and sent by him...

The sea-captain Theon, who became one of the worthy servants of the Lord, is a witness to how the apostle can and should be estimated:... whether you are God or man; but in my opinion, I take you for a servant of God (5). To be sure, 'they' (the Romans) worship Peter like a god, but they have not been enlightened yet. Besides, an elaborate account of Peter's acts of unselfishness and care immediately follows. When he receives two thousand, four thousand and ten thousand pieces of gold, he praises God that the poor could thus be provided for (29-30). Just as these gifts are turned over to the poor, for the well-being of others, so are the wonderful deeds of God performed for the sake of others, for their sanctification (27).

The miraculous in many different forms is the main and essential ingredient of the works and deeds of both the messenger(s) of God and Satan. The apostle's healing miracles cause the deaf to hear, the

---

[4] See also Bremmer, this volume, Ch. I.2.
[5] According to P.J. Achtemeier, 'Jesus and the Disciples as Miracle Workers in the Apocryphal New Testament', in E.S. Fiorenza (ed), *Aspects of Religious Propaganda in Judaism and Early Christianity* (Notre Dame, 1976) 149-86, esp. 159, one of the major arguments in the larger debate on the difference between christian and non-christian miracle workers is that (pagan) miracles or magic is performed for self-aggrandizement through deceit and for the glorification of the performer who charges a fee and does more harm than good. Cf. Poupon, 'L'accusation de magie', 82-3.

blind to see, the lame to walk, the dead to rise. Because of what they witness the weak, including the believers and the neophytes, are strengthened, and many are converted to the Christian faith which promises them life for eternity (28). It is thus that through his servants, 'God cares for his people and prepares for each what is good'.

Simon, who opposes Peter through the works of his father the devil, performs miracles too, but it is made clear that he only seemingly cures the sick and makes dead people alive or makes spirits appear which 'had the semblance of life, but in reality did not exist' (31). He even causes much harm by means of his magical tricks, magic spells, magical arts and incantations. Besides, Simon flatters with words: 'with his soothing eloquence (he) perverted you with (empty) words and spoke of devotion to God with his lips alone, while he himself is wholly filled with wickedness' (17). His followers will have to look forward to the everlasting, unquenchable fire and outer darkness (*et tenebrae exteriores in omnia saecula*, 2, cf. 10, 12, 15, 28).

The differences between Simon and Peter are thus underscored by a dichotomy between magic and miracles. It is not only made manifest that Simon, whom Peter had already exposed as a magician before he came to Rome (*adprobatum magum Simonem*, 5), is indeed a *magus* but terminology related to magic is in the *APt* solely used to define the activities of Simon and his companions[6]. It is the refutation and exposure of all these doings as 'magic', together with, on the other hand, the confirmation of the signs and wonders as acts performed in the power of the Lord, which is at the centre of Peter's mission. This appears most clearly from the vision that contains as it were a summary of the main part of the *APt*:

> But when night came on Peter saw Jesus clothed in a robe of splendour, smiling and saying to him while he was still awake, 'Already the great mass of the brethren have turned back to me through you and through the signs which you have done in my name. But you shall have a trial of faith on the coming sabbath, and many more of the Gentiles and of the Jews shall be converted in my name to me, who was insulted, mocked and spat upon. For I will show myself to you when you ask for signs and miracles, and you shall convert many; but you will have Simon opposing you with the works of his father. But all his (actions) shall be

---

[6] E.g. *Simonem (...) multa mala facientem magico carmine (...) Simonem magica arte usum fuisse et fantasma facta* (17, cf. 5, 6, 8, 16, 23, 28).

exposed as charms and illusions of magic. But now do not delay and you shall establish in my name all those whom I shall send you.' And when it was light he told the brethren that the Lord had appeared to him and what he had commanded (16).

In the *APt* this dichotomy between magic, sorcery and the *mirabilia Dei* is primarily an extension of the good-evil divide, but also functions to rouse and underpin the negative response towards Simon and what he represents. At that time, accusation of fraud was a serious matter and although 'magic' was commonplace, magic and magicians were in fact generally illegal throughout the history of the Roman empire; a *magus* could therefore be feared or considered morally suspect. Consequently, one could try to discredit an opponent as a fraud or a *magus*, which is exactly what Simon's followers do when they call Paul a magician after he has left for Spain and Simon has set out to undo everything Paul has achieved, and to which Albinus, a friend of the Emperor, resorts when Peter has converted many wives who no longer wish to share their beds with their husbands[7]. In general, a conflict over magic was often a matter of labelling. From the standpoint of the accuser the *magus* or *magos* would be in league with 'wrong' powers or the demonic, while from the standpoint of the supporter he or she sanctioned the 'right' powers, representing the 'right' source, entailing the 'right' ends[8]. As has been indicated before, one of the main issues of the *APt* is the question who stakes the rightful claim to the power of God. In the *APt* this power is not to be associated with 'magic'. At the commencement of the big contest in the forum, after the spectators have demanded: 'convince us, both of you, whom we

---

[7] On the subject of the status of the *magus* see D.E. Aune, 'Magic in Early Christianity', *ANRW* II.23.2 (1980) 1507-57, esp. 1518-9; Poupon, 'L'accusation de magie' 71-85; C.R. Phillips III, '*Nullum Crimen sine Lege*: Socioreligious Sanctions on Magic', in C. Faraone and D. Obbink (eds), *Magika Hiera. Ancient Greek Magic & Religion* (New York and Oxford, 1991) 260-76, and his 'The Sociology of Religious Knowledge in the Roman Empire to A.D. 284', *ANRW* II.16.3 (1986) in which he notes that since the laws of the Twelve Tables, various magical practices were considered a crime in Roman law and magicians could face capital punishment.

[8] On the relativity of labelling and 'magic' as a value-judgment on the part of the author see Aune, 'Magic in Early Christianity', 1544; Phillips III, 'Sociology of Religious Knowledge', 2679; Czachesz, this volume, Ch. VII.

should truly believe', Peter speaks and once more underlines: 'For I believe in the living God, through whom I shall destroy your sorceries. Now let him (Simon) do the marvellous things he used to do, here in your presence'. It is an interesting feature of the *APt* that during the final show-down and despite his confidence, self-assurance and status, it is Peter who embodies the belief in and fear of the 'reality' of the magic performed in the power of Satan[9]. When Simon flies over the *Via sacra*, in face of the incredible spectacle Peter cries out for help to Jesus Christ, because, as he says, if he lets the man achieve what he has undertaken, Peter's entire mission will crumble because all those who believe will be scandalized (32). Other moments of flirtation with magic are, for example, the cursing of Simon (12, 14, 15) and the purification of the house of the Roman Senator Marcellus who sprinkles every corner of his house with water, calling upon the name of the Lord (19)[10].

Having sketched this framework of the battle between Peter and Simon, good and evil, I will now look more closely at some of the miracles and, taking up the dictum 'God cares for his people and prepares for each what is good'[11], seek to delineate what is good for whom, in what way and why.

Visions, appearances, voices from heaven, dreams[12]

The many references to visions, appearances, a voice from heaven, a dream, which are prevalent among the signs and wonders recorded in

---

[9] On belief in and fear of magic, which Christians shared with their contemporaries from every level of society, see e.g. Aune, 'Magic in Early Christianity', 1518-9; E.S. Fiorenza, 'Miracles, Mission, and Apologetics: An Introduction', in *Aspects of Religious Propaganda*, 1-25; Poupon, 'L'accusation de magie', 80-2.

[10] On magical power accorded to names and to calling upon names, see e.g. Achtemeier, 'Jesus and the Disciples', 151, who points out that 'already in the first century, the name of Jesus was understood to have a power of its own, e.g. Mark 9:39; Acts 3:6, 16:8 and in a negative context: Matt. 7:22-3; Acts 19:15'.

[11] *P. Berol.* (a): 'Know, therefore, O servant of Christ Jesus, that God cares for his people and prepares for each what is good'; *Cod. Verc.* 22: '(...) for the Lord always takes care of his own'; and cf. 1, 4, 20, 28, 36.

[12] On visions, dreams, etc, as miracles, see e.g. R. Reitzenstein, *Hellenistische Wundererzählungen* (Leipzig, 1906) 9 n. 4: 'Vision und Traum gehören in

the *APt,* are often markers of transition, several times accentuated by an instruction or command. For instance, Paul asks the Lord 'to grant what was good for him', whereupon he sees in a vision the Lord who says to him, 'Paul, arise and be a physician to those who are in Spain (1)!' Peter is instructed in a vision to go to Rome and later to return to the city (5, 36); Ariston is told to flee Rome, Chryse to bring gold to Peter (30), Nero not to persecute the Christians (41). In the vision quoted above, Peter is ordered by Jesus to enter the contest between Simon and himself. However, such wondrous events are also meant to encourage, confirm or strengthen the believers or the apostle, as appears from the following example:

> And when Peter heard this he was the more encouraged, because Marcellus had seen these things; for the Lord is always careful for his own. So cheered and refreshed by these words he stood up to go to the forum (22).

Whosoever receives the vision – ship-captain, inn-keeper, apostle, licentious woman or Emperor – or whatever she is told to do – go to Rome, fight the *magus,* bring money or abstain from persecution –, the Christian community is the main beneficiary, whether directly or indirectly. The visionary is the medium through which God provides for or protects his own.

'*Be helpless again*'

The first two miracles of the *APt,* which are found in the *Papyrus Berolinensis* and the apocyphal Epistle of Titus respectively, stage fathers and daughters and one mother in the margin. The daughters have no names, they do not speak nor do they display any activities; their role is entirely passive. The first girl is the daughter of the apostle Peter. Her father is rebuked because he performs many miraculous cures but leaves his beautiful but paralysed daughter lying helpless in a corner. Thereupon Peter orders her to get up and walk, but next reverses the miracle, ordering the girl to return to her corner and be helpless again. When the onlookers beseech him to reconsider, he

antiker Betrachtung (bei Christen wie Heiden) immer zum Wunder; sie zeigen das Wirken und die Kraft Gottes.'

explains how on the day of the birth of his daughter God had made known to him that the girl would grow up to become a stumbling-block to many if her body remained well. And, so Peter continues, this is exactly what happened. A rich man, named Ptolemy, saw the virgin, wanted to have her, apparently for 'corruption and shame', but finally left her on the doorstep of her parents' house, paralysed from head to foot and dried up[13]. The parents praise the Lord for keeping their daughter from defilement and violation. The attention then shifts away from the fate of Peter's daughter to Ptolemy who is blinded by tears of repentance and wants to commit suicide. He is 'made whole' again by divine intervention, becomes a true believer – one who sees with the eyes of his flesh and with the eyes of his soul' (cf. 21) – and is finally portrayed as both a spiritual and material benefactor of the Christian community.

The second girl is the daughter of a peasant, who asks Peter to offer a prayer for the girl. Peter prays and asks God to give her what is best for her soul. The girl falls down dead, which is interpreted as an escape from the shamelessness of the flesh and the pride of the blood, as heavenly grace and a divine blessing. This time the father asks for the reversal of the miracle and Peter obliges. Some days later, the daughter is seduced by an imposter and disappears.

It appears from these two miracle stories that (total) incapacity or death is deemed expedient for the virgin daughters and their fathers, even though the second father apparently does not understand this at first. Not only is such a fate presented as the only sure means to keep the daughters from defilement and violation, *id est* pure, it will also keep them from harming many souls, *id est* men. Wholeness of body and soul does, however, fall to the man who tried to violate the virgin, because of her became a believer and finally a benefactor through whom God takes care of his own. As there seems to be no other interest in or function ascribed to the daughters themselves besides what they mean in terms of their female body or as an object of male desire, the conclusion must be that the *APt* expounds the view that it is most expedient for the souls of virgins, and even more so for men, that they be no-bodies.

The ascetic notions, contained in this episode, are neither representative of the overall thematic pattern of the *APt*, nor of a special

---

[13] Due to a missing section, it is unknown what exactly happened to the girl or how she came to be paralysed.

concern of the author[14]. Asceticism unexpectedly appears again for a short moment when Eubola is ordered to despise and renounce this world (17); in Peter's prayer for the revival of the widow's son, 'Holy Father (...), who hast given us thy power, that through thee we may ask and obtain, and despise all that is in this world' (27), and in the martyrdom episode, as the immediate cause for Peter's martyrdom. As a result of Peter's proclamation of the *logos tēs agneias*, Nero's concubines Agrippina, Nicaria, Euphemia and Doris, as well as Albinus's wife Xanthippe and 'many other women besides fell in love with the doctrine of purity and separated from their husbands, and men too ceased to sleep with their wives, since they wished to worship God in sobriety and purity' (34). Nero and Albinus, who are furious, conspire and decide to avenge themselves and all those whose wives Peter has alienated, by killing Peter as a trouble-maker.

Two licentious women

In the episode working round to Paul's departure from Rome to 'be a physician to those who are in Spain' (1), a woman named Rufina is present when Paul is preparing to leave. The moment she comes forward to receive the Eucharist, Paul – filled by the Spirit of God – exposes the woman as a sinner because she has come 'from the side of an adulterer', exhorts her to repent, and threatens her with hell and damnation. At once she collapses, paralysed on the left side from head to foot and no longer able to speak. Whether or not the woman repents remains an enigma. Instead the attention is shifted towards the rest of the congregation and the miracle is put to a broader and more general didactic use, for the good of the entire Christian community. The onlookers are taught the lesson that they too are former sinners, which opens the opportunity for Paul to expound to them God's mercy and promises and to pray *inter alia* that the believers, thanking him because he proclaimed to them the word of God, may become established in the faith (2).

Eventually Peter must also deal with a woman of a questionable moral background. On a Sunday, senators, knights, wealthy women and matrons are present when Peter speaks to 'the brethren'. One of

---

[14] Cf. Y. Tissot, 'Encratisme et Actes Apocryphes', in Bovon, *Les Actes Apocryphes*, 109-19, esp. 115-9.

the guests, a very rich woman named Chryse, has been instructed by God in a dream to bring ten thousand pieces of gold to Peter. Some of those present exhort Peter not to accept the gold of a woman who is known for her fornications, but Peter laughs and says:

> I do not know what this woman is regards her usual way of life; but in taking this money I did not take it without reason; for she was bringing it as a debtor to Christ, and is giving it to Christ's servants; for he himself has provided for them (30).

What is the reader to deduce from these two sections of the *APt*, other than the stereotypical view of women as primarily sexual beings? Does Peter advocate an attitude opposed to Paul's view on sexual morals? Probably not. It seems rather that a licentious woman partaking of the Eucharist is the limit, not to be compared with a licentious woman donating money. The fact that it is God himself who provides for his own by miraculously instructing Chryse to bring the money to Peter seems to override everything else and may be the reason for Peter's laughter. None of this explains away the harsh judgement and treatment of Rufina, nor the fact that punitive miracles only hit a woman or the devil and his advocate. Apparently, when there is a way to make the community benefit, the pendulum is allowed to swing quite far, an aspect which this episode has in common with the story about Peter's daughter.

Two patrons of the poor

After Paul has left for Spain, Simon virtually undoes Paul's work, but God calls Peter to Rome to prove that Simon is 'a deceiver and persecutor of good men' (7). When Peter arrives in Rome, Simon is staying at the house of the senator Marcellus, a wise man, a former patron of the poor, for which he was even reprimanded by the Emperor. The evil one, like a ravening wolf, has, however, 'carried of this sheep' (8), whereupon he committed many sins. He beat pilgrims, and committed blasphemies and idolatry by erecting a statue which he dedicated 'To Simon, the young god.' After he has witnessed how a dog sent by Peter spoke to Simon, Marcellus starts to repent. Peter praises God and asks the Shepherd to receive Marcellus among the number of his sheep (10). But a young man, embodying a very bad devil, smashes a statue of Caesar, and Marcellus shows signs of a relapse; his fear of what Caesar might do is apparently greater than the fear of the everlasting fire that frightened him before: 'Pray therefore for me like a good steward of God, that I be not consigned – with the sins of Simon – to eternal fire' (10). He repents again. Both times, he pleads his own case in a stunning flow of rhetoric and convinces even God, for Marcellus is redeemed and rewarded when, as a result, he is allowed to perform his first miracle, which consists of making Caesar's statue (!) whole.

Before the contest in the forum takes place, Peter relates to the 'men and brethren' his first confrontation with Simon in Judaea. This episode, featuring Eubola, is in many ways the counterpart of the Marcellus episode. Both Eubola and Marcellus are rich and respected. Both of them are seduced by Simon and as a result commit the sin of idolatry; Marcellus maltreats the poor and Eubola her slaves, but Peter, supported and guided by prodigies, saves them both, inducing them to repent of their sins. In the end both become, or become again, patrons of the needy and the destitute, which is undoubtedly the aim of the miraculous intervention, or God's way to take care of his own, in these two episodes. This also ends the correspondence between the Senator and the lady. Eubola, the 'simple woman' who had been ordered by Peter to despise and renounce this world, donates her property for the service of the poor, supports the widows and orphans, clothes the poor, 'and after a long time she gained her repose' (17). In other words, her patronage is welcome, but she herself must remain in the background. To Marcellus, the 'wise man', and his house peace is granted. As a patron, a miracle worker, a visionary and an encouragement to the apostle, Marcellus, transforming his house into a *domus communis*[15], continues to play an important active role in the Christian community.

A talking dog, a talking baby and the revival of fish and children

Besides the miracles that can be grouped in pairs, two series of miracles take place, closely related to the contest between Peter and Simon. The first series starts with the miracle of the talking dog that

---

[15] G. Poupon, 'Les "Actes de Pierre" et leur remaniement', *ANRW* II.25.6 (1988) 4363-83, esp. 4374.

has been mentioned earlier. The big talking dog sent to Simon with a message from Peter – not for Simon's sake, but on account of those whom he deceived and brought to perdition (12) – does some more talking on its 'own' initiative. It abuses Simon, returns to Peter and dies. The onlookers are astonished, but some wish to see another miracle that will prove Peter and not Simon to be a servant of the living God. In the name of Jesus Christ, Peter orders a smoked tunny fish to become alive again and to swim like a fish. Very many who witness this do indeed believe and follow Peter (13).

A third miracle takes place in answer to Simon's challenge 'Come down, Peter, and I will prove that you believed in a Jewish man and the son of a carpenter' (14). This time a seven months old baby, assuming a manly voice, held by his mother who is told to remain silent, pours scorn on Simon:

> You abomination of God and men, you destruction of the truth and most wicked seed of corruption, you fruitless one of nature's fruits! But you appear but briefly and for a minute, and after this everlasting punishment awaits you. Son of a shameless father, striking no roots for good but only for poison; unfaithful creature, devoid of any hope (...) Jesus Christ says to you, 'Be struck dumb by the power of my name, and depart from Rome until the coming sabbath' (15).

The three miracles take care of the image of Simon, and at the same time confirm that Peter is the servant of the living God. And, as a result,

> a great number followed him and believed in the Lord, and they assembled by day and by night in the house of Narcissus the presbyter. And Peter expounded to them the writings of the prophets and what our Lord Jesus Christ had enacted both in word and in deeds (13).

Also, the onlookers 'glorified the Lord who had shown these things to men' (15).

The contest between Peter and Simon on the sabbath in the forum of Julius, consists of the next series of three miracles, through which three (young) men are restored to life. Firstly, the prefect Agrippa's slave is killed and revived. The prefect who wished to show his impartiality to both Peter and Simon, had summoned one of his slaves and ordered Simon to kill him, Peter to revive him. As this is exactly what both Simon and Peter achieve, one might say that neither of them fails. But this is not to be the point of this somewhat awkward section. The point is the reaction of the onlookers, the awakening of their faith. After Peter has called upon the Lord to revive the slave in his power and through Peter's voice, and furthermore has commissioned the prefect to restore the boy to life, the multitude does react and cries: 'There is only one God, the God of Peter!' (26). Secondly, in answer to the plea of an aged widow, Peter restores life to her son and commissions the son to take care of his mother after which he will be called to a higher ministry and serve as deacon and bishop. Again, this miracle is performed in view of the spectators, who after all were told by the prefect that they were to judge which of the two contestants was to be accepted before God, he who kills, or he who revives (25). As a result,

> the crowds were astonished at the sight, and the people shouted, 'Thou art God the Saviour, thou, the God of Peter, the invisible God, the Saviour.' And they spoke among themselves, being truly astonished at the power of a man that called upon his Lord by his word; and they accepted it to their sanctification (27).

The third miracle is again initiated upon the request of a mother. The revival of this son called Nicostratus, a respected, noble senator – curiously called a *puer* while the story unfolds[16] – will finally settle who believes in the living God, Simon or Peter. Peter, as the prefect did before him, asks the onlookers to be the judges and challenges Simon to revive the body. Simon fails, and the audience is at last converted from the magic spell he had cast on them. The spectators, consisting of the brethren and all who were in Rome, as well as of senators and prefects and officers, demand that Simon be burned. Peter protests, saying: 'For we have not learned to repay evil with evil; but we have learnt to love our enemies and pray for our persecutors' (28)[17]. Before Peter raises the son, he also stipulates that the mother must promise to set the slaves of her son free and he tells her to divide among the widows that which she meant to spend on the corpse of her son. On the day after the Sabbath, after her son has been restored to

---

[16] But see Bremmer, this volume, Ch. I.3.
[17] These words shed a peculiar light on the abuse and maltreatment Marcellus unleashed on Simon – cf. *c.*14.

her, she brings Peter two thousand pieces of gold. The grateful son offers the double gift and presents himself from then on as a living sacrifice to God (29).

Peter himself explains, as it were, the objective of this series of miraculous events:

> Men of Rome, this is how the dead are restored to life, this is how they speak, this is how they walk when they are raised up, and live for so long as God wills. Now therefore, you people who have gathered to (see) the show, if you turn now from these wicked ways of yours and from all your man-made gods and from every kind of uncleanness and lust, you shall receive the fellowship with Christ through faith, so that you may come to everlasting life (28).

The incomprehensible light

Prior to the contest in the forum, in the purified house of the patron Marcellus, Peter cures a blind widow. He then enters the dining-room where the gospel is being read. He rolls it up and explains that the scriptures contain only what is endurable to be understood by humanity, because no one is worthy to grasp or see the fullness of God's majesty, not even Peter. The words spoken by Peter are confirmed after he has prayed God to help other blind widows. An inexpressible, incomprehensible, indescribable light shines, so bright that it could neither be seen nor endured. The light, however, entered into the eyes of the blind widows. They not only regained their sight, but to each one of them the Lord appeared in a different form, either as an old man, a young man or as a boy tenderly touching their eyes[18].

The visions seen by the widows confirm Peter's words about the fullness of God which humankind can only grasp in fragments, because God is indeed greater than our thought (20).

---

[18] For the suggestion that this episode represents the gnostic view that worldly things lead to ignorance and blindness, a blindness that can only be removed by the light of true knowledge, see 'The Act of Peter (BG 8502,4). Introduced by D.M. Parrott, transl. by J. Brashler and D.M. Parrott', in J.M. Robinson (General ed), *The Nag Hammadi Library in English* (Leiden, 1988³) 528-31, esp. 529. Cf. also the episode in which Ptolemy is 'enlightened' so that he sees with the eyes of his flesh and his soul and the episode in which Nicostratus' mother asks Peter to bestow light upon her son.

In conclusion

An important aspect of the *APt* is that God's care for his people through miracles and other prodigies predominantly transcends the personal; the miraculous must be seen in the light of the well-being of the Church. Miracles strengthen the believers and establish them in their faith; miracles guide the *lapsi* or the lost sheep towards repentance, which will be rewarded by the Shepherd who will receive them among the number of his sheep; and miracles awaken faith, have a missionary function, are meant for the sanctification of outsiders, and thus add to God's own. The apostle, in particular the apostle Peter, fulfils an exemplary role. He who was tempted, betrayed Jesus, lost faith, repented and became a chosen one, is now portrayed as a mighty man of wonders, the apostle of Christ, the servant of the Lord. The miracles he performs are at the same time the legitimation of this apostle, himself not a magician, who outshines as a Christian miracle worker the celebrated *magus* Simon, and therefore ought to be believed.

IX. 'Head Downwards': The Cross of Peter in the Lights of the Apocryphal Acts, of the New Testament and of the Society-transforming Claim of Early Christianity

JÁNOS BOLYKI

In the novel *Quo vadis?* (1896) of the Polish writer, Henryk Sienkiewicz (1846-1916), the apostle Peter asks out of humility to be crucified head downwards, because he does not consider himself to be worthy of dying like his master. Is noble emotion the only reason for Peter's request? At first sight it seems to be. Furthermore, the aspect of humility seems to be strengthened by the other main character of the *Acta Petri* (*APt*), Simon, the magician – an enemy of Peter and of the church[1]. Simon is the type of the man who wants to follow Icarus by flying high – whereas Peter is the humble Christian hanging head downwards. Simon falls from the sky and shatters – the humble Peter is exalted by Christ. Is this not the antithesis between pride and humility depicted by the writer with the aid of an antithetical parallelism[2]?

The matter is not so simple, however. The text of *APt* never mentions that Peter asks his executioners to be crucified head downwards out of humility. We can read, nevertheless, that he justifies his wish in front of the crowd surrounding his cross. From his justification, i.e. from the words uttered from the cross speaking head downwards, we can see how Peter triumphantly embraces his destiny. As we shall explain in our thesis below, this is a self-understanding not only of Peter, but also of the author and of the early Christians – the first

---

[1] E. Haenchen, 'Simon Magus in der Apostelgeschichte', in K.-W. Tröger (ed), *Gnosis und Neues Testament* (Berlin and Gütersloh, 1973) 267-79. For Simon see also Luttikhuizen, this volume, Ch. IV; Adamik, this volume, Ch. V.
[2] K. Berger, *Exegese des Neuen Testaments* (Heidelberg, 1977) 73.

readers. This self-understanding is expressed in the claim that in the cross of Christ as well as in the cross of Peter one can see a turning point in world history, indeed a cosmic turning point. We wish to prove our thesis by first setting Peter's cross in the context of the 'staurology' of the *Apocryphal Acts of the Apostles* (*AAA*)[3], then by comparing our results with the staurology of the New Testament, and finally by showing the characteristics of Peter's cross that differ from the characteristics of crucifixion in the *AAA* and the New Testament.

1. Functions of the motif of the cross in the AAA

As regards the function of the cross within the apocryphal acts, we may observe three aspects: a christological, a martyrological and an abstract-speculative one.

1. We discuss first the christological function of the cross. There is a conversation between Andrew and Jesus which goes back to the historical Jesus of the synoptic gospels and which relates that following Jesus involves the abandoning of everything and the daily taking of one's cross. In a fragment of the *Acts of Andrew* (*AA*) that only survives in the Coptic language, Andrew reports that he always did just that[4]. Jesus acknowledges that this is true. Here the christological function is the obedience to the commandment of the historical Jesus. This obedience is rewarded by the glorified Christ (or even already by the historical Jesus?).

The situation is more complex in the 'Proclamation of John' in the *Acts of John* (*AJ*), especially in *c*.97 and following, where John receives a revelation from the invisible Christ in a cave on the Mount of Olives. The revelation is about the twofold shape of the cross, and about the superiority of the heavenly Christ over the earthly one. Scholarly literature rightly speaks here about the gnostic influence of

---

[3] For a different view see J. Smith, 'Birth Upside Down or Right Side Up?', *History of Religions* 9 (1969-70) 281-303, repr. in his *Map is not Territory* (Leiden, 1978) 147-71.

[4] J.Barns, 'A Coptic Apocryphal Fragment in the Bodleian Library', *JTS* 11 (1960) 70-6, I.verso 26-31, quoted by M. Hornschuh, 'Andreasakten', in E. Hennecke and W. Schneemelcher (eds), *Neutestamentliche Apokryphen II* (Tübingen, 1971[4]) 270-97, esp. 297 (no longer translated in *NTA*[5], but available in J.K. Elliott, *The Apocryphal New Testament* [Oxford, 1993] 271-2).

Valentine[5]. We have to see that the twofold notion of the cross (a cross of light and a cross of wood) points to the twofold existence of Christ. Their separation leads to docetic views according to which Christ had only a spiritual body. The Valentinian Gnosis offers also an evaluation: the Christ of the cross of light is superior to the Christ of the wooden cross. That is why John relates that he did not stay with the crucified Jesus on Good Friday, but fled to the Mount of Olives where the heavenly Christ showed him a cross of light in a cave. Christ also told him: 'First you should know the Logos, then you will know the Lord, and only in the third place will you know the man and what the man has suffered' (*AJ* 101.16-7). It is a characteristic idea that John who was the only one in the Fourth Gospel to stay with Jesus at the cross on Golgotha (Jn 19.26) here is to flee, even though out of compassion. He flees from the wooden cross to the cross of light which he perceives in a vision. This means that the divinity of Jesus and the work of salvation is not shown to the writer of *AJ* after the death and resurrection of Jesus but simultaneously, parallel to the wooden cross on Golgotha, in the cross of light. We have to notice, in short, that a docetic staurology actually implies a docetic christology.

It is different with the cross event of *APt*. Here Peter perceives that by uttering the name of the cross one utters the ineffable name, i.e. that of Jesus. This means that Jesus being the Christ is inseparable from the cross. Although there is a mention of a twofold cross in *APt*, it is done in a different way from that of *AJ*. The twofold character of the cross in *APt* means that for those who have their hope in Christ (37) the visible cross will be transformed into the cross of Christ's suffering. In other words the cross points beyond itself not to another cross but to the secret and salvific role of the actual cross.

2. The martyrological function of the cross is to be examined next. In the *APt* the cross is the symbol and means of martyrdom. Peter takes up the cross out of love for Jesus. Although he once wanted to keep back Jesus from the cross (Mt 16.22), he now takes his cross willingly upon himself although he himself in turn is warned by the congregation

---

[5] M. Hornschuh, 'Die Apostel als Träger der Überlieferung', in Hennecke and Schneemelcher, *Neutestamentliche Apokryphen II*, 41-52, esp. 51 (not in fifth edition); G. Luttikhuizen, 'A Gnostic Reading of the Acts of John', in Bremmer, *AAJ*, 119-52, esp. 145.

not to do so (35). He not only takes up the cross but he wants to testify to it in word and deed. This kind of testimony is the original meaning of martyrdom. The place of this testimony – martyrdom – is the cross (37).

Turning back to the scene of Sienkiewicz in *Quo vadis?*, we remember the occasion when Peter who is about to leave Rome in order to flee execution meets the Lord who is arriving at the city. 'Where are you going?', asks Peter. Jesus answers, 'I go to Rome in order to be crucified in your place.' Peter replies, 'Are you to be crucified again?' 'Yes, Peter, I am to be crucified again,' comes Jesus' answer. From this Peter understood his task. He beheld Jesus ascending to heaven, and then he himself turned back to Rome. He was full of joy and he praised the Lord because the Lord said he was to be crucified, but this now was to happen to Peter instead (end of 35). Peter understood that the second crucifixion of Jesus was nothing other than Peter's own crucifixion: what happened to Jesus happens to Peter. The martyrdom of the apostle continues the suffering of Jesus.

We can see a similar idea in Col 1.24 where Paul says that he fills up that which is lacking in the sufferings of Jesus, for his body which is the church[6]. This idea does not contradict the New Testament view according to which Christ's suffering cannot be repeated: his salvific suffering is carried out once and for all (Heb 9.28, 10.10, 12, 14, 18.18). To this suffering nothing can be added. This view maintains, however, that the suffering of Peter and Paul is a continuation of Christ's suffering in the church, albeit not with a soteriological but with a martyrological aim. The sacrifice of life is a testimony for the sake of mission and for the building up of the church.

In the Greek *AA* the main character longs for martyrdom. He leaves everybody else behind, steps up to the cross and speaks to it (Mart. II.4 and I.14). He and the cross have already waited for one another. When Andrew is to be taken down from the cross after two days' suffering he prays to Jesus and the Father that he should not be

---

[6] The majority of scholars do not think that Paul wrote Colossians, cf. W.G. Kümmel, *Einleitung in das Neue Testament* (Berlin, 1983[11]) 298-306. However, since the city was destroyed in AD 62 and remained uninhabited for a long period, the letter had to be written prior to that destruction by an earthquake. So, if it was really addressed to the Colossians, then from the point of view of dating it could have been written by Paul.

humiliated but that he might receive the glory of martyrdom on the cross. His leaving (*exodos*) in this way may be a help toward other people's entrance (*eisodos*) to eternal life.

In the *Acts of Paul* (*AP*) Thecla on the funeral pyre stands with her body in the shape of a cross (22). This reminds the reader of the fact that the cross is there in every kind of martyrdom[7].

3. The abstract speculative function of the cross is to point beyond itself. We have an example in the personified cross in the Martyrdom of Andrew (I.14f.): 'Hail, Cross...' In a similar way in the *APt* (37) the apostle before his crucifixion expresses the wish that those who trust in Christ should be able to see an invisible meaning behind the visible cross. He refers to Christ's suffering when he tells them that the cross should not simply mean what they can see in it; its meaning is much more than its appearance (*para to phainomenon*). In this way the cross points beyond itself. The cross becomes a mystery (*mysterion, sacramentum*). In *AA* 34, Andrew says in prayer: 'I hang up on your mystery' (i.e. the cross). Among the *AAA* it is the *APt* in which we can observe the character of the cross as mystery most clearly. In cc.37-8 we find the word *mystery* six times. The name (i.e. the essence)[8] of the cross is called a hidden (*apocryphon*) mystery (Greek *APt* ed. 8.2f). The cross is not simply what it seems to be (8.6). It is the secret of salvation (8.15) and indeed of the whole of nature (*physis*). The cross is the secret of everything that was 'in the beginning' (9.4). Peter says on the cross that the Lord had already spoken about the secret of the cross in a mysterious way (*en mysterioi*) (9.13).

How can the secret of the cross be understood? Its meaning is disclosed by revelation. In this context, *APt* uses verbs that are used in the New Testament for the revelation of mysteries of belief (*phainoo, gnorizo, apocalypto, anaggello*, etc.)[9]. Even Peter confesses that once

---

[7] See also Bremmer, *AAP*, 49.
[8] H. Bietenhard, 'Name', in L. Coenen, E. Beyreuther and H. Bietenhard (eds), *Theologisches Begriffslexikon zum Neuen Testament* II (Wuppertal, 1972³) 958-63. In biblical thought, the name carries the essence; it also means the person referred to, the personified object and its power: 'Der Name Jahwes wird (fast) zu einer Hypostase Jahwes' (959) and 'Im Name Jesu ist der ganze Gehalt der in Jesu geoffenbarten Heilswahrheit beschlossen' (962).
[9] G. Bornkamm, 'Mysterion im NT', in *TWNT* IV, 823-31, esp. 827: 'Das Mysterium ist nicht schon Offenbarung, sondern Gegenstand der

he did not understand all this. These things were hidden from him but the Word of Life that is Christ had revealed the secret of the cross to him (9.1-2).

In this way the cross in the *AAA* becomes an ordering principle of the universe (cosmos). It takes up the same role as the Logos in John's Prologue. The cross is explicitly called Logos in *AA* (Mart I.14), *AJ* (98) and *APt* (38). It has a role in keeping the created world together (*AJ* 99 and *AA* Mart I.14). The cross gives structure to the universe. The vertical beam connects heaven with earth. This is nicely expressed in *AA*, 'I have founded you in the depths so that you might connect those things that are under the earth with those things that are in heaven' (Mart I.14). The cross has not only a connecting role, but also a separating one. Its horizontal beam holds back the evil spiritual powers. As we can read at the same place, 'Your other part stretches to right and left so that you might force the awful enemy to flee.' *AJ* expresses a similar idea when it says, 'To the right and to the left are places where there are spiritual powers, demons, evil influences, threats and Satan' (98).

To summarize, we may refer to one of the commentators of *AA* who calls this book 'a Christian Odyssey'[10] and who even wrote an essay about the connection between Odysseus's mast and Andrew's cross. Just as the mast enabled the Greek sailor to cover large distances – and by this means it became a world-unifying principle – so the cross has become the same principle for the writer of the *AA*. In the *AAA* the spirit of Antiquity has been transformed; the mast has been turned into the cross. There is no better way of summarizing the function of the cross in the *AAA*.

2. *The canonical Acts and the Pauline theologia crucis*

If our aim is to observe the development of the teaching about the cross in the *AAA* (historical aspect) and to evaluate its content

Offenbarung: es begegnet darum fast immer in Verbindung mit Ausdrücken der Offenbarung'.
[10] D.R. MacDonald, *The Acts of Andrew and the Acts of Andrew and Matthias in the City of the Cannibals* (Atlanta, 1990) 53-5, esp. 53: 'Several aspects of the AA indicate its authors wanted to write a Christian Odyssey.'

(dogmatic aspect), then we have to compare this teaching with the canonical New Testament texts that precede the *AAA* in time. In the Gospels there is only one occasion where the cross is mentioned in a metaphor: in the saying of Jesus about one's denying oneself for the sake of the following of Christ (Mk 8.34). Otherwise it occurs always in its primary meaning as a means of execution. We do not have to discuss these occurrences for our present purposes. The canonical Acts do not use the term *stauros*, but rather the term *xylon* for the cross (cf. Deut 21.23: cursed is everyone who hangs on a tree). Peter uses the latter term in his two speeches: once before the Sanhedrin (Acts 5.30), and once in the house of Cornelius (10.39). In both places *xylon* means the tree of curse or the tree of shame. Christ was hung there as the consequence of our sins, but God rescued him from there by the resurrection as a vindication. This means that God judged the cross in a different way from men. Thus the cross in the canonical Acts has the function of showing the huge contrast between the judgment of God and that of men. The cross also shows that God's judgment prevailed in the resurrection.

It is well known that in the New Testament it is Pauline theology that says most about a figurative meaning of the cross. *Theologia crucis* is the heart of Pauline teaching[11]. Everything takes its departure from here and returns here. This theme would deserve a separate study, but I will limit myself to three aspects here: a soteriological, an apologetic-polemical and an ethical.

From a soteriological point of view Paul's teaching about the cross emphasises that this was the lowest point in the self-emptying of Jesus and in the humiliation in his human existence: 'He humbled himself and was obedient unto death, even unto death on the cross' (Phil 2.8). It is at the lowest point in the life of Christ that he was able to give most to men: salvation, *soteria*. That is why the apostle holds that the preaching of the cross is 'God's power' to those who are saved. It is the cross which unites the two nations, Jew and Gentile, with one another and which unites them both with God, because Jesus 'put to death the enmity through the cross' (Eph 2.16). Colossians gives a striking teaching about the cross in two places. According to Col 1.20, Jesus achieved peace between things in heaven and things

---

[11] E. Brandenburger, 'Kreuz', in Coenen *et al.*, *Theologisches Begriffslexikon* II, 817-26.

on earth 'through his blood shed on the cross'. Col 2.14 says that Jesus set aside the 'bond which stood against us with its legal demands (because it contained the list of our sins)..., nailing it to the cross.'

Where does the centre of the apologetic-polemical aspect of Paul's teaching about the cross lie? It lies in the twofold role of the cross: by judging men it separates and unites as well. The cross separates believers from non-believers, but it unites believers who come from different national and religious backgrounds. The preaching of the cross separates those who see a 'scandal' or 'foolishness' in it from those who see 'God's power and wisdom' in it (1Cor 1.18-25). Paul presents the cross as power and wisdom to the Corinthians who seek after religious, enthusiastic experiences (1Cor 1.24). But he also presents the cross as the only object of religious boasting to the Galatians who are tempted to turn back to legalism (Gal 6.12-4). If the Galatians are not prepared to suffer for the sake of the cross, then they will inevitably glory in the flesh (Gal 6.12).

Finally, Paul's ethics grow out of his teaching concerning the cross. According to Gal 6.14, it is because of Christ's cross that Paul died for the world and the world for Paul. 'World' in this context means the old self, worldly thinking, sinful nature, an attitude against God, and it also means temptations. Whatever once spelt the world's temptation for Paul, for example his old reliance on pharisaic efforts, is now crucified together with Christ. In the same way, whatever might emerge as a temptation from within – from Paul's instincts, his sinful desires – is now crucified. That is why Paul calls those who refute the ethical power of the cross by their life-style the enemies of Christ's cross (Phil 3.18). Paul can weep about this (ibid.). Thus for Paul the cross is not a form (we do not even know whether he saw before himself a cross *commissa* or a cross *immissa*), but a norm – a norm that shows the depth of God's love and the ethical quality of man's sanctified life. It is important for him that the preaching of the cross should not lose its power (1Cor 1.17b) through human philosophising. Philosophy can only weaken that which was given as a regenerating power to those who believe in Christ. Indeed, the cross can be appropriated only by faith, both from a dogmatic and from an ethical point of view (1Cor 1.21b).

If we compare all this with the teaching of the cross in the *AAA*, we can observe a change in emphasis in comparison with Pauline 'staurology'. The canonical writings start from the general meaning of the term 'cross' (i.e. a place of execution), and from there they approach the concrete, specific meaning (the cross of Christ, the place of salvation). The *AAA* start from the concrete (the cross of Christ), and from there they go on to a transcendent meaning, and eventually they arrive at a world-explaining principle. Furthermore, the canonical writings attach a soteriological and ethical meaning only to the cross of Jesus Christ, whereas the apocryphal writings tend to attribute a cosmological significance to the cross, a significance that started at the creation, i.e. long before Jesus died on the cross. In the canonical writings the cross has primarily a soteriological significance: men believe in the crucified Christ and thereby gain a new existence. In the apocryphal writings the cross becomes an over-arching principle that reveals the structure of the cosmos. Finally, in the *AAA* the cross is the end of ethics in as much as man's supreme ethical deed is to accept martyrdom on the cross. Contrary to this view, for Paul the cross is the beginning of ethics. At the cross the old debts of the sinner are met and man becomes free to live a new life with the strength of the cross of Christ in order to follow the paradigm of the sacrificial life of Jesus.

3. *Wherein lies the special character of Peter's cross?*

In our subtitle above we on purpose avoid using the plural, because we have seen that almost all the elements of the story of Peter's crucifixion can be found in the other apocryphal writings and/or the New Testament. There is only one characteristic that is absent from all other martyr stories or staurological treatises, and that is the fact that he is crucified *head downwards*. We can say then that therein lies the special characteristic of *APt*. In the introductory thoughts we saw that this element is not an expression of humility. On the contrary, behind it lies a conscious embracing of a destiny and a high claim that Peter's crucifixion presents a turning point in world history. How can we make this plain? It is not difficult, because it is Peter himself who discloses the meaning:

> For the first man, whose likeness I have in (my) appearance, in falling head-downwards showed a manner of birth that was not so before; for it was dead, having no movement. He therefore, being drawn down – he who also cast his first beginning down to the earth – established the

whole of this cosmic system, being hung up as an image of the calling, in which he showed what is on the right hand as on the left, and those on the left as on the right, and changed all the signs of their nature, so as to consider fair those things that were not fair, and take those that were really evil to be good. Concerning this the Lord says in a mystery, 'Unless you make what is on the right hand as what is on the left and what is on the left hand as what is on the right and what is above as what is below and what is behind as what is before, you will not recognize the Kingdom'[12]. This conception, then, I have declared to you, and the form in which you see me hanging is a representation of that man who first came to birth. You then, my beloved, both those who hear (me) now and those that shall hear in time, must leave your former error and turn back again; for you should come up to the cross of Christ' (38).

Thus the crucifixion head downwards points to 'the first man', who arrived on earth head downwards. Who is this 'first man'? He cannot be simply the Adam of the Old Testament, because we do not read this about him in Gen 1-3. The 'first man' to whom Peter refers must be the first man of the cosmogonical-anthropological myth of the gnosis[13]. This myth exists in many variations. It speaks about the first man who fell out of the divine sphere. This man became a captive of matter on earth. His redemption will occur when he will be freed from this captivity. As Luttikhuizen puts it: 'A portion of divine light fell apart and came down into the dark world.' Or, in the words of another scholar: 'Der Urmensch... stürtzt hinab und wird von der Natur ergriffen...'[14]

From Peter's words – quoted above – it appears that it was the ancient man, who fell upon earth head downwards, who formed the face of the world. He also formed its concepts as one that is hung up

---

[12] The fullest quotation can be found in the Gospel of the Egyptians, see W. Schneemelcher, 'The Gospel of the Egyptians', in *NTA* I, 209-15, esp. 213. It is also connected with the idea of 'being like little children' in the Coptic *Gospel of Thomas* (logion 37). Apart from *APt* 38, it is also quoted in *ATh* 147 and in *Acta Philippi* 140.

[13] See also Smith, *Map is not Territory*, 166-8.

[14] Luttikhuizen, 'Gnostic Reading', 140; *CHT* 14; K.M. Fischer, 'Adam und Christus', in K.-W. Tröger (ed), *Altes Testament, Frühjudentum, Gnosis* (Berlin, 1980) 283-98, esp. 290; R. Haardt, 'Schöpfer und Schöpfung in der Gnosis', *ibidem*, 37-48, who speaks of 'depravations' and of 'Abfallbewegung' (41).

'head downwards'. That is why in this world everything is the opposite of the heavenly realities. That which should be on the right hand side, is in fact on the left. That which is not beautiful is held to be beautiful. Evil things are said to be good. This means that the 'upside down' world affects man's concepts, his orientation in the cosmos, his aesthetics and his ethics. One can get away from this upside down world – says Peter in his exhortative speech – if one listens to Christ's word. Christ wants us to reverse all that points into a wrong direction, because this turning back is the condition of entering the Kingdom (of God).

Who can be a better example for reversing this world's corrupted order than Peter who is hung up on the cross head downwards? According to the word of the Lord, Peter is able to see the world, its concepts and values in their right order and direction. That which is seen by Peter can – because he is hung up head downwards – agree with the heavenly realities: Peter can see on the right hand side what the others – standing on earth – would see on the left, etc. He has put an end to the ancient 'error', and he has already 'turned back'. At least, this is what he himself claims. What is left to be done is that the others – those present and also the future listeners – should follow him[15]. Those who listen to him and follow his example will change the dimensions of their life and of their whole environment. They will be saved from the upside down world and will know the Kingdom, i.e. they will enter it.

4. *Conclusion*

To summarize, we may affirm that the motif of being crucified head downwards, as well as the words of Peter, express the self-understanding of the author of *APt* and that of the first readers, i.e. certain second-century Christians. It presents a high claim and a program. It

---

[15] This saying directs us toward acknowledging the truth in the movement of reader-response criticism which distinguishes in narratives between a real reader and an implied reader, cf. A.C. Thiselton, *New Horizons in Hermeneutics* (Grand Rapids, 1992) 516-29. In our text Peter himself distinguishes between his present and future listeners (readers). The 'present listeners' are themselves actors in the narrative, but his future readers should become 'ideal' or 'implied' readers by interacting with the text when they read it.

claims nothing less than a 180 degree turning back of the religious, cultural, and ethical life, and indeed the reversal of the values (and perhaps also the changing of the power relations) in the Roman Empire. Did the author and the first readers have in mind a historical change of the grandeur of Constantine's Empire? Did they think of the possibility that Christianity might become an accepted religion and then even the religion of the state? Or did they simply carry out the implications of Jesus' saying about the leaven (Mt 13.33): the gospel will have a permanent effect upon the status quo of every age; the gospel will transform society until it would be 'all leavened', that is, become Christian?

X. Cross and Death in the Apocryphal Acts of the Apostles

MONIKA PESTHY

Anybody reading the story of Peter's death in the *Acts of Peter* (*APt* 36-41) for the first time is bound to be struck by its strangeness: Peter imitates Christ but does so in an inverse way, he addresses the cross as if it were alive, what this all might symbolize, and finally, Peter hangs on the cross head down and carries on a long conversation without showing any sign of uneasiness. Of course, when one becomes more familiar with Christian apocryphal literature one reads the story with a different eye; yet the strangeness remains.

In this chapter, I do not intend to undertake a detailed commentary or analysis of this passage: much has already been said and written about it, and there are numerous details in the story which I cannot explain; all I wish to do is to discuss some of the problems related to the passage. The questions I shall examine are the following:

1. What is the significance of an apostle's death in the *Apocryphal Acts of the Apostles* (*AAA*) in general?

2. What happens in the two unusual instances, in which an apostle is crucified[1]?

---

[1] One question which emerges all the time in connection with these topics and which I shall try to avoid as far as possible is whether the *AAA* or the passages examined are gnostic or not, or to what extent they are gnostic. For example, in connection with the scene of Peter's death, L. Vouaux, *Les Actes de Pierre* (Paris, 1922) 435-59 argues that it is completely orthodox, whereas A. Orbe, *Estudios Valentinianos, V. Los primeros herejes ante la persecución* (Rome, 1956) 176-212 explains it from a Valentinian point of view. It is not the aim of this contribution to take a position on the question.

1. *Painless death*

All of the five major *AAA* constituting the subject of the present series of volumes end with the death of the apostle and, with the exception of John's, it is a violent death: the apostle is executed because of his teaching. Thus it would seem that the apostle, on the one hand, imitates Christ and on the other hand becomes an example for the martyrs; that is to say, his death constitutes a link between the passion of Christ and the death of the martyrs[2]. To verify this statement, let us survey briefly the way each apostle died. My special interest is in the behaviour of the apostle[3].

Arriving at the place of execution, Peter calms the crowd and delivers a speech to them. Then he goes to the cross and, standing there, addresses it. Having finished his prayer, he summons his executioners to accomplish their task and demands that they crucify him upside down. Hanging on the cross in this way, he continues to speak to his listeners for a prolonged period and, with the last 'amen', he delivers his soul to his Lord.

Paul is sentenced to be beheaded. On the way to the place where he is to die he converts and instructs his two guards and he even has to console them because of his death. Nero sends two other persons to determine whether the sentence has been carried out, and they find Paul conversing with his guards. After some conversation, Paul gets up, turns toward the East, and prays at length in Hebrew. Then he offers his neck to his executioners without a word (*MP* 3-5).

Sentenced to death, Thomas is entrusted to four soldiers and their chief, who lead him out of the town. Along the way, and after arriving at the appointed place, the apostle prays and admonishes his disciples. Having finished his last prayer, he calls the soldiers with the words: 'Come and do the will of him who sent you.' At that the four soldiers pierce him with their lances (*ATh* 164-8).

---

[2] A. Hilhorst, 'The Apocryphal Acts as martyrdom texts: the case of the Acts of Andrew', in Bremmer, *AAJ*, 1-14, has shown how little descriptions of the apostles' death have in common with the early historical Acts of Martyrs; they bear much more resemblance to the later epic *AAA*.

[3] For the text and translation of the *AA*, I use D.R. MacDonald, *The Acts of Andrew and the Acts of Andrew and Matthias in the City of the Cannibals* (Atlanta, 1990). I quote the *ATh* according to A.F.J. Klijn, *The Acts of Thomas* (Leiden, 1962). The other translations are my own.

Andrew is sentenced to die on the cross. The soldiers who have to lead the saint to the cross drag him cruelly along, but they are so badly beaten by Stratokles that they run back to their master Aegeates. After this, Andrew and Stratokles walk to the appointed place, followed by the crowd. On their arrival, Andrew, leaving everyone, approaches the cross and greets it in a loud voice. Then he commands the brethren to summon the executioners, standing at a distance, to carry out their orders. They tie him to the cross by his feet and armpits but do not nail him. In this position, Andrew speaks three days and nights on end. On the fourth day Aegeates, urged by the crowd, wants to liberate him. Andrew, absolutely revolted, calls Aegeates an ugly devil and prays to the Lord not to permit this to happen. In the end, nobody is able to seize him and, after a final prayer, he finishes his life (*AA* 52-3).

A comparison of these executions with the passion of Christ and with the Acts of the martyrs, will show three important differences. The first is the lack of suffering. As for Christ, there is no need to prove that he really suffered before and during the crucifixion. As for the martyrs, the authors of their Acts usually seem to find special enjoyment in describing in full detail, and sometimes in quite a naturalistic way, all the tortures, wounds and injuries inflicted on their heroes. In the *AAA*, however, we have nothing of this. The apostle is maltreated or beaten only in a few scenes and when they occur they lack any detailed description of suffering. More often the apostle escapes danger in a miraculous way, as happens to Thecla when she is to be burnt (*AP* 22). When the king wants to make Thomas stand barefoot on gleaming iron plates, the apostle brings a flood on the whole assembly, and they almost perish (*ATh* 140). Here we are very far from the docility of Christ who accepts his fate as a lamb led to slaughter.

In these descriptions of the apostles' deaths we find no trace of suffering. The apostle accepts the sentence of death (which he has more or less provoked) almost triumphantly. He goes willingly to the place of execution, holds long speeches, admonishes his disciples, and prays to God. When he is finished with everything he dies peacefully. This lack of suffering is especially striking in the two cases where the apostles are crucified.

The second difference is that the apostles, when dying, do not have to fight against the powers of Evil. Christ on the cross triumphed over Satan and his hosts. Some of the apocrypha, for example the Gospel of Nicodemus, present a very lively desciption of his fight and of his victory[4]. As for the martyrs, their final agony and suffering is seen as a fight against the Enemy, Satan. In the *Passio of Perpetua and Felicitas*, Perpetua has a dream before her execution in which she has to wrestle with an Ethiopian, clearly the figure of Satan (19)[5]. In the case of the *AAA* this feature is absolutely lacking.

The apostles had to fight the powers of evil during their lifetimes but not in their dying. The evil sometimes appears in the shape of demons, but it is the same Evil one who acts through the human enemies of the apostles, such as Aegeates, Nero, etc. This feature, namely, the fight against the powers of darkness, is especially marked in the *APt*: all along, Peter does not seem to do anything but fight Simon who, as it is clearly stated, is an emissary of Satan. In the end, Peter comes out triumphant and so do the other apostles, though in a less spectacular way. They can die in peace, there is no more battle in their death, and they only pray to escape the demons waiting for their souls on their journey to heaven.

The third difference seems to be that the apostle is not a passive party to these events. On the contrary, it is he who plays the active role while the others, guards and executioners, are completely relegated to the background. The apostle tells his executioners what to do and when. Paul even has to comfort those who must kill him. The apostle dies when he wants to die. In this respect, there is no great difference between the four cases where the apostles are executed, and the case of John, who calls his disciples to dig a grave for him and dies peacefully after prayer (*AJ* 111-5).

We see that the death of the apostle differs considerably from the Passion of Christ as well as from the death of the martyrs. Now we must ask, what happens to the apostle when he dies, or, what is the meaning of his death?

---

[4] Greek text: C. Tischendorf (ed.), 'Evangelium Nicodemi pars II. sive Descensus Christi ad inferos', in *Evangelia Apocrypha* (Leipzig, 1853) 301-11, trans. R. Gounelle and Z. Izydorczyk, *L'Évangile de Nicodème* (Turnhout, 1997).

[5] See also Bremmer, this volume, Ch. I.1.

2. Return to heaven

In their attitude toward death and suffering, Françoise Morand has shown that the apostles bear more resemblance to the gnostic Redeemer than to the Christ of the canonical Gospels[6]. For the gnostic Saviour, suffering is represented as having to enter a human body and our terrestrial world, while death means delivery from this and return to the heavenly country[7]. In the same way, for the apostle, death means the end of all troubles and the beginning of real life. This idea is clearly expressed in all of the Acts:

Peter: 'As long as the Lord wants me to dwell in a human body, I say no word against it, but if he decides to take me out of it, I shall greet it with joy and jubilation' (*APt* 36).

Paul: 'I am no runaway slave of my Christ, but the loyal soldier of the living God. If I thought that I were to die, perhaps I should yield to you [and fly]... but as I can live with God, and I desire what is beneficial for me, I shall depart to the Lord, so as to enter with him into the glory of his Father' (*MP* 3).

Thomas: 'For if I were to pray that I should not die, ye know that I am able (to do so), but this which is seen (by us) is not death, but a release from the world. For this reason I receive it gladly, and for this reason I am delivered, that I may go and receive Him who is comely, Him whom I love, Him who is beloved' (*ATh* 160).

Andrew: 'If you knew that I was released from my bonds and given back to myself, you yourselves would strive to get rid of a lot of things and to dedicate yourself to the Unique one...' (*AA* 61).

We see that for the apostle the real suffering is not death, but life: all the renunciations, hardships and persecution he has had to suffer for Christ. This is expressed by Thomas in a beautiful prayer pronounced in prison: 'Thou deliverer of my soul from slavery of many, because I gave myself to be sold unto one, now, lo, I am glad and

---

[6] F. Morand, 'Souffrance et martyre dans les Actes Apocryphes des Apôtres', in F. Bovon *et al.*, *Les Actes Apocryphes des Apôtres* (Geneva, 1981, 95-108) 101-3.

[7] The most important difference seems to be that, while the Christian Saviour saves mankind through his death, for the gnostic Saviour the saving act consists in his coming into our world and his teaching through which he awakens the fallen spiritual particles.

rejoice... Lo, I shall be without care and without sorrow and without distress, and shall dwell in rest for ever.... Lo, I shall be set free from slavery, and shall go to the liberty unto which I am called, etc...' (*ATh* 142).

The apostle has been sent on a mission and, having completed it, he returns to Him who had sent him, hoping to receive his reward. In this respect, therefore, the apostle bears a certain resemblance to the gnostic Saviour. In some other respects, too, the apostles surpass other human beings. They perform miracles, heal the sick, resurrect the dead; they can foresee the future, read the thoughts of others. After their death, they keep appearing to their friends or their enemies, and this not only in dreams: in certain instances the apostle seems truely to be raised. In relating the feats of their hero, the *AAA* not only imitate the deeds of Christ as described in the canonical Gospels (and it is Christ whom they imitate, not the apostles of the canonical Acts) but aim to surpass them[8]. This tendency might be considered a literary device to render these works more interesting for a not very cultured public. But I think that there are other, and better, explanations. After Christ's departure from earth, it is the apostle who takes over his role so that in a way he becomes a substitute of Christ.

François Bovon presents this thought in a very clear and concise way[9]. According to him there are three patterns: in the first, the apostle is bearer and revealer of the 'beneficent power of the Saviour' and the revelation takes place by miracles, not by teaching. In the second pattern, 'Christ, being absent from the terrestrial world, has a lieutenant, a vicar on earth, the apostle, the image of his divinity'; Bovon adduces Andrew as an example here. There is a third pattern 'which can be integrated into the preceding: the apostle and the Saviour have the same nature, they belong to the same spiritual family. A kinship unites them. Being twins, they accomplish the same salutary activity for the sake of men. So Thomas, named Didymos, that is, twin, becomes the spiritual brother of Jesus in the Acts of this apostle.'

---

[8] See R.J. Bauckham, 'The Martyrdom of Peter in Early Christian Literature', in *ANRW* II.26.1 (1992) 539-95. Quoting the *Apocryphon of James*, Bauckham writes: 'Disciples of Christ are to seek death in order to become "equal with" or even "better than" Christ' (580).

[9] F. Bovon, 'La vie des Apôtres. Tradition et narration apocryphes', in Bovon, *Les Actes Apocryphes des Apôtres*, 150-3.

What Bovon says is perfectly correct. I would only add that the three patterns can be present simultaneously: the same apostle is bearer of the divine power, earthly lieutenant of the Saviour, and twin brother of Christ. Regarding the first two features, it is quite clear that they can be found, at least to a certain degree, in all of the Acts. As for the third, it is obvious in the case of Thomas but much less so in the other cases. Nevertheless, traces of it can be found in all of the Acts. For example, in the *APt* we have two scenes in which Christ and Peter can be confused. The first is the dream of Marcellus, where he sees two Peters, completely identical: the first one, who speaks to him is Peter, and the other, who kills the demon, is Christ (22). The second case is the famous *Quo vadis* scene: we do not really know if Peter is to be crucified instead of Christ, or Christ instead of Peter (35)[10]. And there is one more characteristic little detail: at the beginning of the Acts the captain says to Peter on the ship: 'I am not able to decide whether you are a god or a man' (5).

What is said here about Peter is valid for all of the apostles. They are not divine; Thomas clearly states this: 'I am not Jesus, but I am the servant of Jesus. I am not the Messiah, but I am one who ministereth before him. I am not the Son of God, but I pray and beg that I may be deemed worthy of God' (*ATh* 160). Yet they are not simply human beings either. So it is understandable that they do not consider death as the end of life but, on the contrary, as the beginning of real life. It means the end of a painful mission and arrival in their real home-land. One could say, their return to it. Thus it makes no great difference whether the apostle is executed or dies peacefully.

3. *Peter as second Adam*

What we have said so far has concerned the death of the apostles in general. But in the cases of Peter and Andrew there is the additional circumstance that both die on the cross. I do not insist particularly on the mystery of the cross; what I am interested in is the fate of the

---

[10] See C.M. Thomas, 'Word and Deed: the *Acts of Peter* and Orality', *Apocrypha* 3 (1992) 125-64. Concerning the *Quo vadis* scene Thomas writes: '... the appearance of the Lord turns the ever-irresolute Peter back to Rome and signifies the identification of the apostle with the Lord, over which he rejoices' (154).

apostle on the cross. We have seen before that neither Peter nor Andrew seems to suffer on the cross. This cross is but an instrument of torture; the material cross is only the symbol or rather the outward, visible form of the real cross. This is clearly stated by Peter[11] – and also by John[12] – but there the situation is quite different. The real cross is a living being, addressed as such by both Peter and Andrew; in another apocryphal book we have a passage where the cross itself speaks (*Gospel of Peter* 39-42).

Let us first consider the case of Peter. Vouaux identifies the cross with Christ and holds that Peter is just a descendant of the first, fallen Adam. According to him, what Peter does is merely to provide an example. Thus the meaning of Peter's crucifixion would be the following: Adam by his fall reversed the natural order; Christ by his passion re-established it. Christ raised fallen humanity by uniting it through his person with divinity, and in order to participate in this, we need only to repent. This may well be the lesson the reader has to draw from the story, but my interest lies with what happens to Peter. This question cannot be settled in such a simple way.

First of all, the cross is not simply Christ, it is the logos in its cosmic extension. The cross in its entirety is called extended (*tetamenos*) Logos, horizontal and vertical beams together[13]. Peter's position on the cross symbolizes the situation of fallen humanity, now restored by the cross. But this detail still remains rather perplexing. There seems to be only one parallel: the 23th *Ode of Solomon*, where the thought of the Godhead, that is, the Logos, descends from on high and settles on a wheel (which is the cross, it seems). We then read: 'The head went down to the feet, because unto the feet ran the wheel, and whatever had come upon it' (16)[14]. In this ode the descent of the head

---

[11] 'The cross for you (...) should not be what it seems to be, because it is something different from what it seemed to be at (the time of) the passion of Christ' (37).
[12] 'The cross is not this wooden one which you will see' (*AJ* 99).
[13] Concerning the passage and the cosmic cross in general see J. Daniélou, *Théologie du judéo-christianisme* (Paris, 1991²) 340-53. For Daniélou *tetamenos logos* means that 'la croix est le Logos lui-même dans son extension cosmique' (345). As we know, Justin identified the cosmic X of Plato (*Timaios* 36 B-C) with the cross (*I. Apol* 60.1,5).
[14] J.H. Charlesworth, *The Odes of Solomon* (Oxford, 1973), 95.

signifies the universality of redemption: it is the redeeming act, reaching down as far as possible, perhaps even to the underworld. It is interesting to note that the *Odes* and *APt* were written at practically the same time.

As for Peter's symbolizing the fallen Adam, he is not simply a human being but in a way also becomes the second Adam. We have a few texts (not many, admittedly) where this idea is expressed rather clearly. The first is a fragment from Peter II of Alexandria (died 381) which was discovered not very long ago: 'Then again, he [the resurrected Christ] appeared first to Peter, so that it would be he who becomes a man instead of Adam, that which is firm (*stereon*) and unshakable instead of that which is muddy (*geodes*) and fragile...'[15] The other text is a fragment of the *Gospel of Bartholomew*[16], in which the Virgin Mary says to Peter when discussing who first put questions to the resurrected Christ: 'Chosen stone (*apolekte petra*), is it not on you that he has promised to build his Church? It is you who has to ask him first. You are the image of Adam...'[17] As these two texts are later than the *APt*, there are two possibilities: either all three texts go back to an earlier tradition, or the others have their starting point in our text. However this may be, what is important for us is the fact that a tradition exists in which Peter is considered the second Adam. It is interesting to note the reasons given: the first reason is the name given to him by Jesus, that is, his solidity, and the promise that the Church will be built upon him. The second reason is somewhat surprising: it is because it was Peter to whom Christ appeared first after his resurrection (at least according to one of the traditions). Further, we must not forget that Andrew, too, compares himself to Adam as to his relation to Maximilla (*AA* 37-9). Peter as the second Adam substitutes Christ – at least the human nature of Christ. We have already seen that the apostles in general are in some respect the substitutes of Christ. Thus Peter, the earthly substitute of Christ, is united to the Logos of Christ

---

[15] M. Richard, 'Quelques nouveaux fragments des Pères anténicéens et nicéens', *Symbolae Osloenses* 38 (1963, 76-83) 80.

[16] J.-D. Kaestli and P. Cherix, *L'évangile de Barthélemy* (Turnhout, 1993) 4.1-6.

[17] Both texts are quoted in J. Daniélou, 'Pierre dans le Judéo-Christianisme hétérodoxe', in *San Pietro. Atti della XIX settimana biblica* (Brescia, 1967) 443-56, esp. 455-6.

when hanging on the cross. I dare not say that Peter is here the double of Christ but we are not very far from the idea of the double, which is so clearly expressed in the Hymn of the Pearl (*ATh* 108-13).

4. Andrew

Prieur has shown that Andrew in the *AA* practically takes the place of Christ. We have the impression that it is Andrew who gives salvation to those who follow him, and not Christ through him[18]. Andrew becomes the *salvator salvandus*, a well-known figure in gnosticism[19]. It is worth quoting some relevant parts of his speech to the cross:

> 'Greetings, O cross! Greetings indeed! I know well that, though you have been weary for a long time, planted and awaiting me, even you now at last can rest. I come to you, whom I have known.'[20] '... I study your image for which you stood. I saw mine in you as I etched yours upon me.' 'What should one say to you, alter Andrew?... Well done, O cross, called the 'perfect power'! Well done, intelligent form, born of an intelligent word!' 'So then, cross, pure, radiant, and full of life and light, receive me, the one who for so long has been weary. But how long shall I say these things without being embraced by the cross... Approach, you ministers of my joy and bind the lamb to the suffering, the mortal to its crafter (demiourgos), the soul to its savior.'[21]

What takes place here exactly mirrors what happens to the hero of the Hymn of Pearl when, returning to his country, he receives his garment

---

[18] J.-M. Prieur, 'La figure de l'apôtre dans les Actes Apocryphes d'André', in Bovon, *Les Actes Apocryphes des Apôtres*, 121-39: '... on observe une tendance à identifier les aptitudes et le sort de l'apôtre à ceux de son maître...' (130); '... il joue un tel rôle dans le processus d'acquisition du salut de ses frères qu'on a parfois le sentiment qu'il remplace purement et simplement celui qui l'a envoyé...' (131).

[19] K. Rudolph, *Die Gnosis. Wesen und Geschichte einer spätantiken Religion* (Göttingen, 1994³) 141f.

[20] The Armenian text adds: 'I come to you who long for me', cf. MacDonald, *The Acts of Andrew*, 405 with n.88.

[21] MacDonald, *ibidem*, 411-5, esp. 411 n.6. MacDonald presents a much longer recension of Andrew's speech on the cross based on the Armenian text and on some of the Greek manuscripts. According to MacDonald, parts of this longer version could have belonged to the original *AA*.

that has been waiting for him since his departure (*ATh* 112-3)[22]. As the garment waited for the son of the king, so the cross waited for Andrew. As the garment is a living being which even speaks, brilliant with precious stones and pearls, so is Andrew's cross radiant, full of life and light. As the son of the king sees himself in the garment as in a mirror, so Andrew sees his image in the cross. As the garment and the son of the king have the same form, so is the cross called the 'alter Andrew'. As the son of the king longs to meet the garment and to put it on, so Andrew longs to be embraced by the cross. As the garment itself desires to be put on by the son of the king, so the cross desires that Andrew be hung on it. Putting on the garment, the hero of the Hymn of the Pearl is united to his heavenly self, and so is Andrew when bound to the cross. The Hymn of the Pearl relates the earthly adventures of the *salvator salvandus* and his return to heaven, and as such it is the story of Thomas, the twin-brother of Christ. But it is the story of Andrew as well, and in a way, that of all of the apostles.

---

[22] P.-H. Poirier, *L'Hymne de la Perle des Actes de Thomas* (Louvain-La-Neuve, 1981) presents the most complete analysis of the Hymn of the Pearl with its various interpretations.

XI. *Regulae fidei* and Other Credal Formulations in the *Acts of Peter*

LIUWE H. WESTRA

A layman in the field of the *Apocryphal Acts of the Apostles* (*AAA*) should not pretend to bring new insights to or to provide any solutions for old problems in the *Acts of Peter* (*APt*). This holds particularly true for my introductory statement that the date and place of origin of these anonymous *Acts* are still under discussion. Robert F. Stoops gives 180-190 as a 'commonly accepted dating'[1], but Gérard Poupon puts the *Actus Vercellenses* firmly in the first half of the third century[2]. Léon Vouaux presents a number of earlier suggestions and chooses early third-century Asia Minor for the original *Acts*[3]. As far as I can tell, most modern writers do not venture upon the subject of the date and place of origin of the *APt*[4]. Dennis R. MacDonald only claims that the *APt* are later than the *Acts of Paul* and earlier than the *Acts of John*[5]. Matters are complicated by the possibility that the text as we

---

[1] R.F. Stoops, 'Departing to Another Place: The *Acts of Peter* and the Canonical Acts of the Apostles', *SBL Seminar Papers* (1994) 390-404, esp. 392.
[2] G. Poupon, 'Les "Actes de Pierre" et leur remaniement', *ANRW* II.25.6 (Berlin and New York, 1988, 4363-83) 4381.
[3] L. Vouaux, *Les Actes de Pierre* (Paris, 1922) 203-14.
[4] Thus J.B. Perkins, 'The *Acts of Peter* as Intertext: Response to Dennis MacDonald', in E.H. Lovering (ed), *SBL 1993 Seminar Papers* (Atlanta, 1993) 627-33 and W.J. Stroud, 'Models for Petrine Speeches in the *Acts of Peter*', in E.H. Lovering (ed), *SBL 1994 Seminar Papers* (Atlanta, 1994) 405-14. J. Perkins, *The Suffering Self* (London and New York, 1995) 125, assigns the *APt* to late second-century Asia Minor.
[5] D.R. MacDonald, '*The Acts of Peter* and *The Acts of John*: Which Came First?', in E.H. Lovering (ed), *SBL 1993 Seminar Papers* (Atlanta, 1993) 623-6.

have it may be the result of a revision of an earlier original. We shall refrain from discussing this possibility and just study the text of the *APt* as it is given in Lipsius's edition[6]. The most I can do is try to contribute to this discussion by making a number of observations from the field of credal research.

When relating the *APt* to credal texts, I am following a cue that was provided by Vouaux himself. In his edition of the *APt*, he draws attention to what he calls credal quotations ('les expressions empruntées au symbole romain') more than once. In most cases, this is meant to clear the author of the *APt* of the accusation of gnosticism or heresy, but in at least one instance, he envisages – and rejects – the possibility that these quotations might say something about the origin of our anonymous text[7].

What exactly did Vouaux mean when he referred to the 'symbole romain', the 'Roman Creed'? Writing before the Great War, he can only have had the so-called Old Roman Creed in mind, a term that was coined as early as 1647 by the Irish archbishop James Usher to designate a certain conservative form of the Apostles' Creed[8]. The Apostles' Creed, it is well to remember, is not the creed that is used in the Roman mass and has as such been put to music many times, beginning with the words *Credo in unum deum*, but rather the creed with which all Western Christians have been baptized since the times of the early Church, beginning *Credo in deum patrem omnipotentem*.

What Usher and some of his contemporaries had already discovered in the seventeenth century became a *communis opinio* in the second half of the nineteenth[9]. First: the Apostles' Creed as it is used nowadays may only be a product of the early Middle Ages, but its

---

[6] R.A. Lipsius, *Acta Petri. Acta Pauli. Acta Petri et Pauli. Acti Pauli et Theclae. Acta Thaddaei* (Leipzig, 1891; repr. Darmstadt, 1959).
[7] Vouaux, *Actes de Pierre*, 277n13; 51, 65, 84; 209, respectively.
[8] Usher did so in his study *De Romanae ecclesiae symbolo apostolico vetere...* (London, 1647); his name may also be found in the forms Ussher and Usserius. See F. Kattenbusch, *Das apostolische Symbol* I (Leipzig, 1894) 8, and J. de Ghellinck, *Patristique et Moyen Age. Etudes d'histoire littéraire et doctrinale* I (Brussels and Paris, 1949) 27-9.
[9] The Dutch humanist Gerardus Joannes Vossius should be mentioned here, cf. Kattenbusch, *Das apostolische Symbol*, 6-8; De Ghellinck, *loc. cit.*, and especially N. Wickenden, *G.J. Vossius and the Humanist Concept of History* (Assen, 1993) 116-20.

roots go back to the second or third century AD. In the second place, it is a Western text that has never played a role in the Eastern half of the Church. In the third place, one of its forerunners may be reconstructed from several sources and has been stamped the Old Roman Creed, which runs as follows: *Credo in deum patrem omnipotentem, et in Christum Iesum, filium eius unicum dominum nostrum, qui natus est de spiritu sancto et Maria uirgine, qui sub Pontio Pilato crucifixus est et sepultus, tertia die resurrexit a mortuis, ascendit in caelos, sedet ad dexteram patris, unde uenturus est iudicare uiuos et mortuos, et in spiritum sanctum, sanctam ecclesiam, remissionem peccatorum, carnis resurrectionem*[10]. In Vouaux's days, this creed was believed to have originated in Rome as a Greek text, which was soon translated into Latin. The time of its origin was still being hotly debated, though there was a marked tendency to date it to the second or even first half of the second century[11]. Moreover, many credal scholars believed that this Old Roman Creed had not only given rise to later Latin forms of the Apostles' Creed in the West, but had also influenced the formulation of creeds in the East[12]. In this light, it was entirely natural for Vouaux to look for quotations from the Old Roman Creed in a text which he thought stemmed from Asia Minor.

We should now take a closer look at the relevant passages. Vouaux found quotations from the Old Roman Creed in the following places: APt 2: *Propter quod et uos, fratres, hortor credere in dominum patrem omnipotentem, et in dominum nostrum Iesum Christum filium ipsius spem omnem habere*, 7: *Conuertimini ergo, fratres electi a domino, et confortamini in dominum omnipotentem, patrem domini nostri Iesu Christi, quem nemo uidit umquam neque uidere potest* and further on ... *hortor uos per fidem quae est in Christo Iesu, ut nemo uestrum alium expectet praeter hunc contemptum et*

---

[10] See L.H. Westra, 'A Never Tested Hypothesis: Regional Variants of the Apostles' Creed', *Bijdragen. Tijdschrift voor Filosofie en Theologie* 56 (1995, 369-86) 369-71 with footnotes for more details and secondary literature.
[11] See for two typical statements C.P. Caspari, *Ungedruckte, unbeachtete und wenig beachtete Quellen zur Geschichte des Taufsymbols und der Glaubensregel...* III (Christiania, 1875) iii-vi and A. Harnack, 'Apostolisches Symbolum', in *Realencyklopädie für protestantische Theologie und Kirche... Erster Band* (Leipzig, 1896³) 741-55.
[12] See for example Kattenbusch, *Das apostolische Symbol*, 368-92.

contumeliatum a Iudaeis, hunc Nazarenum crucifixum, mortuum et in tertio die resurgentem, 17: *Per quem tibi ostenditur ut deo uiuo credas... qui est omni ueritate plenus et iustus iudex uiuorum atque mortuorum...,* 20: *... baiulauit et improperia passus est propter nos, mortuus est et resurrexit nostri causa,* 28: *... domini mei Iesu Christi qui est iudex uiuorum et mortuorum.*

Although Vouaux thought otherwise, however, these phrases can hardly be called quotations from the Old Roman Creed. The *APt* more or less consistently call God the Father *dominus* (or *dominus pater*) *omnipotens*, whereas R has *deum patrem omnipotentem*. Similarly, the phrase *dominus noster Iesus Christus*, which frequently occurs in the *APt*, is similar to but not identical with the credal formulation *Christum Iesum, filium eius unicum dominum nostrum*. When we turn to the articles concerning Christ's activities on earth, it is significant that the *APt* make use of the words *passus* and *mortuus*, whereas these were not yet present in the Old Roman Creed. Even the phrase *Iudex uiuorum et* (or *atque*) *mortuorum* cannot be said to be identical with the eighth article of the Old Roman Creed, where we read *Iudicare uiuos et mortuos*. In other words: the *APt* frequently refer to topics that may be found in the Old Roman Creed, but as a rule in a somewhat or even quite different formulation.

Although in the first half of this century such and similar formulations were connected without any problems with the Apostles' Creed or at least with its forerunners, such a procedure is nowadays considered to be highly questionable. Since the middle of this century, as a matter of fact, scholars have become increasingly aware of the fact that the Old Roman Creed was in principle a fixed formula that was in use for baptism and its preparatory rites only, and that as such it can hardly be younger than the end of the second century[13]. Of course, even fixed formulas will change over the course of time and the Old Roman Creed has not escaped this fate, but the differences with the formulations in the *APt* are too considerable to explain them in this way. Moreover, these formulations exhibit some remarkable differences among themselves as well. Vouaux's contention that we find quotations or borrowings from the Old Roman Creed in the *APt* cannot, therefore, be maintained any longer.

---

[13] See especially J.N.D. Kelly, *Early Christian Creeds* (New York, 1976³) 94-9.

Of course, one could try to explain the phrases under discussion as reminiscences of or allusions to the contents of the Apostles' Creed, but then, the contents of the Creed are too generally Christian to be certain that it is the Apostles' Creed and not some other formulation that the author is alluding to.

There is, however, an early Christian formula with which the passages that have been mentioned above may be connected: the *regula fidei*. The *regula fidei* is a rather special kind of text. It differs from the earliest form of the Apostles' Creed in both form and content[14], and may perhaps best be defined as 'an oral composition preserved and handed on by "composition in performance"', probably with an antiheretical purpose, in which the basic contents of Christian faith were formulated according to the needs of the hour[15]. The term *regula fidei* is first found in Irenaeus's *Demonstratio*, probably written after 185[16], but other designations can be found as well[17]. The earliest *regula fidei* we possess is probably found in the *Acts* of Justin Martyr, who died around 165, the latest examples are offered by Origen and Novatian in the middle of the third century[18].

Since this span of time covers most if not all hitherto proposed dates for the *APt*, it is interesting to compare those passages from the

---

[14] As has been seen since D. Van Den Eynde, *Les normes de l'enseignement chrétien dans la littérature patristique des trois premiers siècles* (Gembloux and Paris, 1933). Compare R.P.C. Hanson, *Tradition in the Early Church* (London, 1962) 64-5; Kelly, *Early Christian Creeds*, 63 and 95-6 (though Kelly uses the misleading term 'creeds in the looser, less exact sense of the word' [p. 94] to refer to the *regula fidei*); F.E. Vokes, 'Apostolisches Glaubensbekenntnis I', in *TRE* 3 (1978, 528-54) 532; P. Smulders, '"God Father All-Sovereign". New Testament Use, the Creeds and the Liturgy: An Acclamation? Some Riddles in the Apostles' Creed III', *Bijdragen...* 41 (1980, 3-15) 7-8; A.M. Ritter, 'Creeds', in I. Hazlett (ed), *Early Christianity* (London, 1993, 92-100) 93-4. The *regula fidei* may perhaps best be considered as the forerunner of the fourth-century synodical creeds.

[15] See L.W. Countryman, 'Tertullian and the Regula Fidei', *The Second Century* 2 (1982, 208-27) 226. Similar statements may be found in the literature quoted in the previous footnote.

[16] Irenaeus, *Demonstratio praedicationis euangelicae* 3; for the date, see *Patrologia Orientalis* 12, 752.

[17] See P. Smulders, 'Some Riddles in the Apostles' Creed. II. Creeds and Rules of Faith', *Bijdragen...* 32 (1971, 350-66) 357.

[18] See Smulders, 'Riddles II', 359-61.

Acts which seem to meet the definition of the *regula fidei* with other examples of *regulae*. First of all, I think we may say that the formulations that have been enumerated above do indeed represent *regulae fidei*: they contain a short summary of faith, their wording is apparently free and their context is clearly polemical.

There are, however, a number of other formulas to be found in the *APt* which meet these criteria. These are: *APt* 2: *Deus aeternus, deus caelorum, deus numinis inenarrabilis, qui confirmasti omnia uerbo tuo, qui uinculum inligatum omni saeculo induxisti gratiae tuae, pater filii tui sancti Iesu Christi...*, 7: *... discite cuius rei causa deus filium suum misit in saeculo, aut cuius rei per uirginem Mariam protulit...*, 10: *Tibi, domine noster, gloria et claritudo, deus omnipotens, pater domini nostri Iesu Christi*, 17: *... et ora ad dominum Iesum Christum qui iudicat omnem animam. Ipse enim est inuisibilis dei filius in quem te necesse est saluari...*, 23: *Viri Romani, deus nascitur? Crucifigitur?*, 27: *Tu deus saluator, tu Petri deus, deus inuisibilis et saluator*, 28: *Credis in deum meum per quem filius tuus resurrecturus est?*

Thus, all in all we have twelve passages in the *APt* which may be characterized as *regulae fidei*. It will therefore be worth comparing these with *regulae* that are presented by texts the origins and dates of which we know. In doing so, we shall pay particular attention to the structure of the *regulae* in the *APt*, the wording of their Christological parts, and their way of describing the first person of the Trinity.

First we shall turn to the question of the structure of these *regulae*. It appears that we may distinguish two types. On the one hand, we find a number of *regulae* in which the Father and the Son are mentioned, and something is said of both. These are found in *APt* 2 (second *regula*) and 7 (second *regula*). Following the Dutch scholar Pieter Smulders, the first to try his hand at the history of the *regula fidei*, we shall call this type 'dyadic'[19]. Next, we encounter *regulae fidei* in which the first two persons of the Trinity are both mentioned, but one is clearly dependent on the other. We shall use the predicate 'monarchical' to designate this type[20]. The monarchical type can work in more than one way, however. In *APt* 2 (first *regula*) and 10, the Son is only mentioned in connection with the Father, who receives among others the predicate *pater filii tui sancti Iesu Christi* or *pater domini*

---

[19] Smulders, 'Riddles II', 359.
[20] Another of Smulders's terms (*loc. cit.*).

nostri Iesu Christi (first monarchical subtype). On the other hand, the Father is only mentioned as sending the Son in another *regula*: *discite cuius rei causa deus filium suum misit in saeculo, aut cuius rei per uirginem Mariam protulit* (*APt* 7; second monarchical subtype[21]). The majority of the *regulae* in the *APt*, however, only mention the Son and may therefore be stamped Christological: thus *APt* 17 (twice), 20, 23 and 28 (twice). Finally, we encounter one *regula* in which only God the Father comes to the fore: *Tu deus saluator, tu Petri deus, deus inuisibilis et saluator* (*APt* 27).

Now, it has been known for some time that all these different ways of formulating faith have been used by Christian writers from New Testament times onward[22]. Limiting himself to the study of the *regula fidei*, however, Smulders has shown that in the course of time monarchical and dyadic *regulae* show a marked tendency to disappear in favour of more Trinitarian ones, that is, *regulae* in which not only the Father and the Son, but also the Holy Spirit are given a place. This tendency can already be observed in Irenaeus, writing between 180 and 200[23]. The last author to use purely dyadic *regulae* is probably

---

[21] The only example of this sub-type in Smulders's overview is Clement, *Stromata* 6.15.127.1:... ὅταν τις τὸν υἱὸν τοῦ θεοῦ τοῦ τὰ πάντα πεποιηκότος σάρκα ἀνειληφότα καὶ ἐν μήτρᾳ παρθένου κυοφορηθέντα, καθὸ γέγονεν τὸ αἰσθητὸν αὐτοῦ σαρκίον, ἀκολούθως δέ, καθὸ γεγέννηται τοῦτο, πεπονθότα καὶ ἀνεσταμένον ...

[22] See for example Kelly, *Early Christian Creeds*, 94-5.

[23] Dyadic *regulae* in Irenaeus, *Aduersus haereses* 3.4.2: ... *in unum deum credentes fabricatorem caeli et terrae et omnium quae in eis sunt, et Christum Iesum dei filium, qui propter eminentissimam erga figmentum suum dilectionem eam quae esset ex uirgine generationem sustinuit, ipse per se hominem adunans deo, et passus sub Pontio Pilato et resurgens et in claritate receptus, in gloria uenturus saluator eorum qui saluantur et iudex eorum qui iudicantur et mittens in ignem aeternum transfiguratores ueritatis et contemptores patris sui et aduentus eius* and 16.6: ... *qui est uere deus... huius uerbum, unigenitus qui semper humano generi adest, unitus et consparsus suo plasmati secundum placitum patris et caro factus, ipse est Iesus Christus dominus noster, qui et passus est pro nobis et surrexit propter nos et rursus uenturus in gloria patris ad resuscitandam uniuersam carnem et ad ostensionem salutis et regulam iusti iudicii extendere omnibus qui sub ipso facti sunt. Vnus igitur deus pater... et unus Christus Iesus dominus noster*; Trinitarian *regulae* in *Aduersus haereses* 4.33.7: *et in unum deum omnipotentem*

Tertullian (fl. *c*. 197-220)[24], whereas the last purely monarchical *regula fidei* is probably found in the writings of Hippolytus (*c*. 160-235)[25]. Since the *APt* represent a more conservative state of affairs than is offered by these three authors, it seems reasonable to assume that they are at least no younger than the end of the second century.

There is, however, more to this. The fact that the author of the *APt* only uses monarchical, Christological and dyadic *regulae fidei* implies that he never mentions the Holy Spirit in his *regulae*. The reason for this can hardly be that he is denying the Holy Spirit its divine status as *APt* 5 describes Peter baptizing Theon *in nomine patris et filii et spiritus sancti*[26]. Moreover, the author of the *APt* must have been familiar with the story of Simon asking the Apostles for the power to grant the Holy Spirit to others (Acts 8.18-9). If, then, there can be no doctrinal reason for the author of the *APt* to leave out the Holy Spirit, his taciturnity concerning the third person of the Trinity can only be explained by assuming that his *regula fidei*, even in its most extensive form, just did not mention it. We have seen that from the days of

---

ex quo omnia, fides integra, et in filium dei Christum Iesum, dominum nostrum, per quem omnia, et dispositiones eius per quas homo factus est filius dei, assensio firma quae est in spiritu dei, qui praestat agnitionem ueritatis, qui dispositiones patris et filii exposuit secundum quas aderat generi humano, quemadmodum uult pater, 5.20.1: ... *omnibus unum et eundem deum patrem recipientibus, et eandem dispositionem incarnationis filii dei credentibus, et eandem donationem spiritus scientibus...* and *Demonstratio* 3.
[24] Tertullian, *De praescriptione haereticorum* 36.5: ... *unum deum dominum nouit, creatorem uniuersitatis, et Christum Iesum ex uirgine Maria filium dei creatoris, et carnis resurrectionem...* and *De uirginibus uelandis* 1.3: *Regula quidem fidei una omnino est, sola immobilis et irreformabilis, credendi scilicet in unicum deum omnipotentem, mundi conditorem, et filium eius Iesum Christum, natum ex uirgine Maria, crucifixum sub Pontio Pilato, tertia die resuscitatum a mortuis, receptum in caelis, sedentem nunc ad dexteram patris, uenturum iudicare uiuos et mortuos per carnis etiam resurrectionem*; *De praescriptione haereticorum* 13; *Aduersus Praxean* 2.1.
[25] *Contra Noetum* 4.8: Τοῦτο οὖν ἐσημαίνετο, ἀδελφοί, ὅτι ὄντως μυστήριον οἰκονομίας ἐκ πνεύματος ἁγίου ἦν οὗτος ὁ λόγος καὶ παρθένου ἕνα υἱὸν θεῷ ἀπεργασάμενος (R. Butterworth, *Hippolytus of Rome. Contra Noetum...* [London, 1977] 53). Hippolytus offers a dyadic *regula* in *Contra Noetum* 1.7 and a Trinitarian one in *Contra Noetum* 8.1.
[26] This point has already been made by Vouaux, *Actes de Pierre*, 64.

Irenaeus on, early Christian writers felt the need to include the Holy Spirit in their *regulae fidei*, so that this feature of the *APt* is decidedly conservative. All the authors who have left us more than one *regula* mention the Holy Spirit at least once, so that we may say that the *APt* here represent a tradition that is older than the one we find in the writings of Justin Martyr, who died around 165[27].

Next, we come to the way that the second person of the Trinity is treated in the *regulae fidei* in the *APt*. Three different aspects present themselves here. First of all, one may distinguish a number of general characterizations of the Son: he is, of course, *filius* (2, twice; 7, first *regula*), but also *dominus* (2, second *regula*; 7, second *regula*; 17, first *regula*; 28) and *sanctus* (2, first *regula*). In the second place, something is said about his earthly existence and activities: he was sent to earth and born (7, first *regula*; 23), he ate and drank (20), suffered and was crucified (7, second *regula*; 20; 23), died and rose again (7, second *regula*; 20). In the third place, the importance of Christ for salvation is underlined: he is the future judge and only hope of all mankind (17, twice; 28).

The first of these three elements is rather common in both second- and third-century *regulae fidei*. Its most extensive formulation, *dominum nostrum Iesum Christum filium ipsius* (*APt* 2: second *regula*) comes closest to Irenaeus's *filium dei Christum Iesum, dominum nostrum* (*Adu. haer.* 4.33.7: footnote 23) and Novatian's *filium dei, Christum Iesum, dominum deum nostrum*[28], but also most other *regulae fidei* exhibit either the title 'Son' or that of 'Lord'. It is a typical feature of the *regula fidei* that it avoids putting the name Jesus Christ first[29].

The various formulations of Christ's life and activities on earth are bound to sound very familiar to anyone who is acquainted with any creed, however slightly, and it is no wonder that Vouaux jumped to the end of *APt* 7 to point to the author's acquaintance with the Old

---

[27] For one of the first Trinitarian *regulae fidei* see Justin, *Apologia* 1.61.3: ἐπ' ὀνόματος γὰρ τοῦ πατρὸς τῶν ὅλων καὶ δεσπότου θεοῦ καὶ τοῦ σωτῆρος ἡμῶν Ἰησοῦ Χριστοῦ καὶ πνεύματος ἁγίου τὸ ἐν τῷ ὕδατι τότε λουτρὸν ποιοῦνται.

[28] *De trinitate* 9.1 (46): *Eadem regula ueritatis docet nos credere post patrem etiam in filium dei Christum Iesum, dominum deum nostrum...*

[29] See Smulders, 'Riddles II', 361a-d and 365.

Roman Creed: ... *hunc Nazarenum crucifixum, mortuum et in tertio die resurgentem.* The reason for this familiarity is that Christ's birth, crucifixion, death, resurrection, and future judgement all belong to the so-called Christological sequence or gospel summary, a distinct unit in *regulae fidei* as well as in creeds. As such, it is older than both and probably stems from early second-century Asia Minor[30], so that its presence in the *APt* should not surprise anybody. According to Smulders, the complete sequence, comprising virgin birth, crucifixion, death or burial, resurrection, ascension, glorification and Second Coming, was already a closed unit when the first *regulae fidei* were formulated, and he states that it could be abridged, but not added to[31].

At first sight, this statement seems to hold true for the material in the *APt* just as well as for Smulders's own collection of *regulae fidei*. That the author has frequently abbreviated this sequence is clear enough: in one place he mentions only birth and crucifixion, in another we find the more elaborate chain of passion, death, and resurrection. One feature, however, accords ill with Smulders's theory: the fact that the Last Judgement occurs three times, but never in the Christological sequence. Whenever we meet this element in a *regula fidei* in the *APt* it looks more like a permanent feature of Christ than an element that concludes a narrative: it is usually found in combination with the permanent predicate *dominus* or with a mention of Christ's saving work, and his judging activities are always expressed in the present tense, never in the future: *ora ad dominum Iesum Christum qui **iudicat** omnem animam* (17), *deum... qui **est** omni ueritate plenus et iustus iudex uiuorum atque mortuorum* (17)[32] and *domini mei Iesu Christi qui **est** iudex uiuorum atque mortuorum* (28). It is difficult to imagine why the anonymous author would have separated the final element of a fixed series and only referred to it in isolation from its original context. Instead, it seems more likely that the author of the *APt* knew the role of Christ as a future judge of the quick and the dead as a distinct element of his *regula fidei*. This theory is supported by a number of other *regulae*, where the Last Judgement is also separated

---

[30] See P. Smulders, 'The *Sitz im Leben* of the Old Roman Creed. New Conclusions from Neglected Data', *Studia Patristica* 13 (1975, 409-21) 416-21.
[31] Smulders, 'Riddles II', 363.
[32] One cannot be certain whether Peter is speaking about the Father or the Son here.

from the Christological sequence. In three places, Origen (c. 185-254) offers a *regula fidei* which contains both a Christological sequence and a mention of the Last Judgement, but in which the latter is not given as part of the former but as a more or less autonomous element[33]. Equally instructive are two *regulae fidei* in Irenaeus. In *Aduersus haereses* 3.16.6, the Last Judgement is given in addition to the Second Coming and in 5.20.1 of the same work, the *regula* states that Christ will come again without mentioning any judgement[34].

The combined testimony of Irenaeus, Origen and the *APt* seems to suggest that the famous Christological sequence originally lacked its final element, the Second Coming to judge the quick and the dead. Irenaeus represents a stage in which traces of the process of addition may still be seen, and Origen, though writing later, yields *regulae* that are even more conservative. This implies that, although the complete Christological sequence is already attested in early second-century Asia Minor, a shorter form of the same sequence was still in use in other parts of the Church for some considerable time. The evidence of

---

[33] Origen, *De principiis* 1.pr.4-5: *Corpus assumpsit nostro corpori simile, eo solo differens, quod natum ex uirgine et spiritu sancto est. Et quoniam hic Iesus Christus natus et passus est in ueritate et non per phantasiam, communem hanc mortem uere mortuus, uere enim et a mortuis resurrexit et post resurrectionem conuersatus cum discipulis suis assumptus est... Post haec iam quod anima substantiam uitamque habens propriam, cum ex hoc mundo discesserit, pro suis meritis dispensabitur, siue uitae aeternae ac beatitudinis hereditate potitura, si hoc ei sua gesta praestiterint, siue igni aeterno ac suppliciis mancipanda, si in hoc eam scelerum culpa detorserit...*; *Commentarius in Iohannem* 32.16.187-90: πρῶτον πάντων πίστευσον ὅτι εἷς ἐστιν ὁ θεός ... χρὴ δὲ καὶ πιστεύειν ὅτι κύριος Ἰησοῦς Χριστός ... δεῖ δὲ καὶ εἰς τὸ ἅγιον πιστεύειν πνεῦμα, καὶ ὅτι αὐτεξούσιοι ὄντες κολαζόμεθα μὲν ἐφ' οἷς ἁμαρτάνομεν, τιμώμεθα δὲ ἐφ' οἷς εὖ πράττομεν; *Contra Celsum* 1.7: τίνα γὰρ λανθάνει ἡ ἐκ παρθένου γέννησις Ἰησοῦ καὶ ὁ ἐσταυρωμένος καὶ ἡ παρὰ πολλοῖς πεπιστευμένη ἀνάστασις αὐτοῦ καὶ ἡ καταγγελλομένη κρίσις, κολάζουσα μὲν κατ' ἀξίαν τοὺς ἁμαρτάνοντας γέρως δ' ἀξιοῦσα τοὺς δικαίους. Compare *Homilia in Ieremiam* 5.13.157, *Fragmentum 4 in I Corinthios* (C. Jenkins, 'Origen on I Corinthians', *JTS* 9 [1908] 231-47, 234), and *Commentariorum in Matthaeum series* 33. The contents of all six *regulae* are conveniently presented in Smulders, 'Riddles II', 361c.

[34] See footnote 23.

Origen suggests that Alexandria was at least one such place. A shorter form of the Christological sequence could be found down to the third century, and this opens up new possibilities for the problem of the origin of the *APt*.

A final element in the *regulae fidei* of the *APt* to which I would like to draw your attention is constituted by the predicates of God the Father, the first person of the Trinity. Here we find, not surprisingly, that God is Father and Almighty: *dominum patrem omnipotentem, dominum omnipotentem, patrem...* and *deus omnipotens, pater...*[35] More interesting are the other predicates: *deus aeternus, deus caelorum, deus numinis inenarrabilis* (2, first *regula*) and *inuisibilis*, which is found in two places: Christ is designated *inuisibilis dei filius*, and God is called upon as *deus inuisibilis et saluator* (17; 27). Similarly, we read ... *patrem domini nostri Iesu Christi, quem nemo uidit umquam neque uidere potest...* (7, second *regula*). All four places seem to stress God's transcendence, as has already been pointed out by Vouaux[36]. When one examines Smulders's collection of *regulae fidei*, however, no such predicate can be found[37]. Nevertheless, the double use of *inuisibilis* as well as the more elaborate phrases *deus aeternus...* and *quem nemo uidit...* seem to make certain that for the author of the *APt*, God's transcendence belonged to the predicates of the first person of the Trinity that could be used in a *regula fidei*. Now, is there any way of accounting for this situation?

As a matter of fact, there is a group of documents that exhibit the same feature when speaking about God the Father. These are the forms of the Apostles' Creed that were used by Augustine of Hippo in the first third of the fifth century and by Fulgentius of Ruspe in the early sixth, and it seems possible that there may be a connection with our anonymous *APt*.

---

[35] *APt* 2 (second *regula*), 7 (second *regula*) and 10. The use of *dominus* instead of the more normal *deus* in two out of three places seems to be typical of the *APt*. The closest parallel to this wording from another *regula fidei* is perhaps Novatian, *De trinitate* 1.1 (1): *Regula exigit ueritatis ut primo omnium credamus in deum patrem et dominum omnipotentem...*

[36] Vouaux, *Actes de Pierre*, 66.

[37] Origen, *De principiis* 1. pr.4 (*Primo, quod est unus deus, qui omnia creauit atque composuit quique cum nihil esset esse fecit uniuersa, deus a prima creatura et conditione mundi...*) comes closest to the formulations in the *APt*.

As has been indicated above, we may postulate an early form of the Apostles' Creed, which was considerably shorter than the formula we use nowadays, to have been in use for baptism and its preparatory rites in Rome around 300. One century later, we find slightly longer variants of essentially the same formula all over the Latin-speaking Church. It is important to notice that each region tends to make its own set of additions and other changes to the original form[38]. Now, one of the typical features of the form of the Apostles' Creed in North Africa is the addition *Vniuersorum creatorem, regem saeculorum, immortalem et inuisibilem* to the first article. Augustine testifies to its use in Hippo probably as early as the late fourth century[39], and Fulgentius of Ruspe shows, albeit a hundred years later, that this was not a purely local phenomenon[40]. Also, Quodvultdeus, bishop of Carthage in the first half of the fifth century, shows his familiarity with a similar formula[41]. It is tempting to consider the possibility, then, that a mention of God's transcendence was a distinctive feature of the *regulae*

---

[38] See for a recent overview L.H. Westra, 'A Never Tested Hypothesis. Regional Variants of the Apostles' Creed. II', *Bijdragen...* 57 (1996) 62-82.

[39] Augustine, *Sermo* 215.2: *Fides ergo haec et salutis est regula, credere nos in deum patrem omnipotentem, uniuersorum creatorem, regem saeculorum, immortalem et inuisibilem* (P. Verbraken, 'Les sermons CCXV et LVI de saint Augustin *de symbolo* et *de oratione dominica*', *Revue Bénédictine* 68 (1958) 5-40, 19).

[40] Fulgentius, *Contra Fabianum* 36.3: *Pater enim sic omnipotentem filium genuit sicut est ipse pater omnipotens, sic uniuersorum creatorem sicut ipse uniuersorum creator est, sic regem saeculorum sicut ipse rex saeculorum est, sic immortalem et inuisibilem sicut ipse immortalis est et inuisibilis. Omnia igitur quae deo patri dantur in symbolo, ipso uno filii nomine naturaliter tribuuntur et filio.*

[41] Quodvultdeus, *De symbolo* 2.3.2 and 14: *... sed credamus in deum patrem omnipotentem, uniuersorum creatorem, regem caelorum* and *Credimus ergo deum immortalem et inuisibilem, De symbolo* 1.4.35: *Fides itaque catholica haec est: omnipotentem, immortalem atque inuisibilem credere deum patrem..., De symbolo* 3.2.22: *Confiteamur, intelligamus habere nos regem immortalem et inuisibilem*. Rufinus, quoting the Aquileian form of the Creed with which he was baptized at the end of the fourth century, yields a similar addition to the first article in his *Expositio symboli* 4-5: *Credo, inquit, in deo patre omnipotente... his additur: inuisibile et impassibile.* But there is evidence that this was the result of a local measure against Sabellianism, which would make it too late to be of any use for our purposes.

fidei that were in use in North Africa, and that it manifested itself later on as a typical African addition to the Apostles' Creed.

All in all, then, we may conclude that the *APt* seem to witness to a *regula fidei* of a markedly conservative character: nowhere do we find any mention of the Holy Spirit, and the Christological sequence is shorter than in most other *regulae*. This pleads for a second-century rather than a third-century origin of the text, whereas the latter fact seems to rule out Asia Minor as a possible place of origin for the *APt*. Moreover, we have seen that certain features of the *regulae fidei* in the *APt* seem to point to North Africa as their home. The stress on God's transcendence has a possible parallel in a typical African extension of the first article of the Apostles' Creed, and the form of the Christological sequence that comes closest to that in the *Acts* is probably found in Origen, who started his theological career in Alexandria. If Africa is indeed the place to look for the origin of the *APt*, the text must have been written at least ten or twenty years before the start of Origen's teaching activities in 203[42].

It is important to remember, however, that research in the field of the *regula fidei* is still very young, and that the *APt* themselves have not yet received the attention that is their due either. Perhaps our guesses may help to say something more definite about the origin of the *APt* in the future.

---

[42] See also Bremmer, this volume, Ch. I.3; Poupon, this volume, Ch. XV.

XII. The Text of the *Actus Vercellenses*

A. HILHORST

As Gérard Poupon remarked in his 1988 review of the textual problem of the *Acts of Peter* (henceforth *APt*), the Vercelli manuscript remains by far the principal source for our knowledge of that apocryphon[1]. Therefore it may be justified to devote some pages to that witness once more. In this contribution, I shall firstly discuss the backgrounds of the editions by Lipsius and Vouaux and, secondly, examine a number of difficult passages. While preparing my paper, I had the benefit of a microfilm of the manuscript.

Editions

The manuscript is preserved in the Chapter Library of Vercelli[2]. It dates from the seventh century and contains two writings on Peter and Simon Magus[3]. The first of these, which occupies the lion's share of the manuscript, 321 leaves, are the *pseudo-Clementine Recognitions*. The second, which occupies 46 leaves, is the text which interests us here, the *APt*[4]. Both texts are written by the same scribe in an uncial

---

[1] G. Poupon, 'Les "Actes de Pierre" et leur remaniement', *ANRW* II 25.6 (1988, 4363-83) 4367.
[2] For a description see R.A. Lipsius and M. Bonnet, *Acta Apostolorum Apocrypha* (Leipzig, 1891, 1898, 1903, reprint Darmstadt, 1959) (henceforth this work is referred to as LB) I, xxxiii-xxxvi; E.A. Lowe, *Codices Latini Antiquiores* IV (Oxford, 1947) 18 and 37 (further bibliography); B. Rehm, *Die Pseudoklementinen* II, *Rekognitionen in Rufins Übersetzung* (Berlin, 1965) xxxvi-xxxvii.
[3] Lowe, ib. 18, Rehm, ib. xxxvi.
[4] The manuscript does not provide a title. Often the work is referred to as *Actus Petri cum Simone*, a title introduced by R.A. Lipsius on the basis of the colophons (LB I, 45, critical apparatus).

script without word-division (except for foll. 359-62, written by a different scribe, who did divide words). On a number of pages, the ink of the manuscript has faded, which makes deciphering difficult.

Our text will always be connected with the name of Richard Adelbert Lipsius, to whom we owe the *editio princeps*. Lipsius was a Lutheran theologian born in Gera in Eastern Germany in 1830. He came from a Saxon family long noted for producing theologians. From 1871 until his death in 1892, he was professor of systematic theology at Jena. He still counts as one of the prominent liberal Protestant theologians of the nineteenth century[5]. Besides his work on systematic theology and the part he took in practical Church affairs, he was interested in Biblical and patristic studies, and his monumental *Apokryphe Apostelgeschichten und Apostellegenden: Ein Beitrag zur altchristlichen Literaturgeschichte* is still of great value for our present studies[6]. He had an excellent command of Latin, not out of place for the son of a professor of classical literature at Leipzig, and in his edition he shows himself an accomplished textual critic.

His *Apokryphe Apostelgeschichten* was a pioneering work, and even if its main thesis of the Gnostic character of most of the *AAA* now seems to be antiquated, we cannot but be filled with awe when realizing the circumstances in which it had to be prepared. Indeed, not only were most of the texts either unpublished or badly published, but moreover one could not simply command photographs or xerox copies of a manuscript. As a rule, there was nothing for it but to transcribe or collate a text, either by oneself or, more normally, since travelling was much more difficult than it is nowadays, by the good offices of friends. Many of the writings discussed in the *Apokryphe Apostelgeschichten* were known to Lipsius in this way. He himself tells how he had to get hold of the Vercelli text[7]. Encouraged by Lipsius and Heinrich Holtzmann, Wilhelm Studemund copied the Vercelli text, probably in 1867[8], and lent the transcript to Lipsius. Later on he

---

[5] On Lipsius, see M. Scheibe in *Allgemeine Deutsche Biographie* 52 (Leipzig, 1906) 7-27.
[6] Braunschweig, I 1883; II 1 1887; II 2 1884; *Ergänzungsheft* 1890. A reprint was published in Amsterdam in 1976. See D. Ritschl in *New Catholic Encyclopedia* VIII (New York etc., 1967) 784, with further bibliography.
[7] Lipsius (n. 6) 1883, 631; 1887, 97 n. 1; id., LB I, xxxiii-xxxiv.
[8] In that year he collated the *Pseudo-Clementine Recognitions* in the same manuscript on behalf of J.B. Lightfoot, who was preparing an edition of

prepared an edition of the *APt* as part of a collection of Anecdota varia, printed foll. 327r-362r l. 22 (= LB I, 45,2-77,23), and asked for Lipsius' comments on the proofs. Lipsius granted the request, but subsequently heard nothing from Studemund. When eventually he himself needed the text for his *Apokryphe Apostelgeschichten*, Studemund refused to put his transcript at Lipsius' disposal[9]. Still hoping to receive the text of the chapters on which he had commented on behalf of Studemund, he called in his brother Hermann for a transcript of the remaining chapters and his colleague Friedrich Kluge for a decipherment of passages which had remained obscure to his brother; they did this for him in 1885 and 1886, respectively. He could use their work in *Apokryphe Apostelgeschichten* II 1, which appeared in 1887. In the meantime Hermann Mendelssohn, the publisher of Constantin Tischendorf's *Acta Apostolorum Apocrypha* (1851), invited him and Max Bonnet to produce a new edition of that collection of texts, which they accepted[10]. Since no more cooperation from Studemund could be expected, Lipsius asked Gotthold Gundermann to make a transcript of chapters 1-28 and to check the remaining part. He did so in the autumn of 1888[11]. Thanks to the skill of Gundermann, Lipsius finally had *his* transcript of the text and was able to produce the excellent edition of the text that is still the basis of scholarship concerning the *APt*.

them, cf. Rehm 1965 (n. 2) ix and xxvii. That edition was not to appear, cf. B.F. Dunelm in J.B. Lightfoot, *The Apostolic Fathers*, Part I, *S. Clement of Rome. A Revised Text* I (London and New York, 1890) vi n. 1. On Studemund (1843-1889), see Leopold Cohn in *Allgemeine Deutsche Biographie* 36 (Leipzig, 1893) 721-31.

[9] Studemund's unwillingness seems to be the consequence of a philological scrupulosity, on which cf. Cohn (n. 8) 722-4. He had obtained the Greek text of part of *APt*, cf. Lipsius (n. 6) II 1, 97 n. 1, and no doubt wanted to compare both versions thoroughly before handing over the texts.

[10] LB I, vii. The invitation was extended in 1890 at the latest, cf. ib. II 1, vii. Max Bonnet (1842-1917) was a Swiss classicist from French Protestant extraction born in Frankfurt-on-the-Main. In 1874 he moved to Paris, was naturalized as a Frenchman, and from 1881 worked in Montpellier, where he was appointed in 1891 as a professor of Latin literature after his doctoral thesis entitled *Le latin de Grégoire de Tours* (1890), still a standard work. He was a great admirer of the German *Altertumswissenschaft*.

[11] Gundermann (1856-1921) was an outstanding palaeographer, see G. Goetz in *Biographisches Jahrbuch für die Altertumswissenschaft* 42 (1922) 1-10, esp. 3-4, where his work for Lipsius is also mentioned.

How did he proceed? His starting-point was that the text was translated from the Greek some two centuries before the Vercelli manuscript was written. It was clear to him that the translator had used a far from elegant sort of Latin, but at the same time that not all of the flaws were his: the scribe had contributed his part to the careless appearance of the Vercelli text. But how could he distinguish between them? This proved simply impracticable. Therefore he decided to follow a different method from the other texts he was editing: not to offer the reconstructed text of the translator but, instead, to provide the uncorrected text of the manuscript including an indication of folios and even lines. As for textual corrections, they were all accommodated in the critical apparatus. Consequently, this apparatus is of vital importance to the user of the edition, as anyone who has worked with it knows. Whereas in other editions the critical apparatus is a sort of luxury for the average reader and can be left uninspected as long as he has confidence in the text established by the editor, here he has to consult it continually in order to make sense of the text.

This procedure is aimed at making no prejudgements about the authentic text[12]. But why not emend in the text what is declared to be in need of emendation in the critical apparatus? To this Lipsius would respond, I suppose, that his method has two advantages: firstly, he is not obliged to be exhaustive. Where he sees fit to propose a correction, he makes a remark; where he is not sure, he leaves the matter open and does not prescribe what we should suppose was written in the original text. Secondly, he is able to make nuances. In some cases he is categorical: '*corrige* unam', '*scribe* dicentes', in others he records suggestions by others: 'pateat *conicit HUsener*', 'sensu *corrigunt HUsener et MBonnet*', in still others he gives his own proposal: '*emendo* proditum' or surmise: '*expectes* aliae'[13].

Lipsius' method has the healthy effect of constantly reminding the reader of the problems of the text. Yet his edition is not a diplomatic one. He does not keep the *scriptio continua* but separates the words, he introduces a modern punctuation, he capitalizes the proper names, he spells out the abbreviations, he fills the lacunae and he adds chapter numbers. All this involves interpretation. Words can sometimes be separated in different ways. Abbreviations are not always

---

[12] LB I, xxxvii.
[13] All examples are from pp. 68-9.

unambiguous. Punctuation can make all the difference. A division into chapters betrays a view of the text. Even the capitalization of proper names may be arguable. And as for filling the lacunae, this is simply a form of emending. So Lipsius cannot entirely withdraw from interpreting.

In Lipsius' critical apparatus, we regularly meet not only the name of Gotthold Gundermann but also those of Max Bonnet and Hermann Usener[14]. They probably were the expert friends mentioned on p. xxxvii of the 'Prolegomena' who had persuaded him to follow the procedure just discussed[15]. He had already been in close contact with Bonnet and Usener for years; in the preface of the first volume of his *Apokryphe Apostelgeschichten*, dated September 1882, he states:

> Neben den gedruckten Quellen standen mir reiche handschriftliche Schätze zu Gebote, deren Benutzung ich zum grösseren Theil der Liberalität des Herrn Professor Max Bonnet in Montpellier, früher in Paris, verdanke. Vielen Dank schulde ich auch Herrn Professor Usener in Bonn[16].

The collaboration with Bonnet was further consolidated by the *Acta Apostolorum Apocrypha* project. Lipsius, however, hardly survived the publication of his share: volume I of LB appeared in 1891, Lipsius died the next year.

The Vercelli text received preferential treatment in Lipsius' edition. First of all, he (or was it Gundermann, who transcribed the text for him?) wrote a very complete survey of the grammar of the *Vercelli Acts*. Secondly, he compared the proofs of this text several times with

---

[14] 33 x G. Gundermann, 19 x Bonnet, 35 x Usener. In addition 2 x G. Götz (pp. 46 and 49), a friend of Gundermann; they had worked together on the *Corpus glossariorum latinorum*. On Usener, see J.N. Bremmer, 'Hermann Usener 23 October 1834-21 October 1905', in W.W. Briggs and W.M. Calder, III (eds.), *Classical Scholarship: A Biographical Encyclopedia* (New York and London, 1990) 462-78. On Götz, see K. Barwick, 'Georg Götz. Geboren 3. November 1849, gestorben 1. Januar 1932', *Jahresbericht über die Fortschritte der klassischen Altertumswissenschaft* 245 = 60.4 (1934) 146-71.

[15] Cf. also LB II 1, viii-ix.

[16] Cf. LB II 1, 40; II 2, 414-5 and 426.

the transcript, corrected them accordingly and sent the corrected ones to Gundermann, who compared them directly with the manuscript once more. Furthermore (but this is true of all of the texts he edited), Usener and Bonnet revised the proofs[17]. Finally, Lipsius deposited many observations in the 'index latinus' at the end of the book.

In 1922 a new edition by Léon Vouaux appeared, together with a translation and commentary. Vouaux was a Catholic priest from the diocese of Nancy. He was a great student, who produced valuable studies of fungi and insects, until he was persuaded to work on early Christian literature. This resulted in his two editions of apocryphal Acts, the *Actes de Paul* of 1912 and the *Actes de Pierre* of 1922. The latter work, however, appeared posthumously: when his younger brother, who was a parish priest, was mobilized, he took his place in July 1914, was taken hostage in August by the Germans and soon after summarily executed by a firing-squad[18].

Vouaux had finished his work in 1914. Then the work was held over, owing to Vouaux's death and the war. It could finally appear in print in 1922, thanks to the good offices of Émile Amann. Vouaux's edition is an independent piece of work of a remarkable quality. Although no traces of hasty work are visible, Vouaux must have familiarized himself with the problems in a very short time, and Amann is probably right in supposing that he would have modified some of his views had he lived to supervise the edition in its final stage[19]. True, he relied on the information offered by Lipsius' edition and, as far as I am aware, did not investigate the manuscript himself, no more than Lipsius himself, for that matter. On the other hand, he did not follow Lipsius' policy of presenting the uncorrected manuscript text, but introduced most of the corrections from Lipsius' critical apparatus along with a number of his own into his text. In his apparatus, he discusses many textual problems, and his name regularly recurs in the footnotes of Schneemelcher's translation.

---

[17] LB I, 284.

[18] I owe these details to the preface E. Amann contributed to L. Vouaux, *Les Actes de Pierre* (Paris, 1922). According to *Dictionnaire de Théologie Catholique, Tables Générales* III (Paris, 1972) 4400, Vouaux's year of birth was 1870. As Jos. van der Straeten, S.J. (Brussels) kindly informs me (letter of 20.viii.1997), there seems to be no article devoted to him in the current biographical reference works.

[19] Vouaux 1922 (n. 18) ix.

One more contribution to the textual criticism of the Latin of the *Vercelli Acts* deserves to be mentioned, although it is not an edition. It is by C.H. Turner (1860-1930), well-known among New Testament students for his articles on 'Marcan Usage'[20]. In a posthumous article in the *Journal of Theological Studies* of 1931, he offers a large number of suggestions for the improvement of the text, using Lipsius' edition. Many of these have been adopted into the translations published since.

Problematic passages

As previously mentioned, the text of the Vercelli manuscript is not always easily interpretable. Apart from the passages where the manuscript has faded, there are the difficulties of late Latin, literal translation, and misunderstanding on the translator's part. In his critical apparatus, Lipsius solved a large number of obscurities in the Vercelli text, but it is only natural that later scholars, especially Vouaux and Turner, could shed further light on the text. However, some puzzles still remain, and it is somewhat disquieting that modern translators tend to render them as if nothing were the matter. Let us review a number of them[21].

1. ch. 2, p. 46,12 **optulerunt autem sacrificium Paulo pane et aqua**: The passage is invariably rendered 'And they brought bread and water to Paul for the sacrifice' (Elliott). This seems to go back to Gerhard Ficker 408, who is fair to the text and observes: 'Um jedes Mißverständnis auszuschließen, übersetze ich, als ob für die Worte

---

[20] On him, see H.N. Bate in *The Dictionary of National Biography, 1922-1930* (London, 1937) 861-4.

[21] From now the names of authors mentioned in the text stand for editions: Lipsius (n. 2), Vouaux (n. 18), and translations: Vouaux, James, Erbetta, Moraldi, De Groot (in Klijn), Schneemelcher, and Elliott, on which see the general bibliography of this volume. In addition, Blaise = A. Blaise, *Dictionnaire latin-français des auteurs chrétiens* (Turnhout 1962), Ficker = G. Ficker, 'Petrusakten', in E. Hennecke (ed.), *Handbuch zu den neutestamentlichen Apokryphen* (Tübingen, 1904) 395-491, Szantyr = A. Szantyr, *Lateinische Syntax und Stilistik* (Munich, 1965), Turner = C.H. Turner, 'The Latin Acts of Peter', *JTS* 32 (1931) 119-33. The page and line numbers after the chapter numbers refer to Lipsius' edition.

des Textes: *sacrificium Paulo pane et aqua* stünde: *ad sacrificium Paulo panem et aquam'*. But perhaps *sacrificium* has a concrete sense, 'the material for the eucharist' and the ablatives *pane et aqua* mean 'consisting in bread and water'[22]. This meaning of *sacrificium* is mentioned in the dictionary of Blaise, under no. 3: 'ce que les fidèles apportaient pour la messe (pain, vin), offrandes'; it occurs in Cyprian, Isidore, and the *Sacramentarium Gregorianum*.

2. ch. 4, p. 49,5-7 **et postea apparuit in medio populo stans, quemque uniuersi adornantes et cognoscentes quia ipse esset**: Already Lipsius felt that *adornantes* should be read as *adorantes*; indeed the superfluous *n* may be the result of an error of anticipation. What, however, of *quemque* and the participles? Both may be explained from late Latin. Then *quemque* may be the accusative not of *quisque* but of *quique* = *qui*[23], and the participles may be used as finite verbs (*adorauerunt* and *cognouerunt*); this occurs especially in main sentences or, as in our case, in relative clauses[24]. James's rendering: 'and thereafter he appeared, standing in the midst of the people; whom they all worshipped, and took knowledge that he was the same' is in accordance with this interpretation. If it is right, *adorare* and *cognoscere* are in the *hysteron proteron* order.

3. ch. 6, p. 53,6-9 **fiet autem non tantum lapis molaris, sed quod deterius est, contrarium longe ab eis qui in dominum Iesum Christum crediderunt, in hunc persecutorem seruorum suorum consummari**: This is a real *locus desperatus*. Most translators follow Ficker 421-2, who hesitatingly connects *contrarium* with *in hunc persecutorem* and adds *me* to *suorum*. Thus Elliott has (adding 'Text corrupt'): 'Not only would it be a millstone, but what is worse, I the opponent of this persecutor of his servants would die far away from those who have believed in the Lord Jesus Christ.' In that case, as Erbetta points out, Peter states that he is still more concerned about the collapse of the faithful than about his own; he compares Rom. 9.3: 'I would willingly be condemned and be cut off from Christ if it could help my brothers of Israel' (Jerusalem Bible). But *contrarium* is too far from *in hunc persecutorem* and *contrarius in* can hardly mean

---

[22] Ablativus materiae, cf. Szantyr 106-7.
[23] Cf. Szantyr 475.
[24] See Szantyr 389. This occurs frequently with our text, see LB I, 1, even in subordinate clauses (54,8; 67,5-7; 74,7).

'opponent of'. Turner has another idea. He isolates the words *contrarium longe ab eis qui in dominum Iesum Christum crediderunt*. Then the remaining words from *fiet* can be taken to apply to Simon, the persecutor: if Peter can meet this enemy of our Lord, 'then not only the millstone but what is worse shall come to be accomplished on this persecutor of his servants.' The excised words are supposed to precede that statement as an exclamation, taken for granted that *contrarium* should be emended to *conmorari me*: 'That I should stay on here far from these believers in their peril!'[25] But Turner's proposal entails serious interventions in the text and is commented upon by its own author with the words 'But the true restoration of the whole passage is still to be found.' Perhaps we may take *contrarium* as a neuter subject of *consummari* and suppose Peter designating himself as a persecutor because of his deserting the faithful. This is the interpretation of De Groot; his rendering would run in English: 'Not only the (case with the) millstone will occur, but also, what is worse, the opposite of what will happen to those who have believed in the Lord Jesus Christ will happen to this persecutor of his servants.' That 'opposite' may be eternal damnation; it is a topos of martyrdom texts to contrast temporal and eternal punishment.

4. ch. 7, p. 53,16-18 **concurrit itaque multitudo omnis ut uiderent domini apostolum fundari in Christum**: The passive *fundari* is a slip of the pen for *fundare* according to Lipsius xliv. Then an object is supplied: either himself or the congregation. But even then it is awkward: confirming oneself or a congregation is hardly an act capable of enthralling a crowd looking for sensation. I suggest reading *fundati*: the multitude came together to see the apostle who, unlike them, was built on, that is, inseparable from Christ. Similar expressions may be found in the New Testament (I quote from the Vulgate): Eph. 3.17 *in caritate radicati et fundati*, Col. 1.23 *in fide fundati*, 2.7 *radicati et superaedificati in ipso* (sc. *Christo*). The scene is familiar from other *AAA* and also from martyrdom texts. Erbetta and Moraldi render similarly, but seem to start from *fundari*, which does not allow this translation.

5. ch. 7, p. 53,24-25 **uolens omne scandalum et omnem ignarantiam et omnem inergaemam diaboli, initia et uires infirmes**: God certainly does not will 'every offence and every ignorance' etc.; so an

---

[25] Turner, 122.

infinitive meaning 'taking away' is needed. Lipsius offers two solutions: adding a verb like *dissoluere* or changing *infirmes* into *infirmare*. In itself, the latter is clearly preferable: it is more economic, and it can be explained as an error of perseveration, the ending *-es* of *uires* supplanting *-are*. Such errors occur frequently in manuscripts and indeed in human speech generally. In our manuscript, it occurs for instance in ch. 5 (p. 50,27) *si ui* for *si uis*. There is, however, an important reason for preferring the addition of *dissoluere* (or rather *reddere*, as Ficker advises): chapter 24 of the *Life of Abercius* (19,15-16 Nissen), which textually follows our text here, has ἀσθενῆ ποιῆσαι.

 6. ch. 7, p. 53,27-29 **qui multis et uariis infirmitatibus per ignorantiam in mortem ruebant, motus misericordiam deus omnipotens misit filium suum**: *qui* is not in need of correction to *quia*, although that emendation, suggested by Usener, is a small one, but can be interpreted as *eorum qui* dependent on *misericordiam*. Cf., in ch. 1 (p. 45,10), *qui in Spania sunt corpori tuo medicus esto*, where *qui* stands for *eis qui*, as Lipsius remarks. (For *corpori tuo*, Vouaux reads *corpore tuo*, 'par ta présence corporelle'.)

 7. ch. 9, p. 57,11-12 **audiens enim haec Simon et respiciens incredibilem uisum excidit a uerbis**: Vouaux 291 gives *enim* a causal value: 'Aussi, Simon... en oublia les discours', but this is highly improbable in view of the context, and *enim* does not mean 'consequently'. Ficker honestly admits that he renders 'aber' in spite of the manuscript's *enim*. But indeed, *enim* in late Latin quite often is an equivalent of *autem* (Blaise s.v. *enim*, Szantyr 505-6, 508-9).

 8. ch. 9, p. 57,19-20 **ne in animo inducas delictorum meorum**: In his 'Prolegomena' (xlix), Lipsius mentions the genitive as an anomaly. It may be a Graecism, cf. the similar expression in Psalm 78(LXX).8: μὴ μνησθῇς ἡμῶν ἀνομιῶν ἀρχαίων. But there are also good Latin parallels on the basis of the genitive with verbs of recalling (Szantyr 81), e.g. Cicero *Verr.* 5.180 *uenit mihi in mentem M. Catonis*.

 9. ch. 19, p. 66,6-7 **domum meam permundaui a uestigiis Simonis et scelesti pulueris ipsius perstirpaui**: Lipsius here mentions emendations by Gundermann and Usener, both unconvincing. Vouaux adds two more of them, which are much simpler. But perhaps we can do without changing the text. The verb *perstirpare* is extremely rare; indeed, I am not aware of a second occurrence in

antique or medieval literature. But there does exist a verb *exstirpare*, 'to root out', which our text uses in ch. 6 (51,33): *extirpauitur omnis seductio a seruis eius* or 'to clear by rooting out', e.g. Jerome *Tr. II in Ps.* 84.13 (CCSL 78,398) *terra nostra... a ueteribus uitiis exstirpatur*. Supposing *perstirpare* having the latter sense, 'to clear of, cleanse of', the sentence is tolerable if we put a comma or insert an *et* after *permundaui*.

10. ch. 20, p. 67,2-4 **quae gratia ipsius quod coepimus, scribsimus, etsi adhuc uobis infirma uidentur, capaciter tamen quae perferuntur in humana carne inferre**: This sentence is provided with four emendations by Lipsius, briefly discussed by Vouaux 338 and treated in a page and a half by Ficker 445-6. The words *quod coepimus, scribsimus* have been transmitted in Greek in a quotation by Isidore of Pelusium *Ep.* 99 (PG 78,544): ἃ ἐχωρήσαμεν ἐγράψαμεν. Usually, *quod coepimus* is understood as *quoad cepimus*, 'as far as we were able', which seems reasonable. The real problem resides in *capaciter* etc. Ficker reads these words as if they ran *capacia tamen <sunt>, quae proferuntur, in humanam carnem inferri*, 'yet the things brought forward are capable of being brought into human flesh (i.e. 'are endurable to be understood by humanity', to borrow from Elliott's translation)'. This may mean two things. Either it is an answer to the objection that the apostle's written words, even if feeble, are at least not beyond human comprehension, which would be a remarkably weak defence. Or it points out that even if Peter's audience regards his words as feeble, they contain the maximum the human mind can grasp. But it would be curious if that audience should have expectations here that are beyond human comprehension. Other scholars divide between *tamen* and *quae*. They read *capaciter tamen* as *capaciter tamen scripsimus*, 'yet we have written according to our power', and take *quae perferuntur in humana carne inferre* as a further characterization of Peter's statements, a characterization which works out the notion of either Peter's or humanity's restricted comprehension. Thus Schneemelcher, who also reads *inferri* for *inferre*: 'What we have written by his grace, so far as we were able, although it seems weak to you as yet, yet (we have written) according to our powers, so far as it is endurable to be implanted in human flesh.' The same criticisms here apply; in addition, one may ask whether *capaciter* can mean 'according to one's power'.

11. ch. 20, p. 67,7-9 **motus dominus misericordiam suam, in alia figura ostendere et effigie hominis uideri, quem neque Iudei**

neque nos digni inluminari possimus: The first four words are generally read as *motus est dominus misericordia sua*[26], and *ostendere* as *ostendere se*. Both may be right. What, however, about the relative clause? Here the difficulties are considerable, and it is not to the credit of the translators that they offer smooth renderings without sufficiently justifying their choices. Let us take for granted that *digni inluminari* stands for *digne inluminare*, as is claimed by Vouaux and some translators, and *possimus* for *possumus*, on which no one offers any comment (although the subjunctive is in pressing need of an explanation): what does *quem neque Iudei neque nos digne inluminare possumus* mean? According to Lipsius (xliv and 314) and Ficker, *inluminari* means *conspicere*, but this meaning is not in the dictionaries. Vouaux takes *inluminare* as 'éclairer', 'faire connaître dans sa lumière' (cf. Moraldi: 'illustrare'). But is it the task of Jews to 'reveal' Jesus 'in his light'? A solution followed by James and others is to explain *quem* as an accusative of respect ('concerning which') and keeping the passive *inluminari* in the sense of 'to be enlightened'. This fits the context up to a point, for the next sentence runs *unusquisque enim nostrum sicut capiebat uidere, prout poterat uidebat*, but the accusative of respect with a masculine relative pronoun is most unusual.

12. ch. 20, p. 67,17-18 **et dixi: et haec tua uoluntas est, non contradico**: According to Lipsius, we should read *si* instead of *et*. His reason may have been *forsitan* in the preceding sentence, which suggests more than one possibility. Yet this is not strictly necessary; we can translate: 'This too is your will, I do not resist', as is actually done by Vouaux (in spite of his reading *si*). If, however, we prefer taking the former sentence as a conditional clause, we may suppose a haplography: *dixi* instead of *dixi si*.

13. ch. 24, p. 72,14-15 **per quas necesse erat per mysterium et regnum dei consummare**: The antecedent of *quas* is *profeticas scribturas*. Elliott renders the sentence as follows: 'It was necessary that through them it should be a mystery and the Kingdom of God be completed'. This is highly unsatisfactory. Why should the Kingdom of God be completed *through* the prophetical writings? And what about *per* before *mysterium*? But the addition of *locutum esse* after *mysterium*, as done by Vouaux and adopted by Schneemelcher, is not much better; one cannot simply add words till the sentence is comprehensible.

---

[26] For the participle see LB I, 1; for *-am* read as an ablative ending ib. xlviii.

Moreover the deponent verb *locutum esse* cannot have the passive meaning they ascribe to it. I tentatively offer an interpretation of the words as they stand: *per quas* meaning 'as far as they are concerned' or 'according to them' and *per mysterium* being an elucidation of the way of speaking of the prophetical writings and meaning 'in a symbolic or allegorical way' (cf. Blaise s.v. *mysterium* 4). As for *consummare*, this may be either a lapse for *consummari*, as Lipsius xlv and 72 would have it, or have an intransitive value here. Then the words may be rendered as follows: 'according to which (prophetical writings), <which expressed themselves> in a symbolic way, it was necessary that also the kingdom of God should be completed'.

14. ch. 29, p. 78,6-7 **adorabant eum tamquam deum pedibus eius deuoluti, et quos habebant in domo infirmos ut curaret eos**: Lipsius feels that before *ut curaret eos* something like *adportantes* has been left out. Vouaux 394 disagrees, for the prefect indicated to Peter to depart; so it would be useless to bring the sick. There is also a linguistic reason for accepting the text as it stands. Under stress we tend to loosen the bridles of logic and throw out first what we are full of. That is *quos habebant in domo infirmos*. Then comes what the hearer needs in order to make sense of it. That is *ut curaret eos*. After that there is no more energy or indeed need to supply words that could make the words into a logically correct statement.

Much more should be done for the elucidation of the text, but hopefully the observations made will contain something of benefit for the edition by Gérard Poupon which we all look forward to.

XIII. The relation between the *Acts of John* and the *Acts of Peter*

PIETER J. LALLEMAN

The mutual relations between the *Apocryphal Acts of the Apostles* (*AAA*) are still a very thorny subject, which was largely ignored in the first two volumes in the present series[1]. In this volume I have the honour to be in the company of professor Willy Rordorf in my attempt to attain some progress. Comparing the relationships between *Acts of Peter*, *Paul* and *John* (*APt*, *AP*, *AJ*) to a triangle, we can say that I will describe one side of this triangle and professor Rordorf another one. The question is, which end of the triangle points upwards. Indeed, some would have urged that we dealt with the relations between the *AAA* in the very first volume. In his important essay on this subject, Stanley Jones goes so far as to suggest that the mutual relations are just as important for our reading of these texts as the Synoptic comparison is for any understanding of the first three canonical gospels[2].

The question of the connection between *AJ* and *APt* seemed to have received a definitive answer long ago in the work of the great specialist on the *APt* and *AP*, Carl Schmidt. His view that the *AJ* are the oldest of the two texts and that the *APt* depend heavily on them received much support and was undisputed from the year he published it, 1903, until after the Great War[3]. Schmidt effectively combatted the

---

[1] I wish to thank Jan N. Bremmer and Peter W. Dunn (Ontario) for suggesting improvements to this paper.
[2] F.S. Jones, 'Principal Orientations on the Relations between the Apocryphal Acts', in E.H. Lovering (ed), *SBL 1993 Seminar Papers* (Atlanta, 1993) 485-505, esp. 486.
[3] C. Schmidt, *Die alten Petrusakten* (Leipzig, 1903); J. Flamion, 'Les Actes apocryphes de Pierre', *RHE* 10 (1909) 248-70; L. Vouaux, *Les actes de Pierre* (Paris, 1922) 70, 443, 459; P. Weigandt, *Der Doketismus im Urchristentum* (Dissert. Heidelberg, 1961) 86; E. Junod & J.-D. Kaestli, *Acta Iohannis* II (Turnhout, 1983) 697-700.

earlier idea that *AJ* and *APt* stem from one and the same author[4]. But the consensus over the correctness of Schmidt's insights gradually eroded and was replaced by the conviction that direct relations cannot be proven[5]. Recently even the contrary view, that the *APt* are older and in turn influenced the *AJ*, was voiced by members of the group of American scholars who have dealt with the *AAA* at several annual meetings of the Society of Biblical Literature. It is remarkable that one of them, Dennis MacDonald, needs only four pages to conclude that we have always been wrong and that in reality the *AJ* depend on the *APt*, whereas Stanley Jones is much more cautious, merely points to the weaknesses in Schmidt's position, and leaves the matter open[6]. MacDonald does offer three sensible criteria that can be used in the comparison, but in practice his own work is not convincing[7].

1. *Sources of the Apocryphal Acts*

When two texts seem to be related, it is always difficult to say with certainty which text is the original. For example, the priority of Mark

---

[4] So M.R. James, *Apocrypha anecdota*. Second Series (Cambridge, 1897) 24f; Th. Zahn, 'Die Wanderungen des Apostels Johannes', *Neue Kirchl. Zs.* 10 (1899) 210.

[5] G. Ficker, 'Petrusakten', in E. Hennecke, *Handbuch zu den Neutestamentlichen Apokryphen* (Tübingen, 1904) 395-491 always remained sceptical; W. Schneemelcher, *Neutestamentliche Apokryphen* II^3 (Tübingen, 1964) 180; Schneemelcher in *NTA* II, 274-5; Ph. Vielhauer, *Geschichte der urchristlichen Literatur* (Berlin and New York, 1975) 696.

[6] Jones, 'Orientations'.

[7] D.R. MacDonald, '*The Acts of Peter* and *The Acts of John*: Which Came First?', in E.H. Lovering (ed), *Society of Biblical Literature 1993 Seminar Papers* (Atlanta, 1993) 623-6. His treatment is superficial: 1. In dealing with the Transfiguration episodes he overlooks that the *AJ* know this story from one or more gospels and thus cannot depend solely on the *APt* even if the *APt* were older. 2. He overlooks that *APt* 20-2 (about women) is a different scene from 23-7 so that a comparison with *AJ* 30-7 (about women) is more complicated than he assumes. 3. *AJ* 30-7 cannot be classified as a 'miracle contest'. MacDonald and J.B. Perkins ('The *Acts of Peter* as Intertext' [*ibidem*, 627-33]), who follows him without much criticism, do not convincingly prove dependence on the side of the *AJ* but merely reveal parallels. For MacDonald's criteria in his '*The Acts of Paul* and *The Acts of John*: Which Came First?' (*ibidem*, 506-10) 506-7, see Rordorf, this volume, Ch. XIV.

among the Synoptics has never been unanimously accepted, and in the relation between the Second Epistle of Peter and the Epistle of Jude dependency can still be thought to go either way. Of course, the possibility that a third text, unknown to us, functioned as a source for both related texts must also be taken into account.

In the present case, it is clear that there are two literary sources from which both *AJ* and *APt* draw. First, the Synoptic Gospels were a source. Both Acts display a special interest in the story of the Transfiguration. The study of their mutual relations is complicated by the fact that both had independent access to the Gospels. Relatively new is the insight that both *APt* and *AJ* do have another common source, although in this case the word 'source' can only be used with qualifications. I mean the canonical Acts. For the *APt* it is again American scholars who have adduced evidence that the author of *APt* was well acquainted with and influenced by Luke's book[8], whereas the relation between Acts and the *AJ* is one of the subjects of the dissertation that I am preparing. Yet the relations of both Apocryphal Acts with canonical Acts leave open the possibility that the two are also mutually related or have still other sources.

For the *AJ* no other sources have been found than those just discussed, the Synoptics and Acts, plus the Fourth Gospel; and even these have been used in a very independent way. The *APt* on the other hand may have drawn on the *Kerygmata Petri* and certainly used Justin Martyr[9]. Moreover, they clearly quote from the OT as well as the NT: Gospels, Acts, but also Pauline and Petrine letters.

Another recent insight, which we owe to Junod and Kaestli, is that the *AJ* consist of two different parts which had different origins. This view lies at the basis of the first volume of the present series and I will come back on it below[10].

---

[8] R.F. Stoops, 'Departing to Another Place: The *Acts of Peter* and the Canonical Acts of the Apostles', in E.H. Lovering (ed), *Society of Biblical Literature 1994 Seminar Papers* (Atlanta, 1994) 390-404; W.J. Stroud, 'Models for Petrine Speeches in the *Acts of Peter*', *ibidem*, 405-14.
[9] See Adamik, this volume, Ch. V.
[10] The homogeneity of the *APt* is also disputed. L. van Kampen, *Apostelverhalen* (Diss. Utrecht, 1990) 42, 63-4, doubts if the Martyrium (*cc*.33-41) belonged to the original *Acts* because it has another theme (chastity) than the rest of the text (power over Rome). Also, what I said above about the use of the Scriptures does not apply to the *MartPt* which contains no quotations

2. Differences

While I intend to show that *AJ* and *APt* are indeed closely related, it is also possible to list significant differences between the two texts such as varying views of the church, its leadership, and the sacraments. The *AJ* know no baptism and a 'eucharist' with bread only (cf *APt* 5), whereas in the *APt* Peter baptizes, and bread and water are used for the eucharist. The *AJ* know no organized church and no hierarchy, whereas the *APt* mention bishops and elders (6, 13, 27) and an organized church life. Peter fasts (5, 18), but the *AJ* know no fasting. Secondly, the *AJ* cluster all they say about Jesus in a veritable 'gospel' and can do so because the NT gospels are not recognized as authoritative. The *APt* do recognize written gospels and have only scattered pieces about the life and death of Christ. A third major difference concerns the theology of the texts. The *AJ* contain a Gnostic interpolation, while the rest of the text shows a consistent ideology which is best described as Ultra-Johannine. The theology of the *APt* on the other hand cannot be sharply delineated. It is a layman's theology, an uneven mixture of docetic and incarnational elements[11]. In several places a proto-Orthodox Christology can be found[12], but, e.g., *c*.20 and the Coptic fragment are docetic. Remarkable in comparison with the *AJ* are the references to the resurrection of Christ (7) and the expectation of his second coming (1, 36).

It is necessary to say something more about the alleged Gnosticism of the *APt*. It is soon evident that *cc*.1-36 and 40-1 contain no gnostic ideas at all. This leaves us with *cc*.37-9, which narrate the words of Peter from and to the cross[13]. But although these chapters 37-9 contain reminiscences of gnostic language, what is actually expressed is not gnostic at all[14]. The fact that the significance of

---

from the OT and hardly refers to the NT. The *MartPt* may be a (gnosticizing – see below) addition to the *Acts of Peter and Simon* (*cc*.1-32). If this is correct, the situation with the *APt* resembles the way in which *cc*.94-102 are an addition to the *AJ*. A weak spot in Van Kampen's argument is that he has to leave the Coptic fragment out of his considerations. See also Luttikhuizen, this volume, Ch. IV.

[11] Schmidt, *Petrusakten*, 91-4, and Schneemelcher, in *NTA* II, 282-3.
[12] E.g. in 2.36-8, 44-6; 7.8-11.
[13] C.L. Sturhahn, *Die Christologie der ältesten apokryphen Apostelakten* (Diss. Göttingen, 1952) 153-9 states that in *cc*.37-9 gnostic elements dominate, whereas the rest of the text has a more "middle-of-the-road" theology.

events is not located in what is physically visible, but in their deeper, spiritual meaning is common to all religions and not foreign to the Old Testament and Early Christianity. Although Peter admittedly goes rather far in his spiritualization, that does not make his words gnostic. After all, ἐν μυστηρίῳ in the *APt* only means 'allegorical'[15]. Contrary to what we see in the *AJ*, neither the factuality nor the importance of Christ's appearance on earth, his death and resurrection, are denied. *C*.38 even implies that the first man was created good and later became a sinner[16]. The above is sufficient to exclude the idea of common authorship once and for all.

3. *Similarities*

But what interests us here are the similarities. The list of parallel passages at the end of the present chapter, which follows the order of the *APt*, is rather impressive[17]. I have left out the agreements in areas like Christology and asceticism, mainly because arguments based on them can usually easily be reversed. A can depend on B, but also B on A. Closer inspection of this list leads to several conclusions.
I. First and foremost, the parallels are so numerous and so direct that the hypothesis of a common environment falls short to explain them. The least we must posit is a common written source, if not direct literary dependence.
II. The parallels are not equally spread, but concentrated in specific chapters. On the side of the *APt* these chapters are especially 20-1 and 36-9. On the side of the *AJ* we used to point to *cc*.87-93 and 94-102 + 109, that is the gospel-like part of the text, but my research also brings to light numerous parallels with *cc*.106-13. The passages in which the parallels occur can be characterized as didactic or homiletic over against the more novelistic parts of the texts. In the narratives the *APt* and the *AJ* are far more independent of each other than in their sections of teaching.

---

[14] Cf. A. Hamman, *Das Gebet in der Alten Kirche* (Bern, 1989) 105-7.
[15] A. Harnack, as quoted by Vouaux, *Actes de Pierre*, 267.
[16] Sturhahn, *Christologie*, 184-94 is a useful discussion of the idea of revelation in *APt*.
[17] Cf. the lists in James, *Apocrypha anecdota*, xxv-xxviii; Flamion, 'Actes de Pierre', notes to 249-53; Jones, 'Orientations', 503-4.

III. Lists of christological predicates, such as 'word', 'door', 'light' and 'life', occur in *AJ* 98 and 109 and in *APt* 20 (**14** in the list). In the first mentioned passage they are applied to the cross of light, in the other two to Jesus. But similar lists occurs in other second-century texts[18]. This circumstance complicates the determination of dependence.

IV. The parallels are nevertheless rather diverse in kind. Not only ideas or concepts are similar, but sometimes there are phrases which are literally the same (**28**), and sometimes the rough lines of an episode are similar (**1, 18**). Peter's last farewell (**20**) uses many the same words as that of John.

An interesting remark which I have nevertheless not included in my list is offered by Gérard Poupon and Judith Perkins. They hold that there are parallels between the senator Marcellus in the *APt*, who had lapsed from the faith but was reconverted by Peter, and the necrophiliac Callimachus in the *AJ*. Perkins goes even further and suggests that Fortunatus, the wicked steward who helps Callimachus and who was unwilling or unable to convert, was created as a kind of double of Callimachus in order to polemize against the *APt*. She suggests that the *AJ* want to combat the notion of unlimited forgiveness for *lapsi* in the *APt* by showing the awful end of Fortunatus. The *AJ* are therefore the later text[19]. But this is not convincing. The comparison overlooks that Callimachus and Fortunatus never were believers; especially the former is explicitly introduced as a heathen[20]. Consequently he can neither be a *lapsus* nor an exact counterpart of Marcellus, although the descriptions of the two may have some resemblances.

4. *Hypothesis*

I must now try to formulate a hypothesis concerning the intertextual relations, which adds something to our insight in at least one of the

---

[18] E.g. Justin, *Dialogue* 61, 100, and Melito, *Peri Pascha* 7, 8, 103, 105.
[19] G. Poupon, 'Les "Actes de Pierre" et leur remaniement', in *ANRW* II.25.6 (1988) 4363-83, esp. 4376; Perkins, 'Intertext', 630-1. Poupon's suggestion (4379) that the problem of the *lapsi* is a theme in the *APt* is in itself illuminating, but I fail to see it in the *AJ*.
[20] 63.1-4 (Callimachus; his name appears no earlier than 73.10), cf. 76.32-40 (his conversion); 70.4-5 (Fortunatus; his name in 73.12).

texts involved. When one notices the polemical tone in the gospel part of the *AJ*, one might be inclined to think that it is the *AJ* which direct a polemic against the *APt*. But although we certainly have a polemic in the *AJ*, it is directed against the canonical gospels and can be fully explained as such. I would say that the reverse is true. Indeed, the hypothesis that the *APt* depend on the *AJ* can serve to explain several features.

1. There are ideological inconsistencies in the *APt*. What I mean is: whenever the author of the *APt* independently tells his own story, his theology is more or less middle of the road and can never be labeled clearly 'heretic'; but whenever it seems that the author leans on the *AJ*, his theology changes and becomes quasi-gnostic, spiritualizing. In this way his Christology becomes docetic in *cc*.20-1 and his soteriology in *cc*.37-9[21]. That an author who knows the *regula fidei*[22] can say that Christ did not eat (**11**) must be due to dependence on another text: the *AJ*.

2. It is noteworthy that the instruction not to recompense evil with evil (**19**) occurs in both Acts together with the verb 'we have learned'. The instruction also appears in three NT epistles including 1 Peter[23], and it almost certainly reflects Jesus' denunciation of the ἀντί-principle in Mt 5:38-39a which was well-known in the early church[24]. The verb 'to learn' which both Acts use normally applies to ecclesiastical tradition[25]. In this case the source of the words could be none other than the Scriptures. But the *APt* would never use the abstract expression 'we have learned' with reference to the Scriptures which they otherwise quote openly. This strongly suggests that the *AJ*, the main part of which consciously avoids references to the NT books, first used the words and coined the introduction 'we have learned', which was then copied by the *APt*.

---

[21] Schmidt, *Petrusakten*, 90-6; Harnack, quoted by Flamion, 'Actes de Pierre', 260 n.3.
[22] Westra, this volume, Ch. XI.
[23] Rom 12:17, 1 Th 5:15, 1 Pe 3:9. The saying also occurs in Polycarp, *ad Phil*, 2.2, and several times in the Jewish novel *Joseph and Aseneth* 23.9; 28.5,10,14; 29.3, which stems from roughly the same period.
[24] J.Piper, *"Love your enemies". Jesus' love command in the synoptic gospels and in the early Christian paraenesis* (Cambridge, 1979) 53, 49.
[25] K.H. Rengstorf, in *TWNT* IV, 414ff. See e.g. 1 Clem 21:8; IgnRom 4:3; IgnMagn 10:1; Barn 9:9, 21:1; *Epistle to Diognetus* 4:6.

3. *APt* 20 is closely akin to the *AJ*: the list contains no less than eight similarities. This suggests that the chapter is a kind of summary of *AJ* 87-93. In my opinion this explanation is better than the reverse option, viz. that this chapter inspired the author of the *AJ* to a whole series of short episodes. And this brings us to the fourth point, which I consider decisive.

4. The *AJ* consist of two parts that were written by different authors who had different convictions. The first wrote a text which generically resembles the other *AAA*. The second author wrote a kind of gospel in which he polemizes against the NT Gospels and which has gnostic convictions. These authors worked at different moments and probably the second did not know the first. Yet in both parts of the text similarities with the *APt* occur. I deem it very unlikely that two authors so different would have undergone the influence of the same text, the *APt*.

In view of the composite character of the *AJ*, the only plausible hypothesis is that the *AJ* in their final form were known to and used by the author of the *APt*. My tentative conclusion is therefore that the author of the *APt* knew the *AJ* in roughly the same form in which we have that text, namely including *cc*.94-102, and that for him it was one of the sources from which he drew. Thus I uphold the opinion of that great scholar, Carl Schmidt. The current datings of the texts, viz. middle of the second century for the *AJ* and end of that century for the *APt*[26], are not in need of revision.

---

[26] See also Bremmer, this volume, Ch. I.3.

5. List of parallels

ACTS OF PETER
(line numbers according to ed. Vouaux)

1   Coptic Fragment, end
    Ptolemy learns chastity by means of blindness

2   2.21-5 forgiveness of previous sins if good henceforth
    si non permanseritis in pristinis operibus... <u>dimittet</u> vobis Jesus deus vivus <u>quae ignorantes egistis</u>

3   3.15 (cf. 4.30; 10.37; 30.4; 40.16) strong in faith
    perstabilitus, constabilitus, στηριζόμενος

4   10.27 word of the Lord quoted by Marcellus
    qui mecum sunt non me intellexerunt

5   15.12
    qui numquam in bono, sed in veneno radices emittis

6   18.6-11 call to thank the One who is there
    flectamus ergo genua Christo: obaudiens non, etsi non clamaverimus; est qui videat nos, etsi non videtur istis oculis, sed in nobis est: si volumus, non recedet a nobis

7   20-21 old women (widows) healed

8   20.11-3 the written gospel is according to capacity
    quae gratia ipsius coepimus (cf 20.19, 29), scribsimus [sc. in Scriptura], etsi adhuc vobis infirma videntur, capaciter tamen quae perferuntur in humana carne inferri

9   20.16-9 discusses the Lord's polymorphy
    motus dominus misericordia sua in alia figura ostendere se et effigie hominis videri, quem neque Judaei neque nos

ACTS OF JOHN
(line numbers according to ed. Junod-Kaestli)

1   113 John learns chastity by means of blindness

2   107.14-5 forgiveness of previous sins if good henceforth
εἰ μὲν οὖν μηκέτι ἁμαρτάνετε <u>ἃ ἐν ἀγνοίᾳ ἐπράξατε ἀφίησιν ὑμῖν</u>

3   45.7; 87.4; 106.10 strong in faith
στηρίζω

4   92.6-8 word of the (double of the) Lord
Ἰησοῦ, οὓς ἐξελέξω ἔτι σοι ἀπιστοῦσιν – ἄνθρωποι γάρ εἰσιν

5   98.18
ἡ κατωτικὴ ῥίζα

6   103 call to thank the One who is there
.2 προσκυνῶμεν αὐτῷ
.9-11 ἅπασιν ἡμῖν συνὼν πάσχουσι συμπάσχει καὶ αὐτός· ἀδελφοί, ὑφ' ἑκάστου ἡμῶν καλούμενος οὐχ ὑπομένει παρακοῦσαι ἡμῶν, ἀλλ' ὡς πάντῃ ὢν πάντων ἡμῶν ἀκούει κτλ.

7   30-36 old women healed (end of the story lost)

8   88.1-8 the written gospel is according to capacity
ἐγὼ μὲν ὑμῖν οὔτε προσομιλεῖν οὔτε γράψαι χωρῶ ἅ τε εἶδον ἅ τε ἤκουσα· καὶ νῦν μὴν (...) καθ' ἃ χωρεῖ ἕκαστος ἐκείνων ὑμῖν κοινωνήσω ὧν ἀκροαταὶ δύνασθε γενέσθαι κτλ.

9   88-93 twelve descriptions of polymorphous appearances

*digne inluminare possimus. Unusquisque enim nostrum
sicut capiebat videre, prout poterat videbat*

10 20.20-9 the Transfiguration

11 20.36-7 Christ needs no food
*manducavit et bibit propter nos, ipse neque esuriens
neque sitiens*

12 20.40-2 antitheses about the appearance of Christ
*hunc magnum et minimum, formosum et foedum, juvenem
et senem, tempore adparentem et in aeternum utique
invisibilem*

13 20.42-9 antitheses about the being of Christ, e.g.:
.42-3   *quem manus humana non detinuit et tenetur a
       servientibus*
.44   *quem obauditum verbum sed nunc cognitum.*
.45   *quem impassibilem et nunc est tamquam nos
       passionem expertus*
.46   *castigatum numquam sed nunc castigatum*
.47   *qui ante saeculum est et tempore intellectus est*

14 20.50-3 list of predicates
januam, lumen, viam, panem, aquam, vitam, resurrectionem, refrigerium, margaritam, thensaurum, semen, saturitatem, granum sinapis, vineam, aratrum, gratiam, fidem, verbum

39.12-5 list of predicates
πατήρ, μήτηρ, ἀδελφός, φίλος, δοῦλος, οἰκόνομος,
τὸ πᾶν, τὸ ὄν.

15 21.17-20 appearance of light
*nec tale lumen quod est interdiu, inenarrabilem,
invisibilem, quod enarrare nemo hominum possit.*

10 90.1-4 the Transfiguration

11 93.4-10 Christ needs no food
τὸν [sc. τακτὸν ἄρτον] δὲ αὐτοῦ εὐλογῶν διεμέριζεν ἡμῖν.

12 88-90 antitheses about the appearance of Christ
88.12   James sees a παιδίον – 88.16 John an ἄνδρα εὔμορφον
89.2-4   πάλιν ὤφθη ἐμοὶ τὴν μὲν κεφαλὴν ὑπόψιλον ἔχων, τὸ δὲ γένειον δασὺ καταγόμενον, τῷ δὲ Ἰακώβῳ ἀρχιγένειος νεανίσκος.

13 95, 101.6-11 antitheses about the being of Christ
95.4-5   λυθῆναι θέλω καὶ λῦσαι θέλω
95.12-3   ἀκούειν θέλω καὶ ἀκούεσθαι θέλω
101.7   με παθόντα καὶ οὐκ ἔπαθον, μὴ παθόντα καὶ ἔπαθον
95.6-7   τρωθῆναι θέλω καὶ τρῶσαι θέλω
95.14-5   νοηθῆναι θέλω νοῦς ὢν ὅλος

14 98 list of predicates of the cross:
λόγος, νοῦς, Χριστός, θύρα, ὁδός, ἄρτος, σπόρος, ἀνάστασις, υἱός, πατήρ, πνεῦμα, ζωή, ἀλήθεια, πίστις, χάρις.
109 list of predicates of Christ:
υἱός, θύρα, ἀνάστασις, ὁδός, σπόρος, λόγος, χάρις, πίστις, ἅλας, μαργαρίτη, θησαυρός, ἄροτρον, σαγήνη, μέγεθος, διάδημα, υἱὸς ἀνθρώπου, ἀλήθεια, ἀνάπαυσις, γνῶσις, δύναμις, ἐντολή, παρρησία, ἐλευθερία, καταφυγή.

15 90.3-4 light beyond description
φῶς τοιοῦτον ὁποῖον οὐκ ἔστιν δυνατὸν ἀνθρώπῳ χρωμένῳ λόγῳ φθαρτῷ ἐκφέρειν οἷον ἦν.

16 21.27-31 polymorphy in three forms
seniorem, iuvenem adulescentem, puerum

17 22.33-6 Marcellus sees the Lord in the stature of Peter
tibi similis, Petre... ut intenderem ego vos ambos... tam similes

18 26 resurrection story
.2-3 *... Petrum dixit: quid dicis, Petre? Ecce puer mortuus jacet*
.6 *non temptatur Deus neque extimatur*
(*P.Oxy*) οὐ πειράζεται θεὸς οὐδὲ δοκιμάζεται
.8-11 *sed quoniam nunc temptatur inter vos Deus et dominus meus Jesus Christus, et tanta signa et prodigia faciens per me in conversatione peccatorum suorum*
.14-6 another person raises the dead
.17 *unus Deus, unus Deus Petri*

19 28.74-5 *malum enim pro malo non novimus retribuere*

20 36-9 last farewell
36.9 (41.13)   ἀγαλλιῶμαι
36.10 (41.13) εὐφραίνομαι
36.5-6   στηρίξαι ... ἐν αὐτῷ
36.21 (37.9)   οἱ ἐπὶ Χριστὸν ἐλπίζοντες
36.22   μέμνησθε ... δι' ἐμοῦ σημείων
               καὶ τεράτων, μέμνησθε τῆς
               συμπαθείας ... πόσας ἰάσεις
37.12   χωρίσατε
37.13,14   πηρώσατε
38.15   βασιλεία

21 37-8 speculation about the cross (= logos, see 39.2 λόγε)
37.8-10 σταυρὸς μὴ τοῦτο ὑμῖν ἔστω τὸ φαινόμενον ... ἕτερον γάρ τί ἐστιν παρὰ τὸ φαινόμενον τοῦτο κατὰ τὸ τοῦ Χριστοῦ πάθος.

22 38.5,17, 23 ὁ πρῶτος ἄνθρωπος

ACTS OF JOHN AND ACTS OF PETER

16 88-93 polymorphous appearances in two forms (cf. **12**)

17 87.2-3 Drusiana sees Christ in the stature of John
μοι ὁ κύριος ὡς Ἰωάννης ὤφθη

18 81 resurrection story
.1-2 (εἶδε) τὸν Φορτουνᾶτον κείμενον καὶ εἶπε πρὸς τὸν Ἰωάννην· Πάτερ κτλ.
(90.22 μὴ πειράζειν τὸν ἀπείραστον)

.10-2 καὶ γὰρ ὁ θεὸς ποιησάντων ἡμῶν εἰς αὐτὸν πολλὰ κακὰ καὶ οὐχὶ καλὰ ἀντιμισθίαν ἡμῖν οὐκ ἀπέδωκεν ἀλλὰ μετάνοιαν.
.20-2 (83.1-4) another person raises the dead
79.8-9 τὸν μόνον θεόν σε ὄντα ἐπικαλοῦμαι (42.7-8)

19 81.9-10 οὐκ ἐμάθομεν κακὸν ἀντὶ κακοῦ ἀποδοῦναι

20 106-13 last farewell
106.1   ἀγαλλιώμενος
107.5   εὐφραινέσθω
106.10 στηρίζεσθε οὖν ἐν αὐτῷ
108.10 ἐπὶ σὲ [Χριστὸν] ἐλπίζοντας
106.5-6 γινώσκετε ... πόσας δυνάμεις δι' ἐμοῦ ... ὅσα τέρατα, ὅσα σημεῖα, ἰάσεις πόσας.
113.13 χωρίζω
113.7   πηρώσας
106.5   βασιλεία

21 97-101 speculation about the cross = logos (98.8)
99.1-4 οὗτος οὖν ὁ σταυρὸς ... οὐχ οὗτος δέ ἐστιν ὁ σταυρὸς ὃν μέλλεις ὁρᾶν ξύλινον.

22 101.14, 15-6 speculation on ἄνθρωπος

23 38.25 (at end of pericope)
ἡ ἐπιστροφὴ καὶ ἡ μετάνοια τοῦ ἀνθρώπου

24 39.2 λόγε, ζωῆς ξύλον νῦν ὑπ' ἐμοῦ εἰρημένον

25 39.2-12 inner voice and inner hearing
εὐχαριστῶ σοι οὐκ ἐν χείλεσιν τούτοις τοῖς προσηλωμένοις, οὐδὲ γλώσσῃ ... οὐδὲ λόγῳ τούτῳ ὑπὸ τέχνης φύσεως ὑλικῆς προερχομένῳ, ἀλλ' ἐκείνῃ τῇ φωνῇ ... τῇ μὴ <u>δι' ὀργάνων σώματος</u> προϊούσῃ κτλ.

26 39.15-6 καταφεύγω ἐπὶ Χριστόν

27 39.17-8 (1 Cor 2:9)
ἃ οὔτε ὀφθαλμὸς εἶδεν οὔτε οὖς ἤκουσεν οὔτε ἐπὶ καρδίαν ἀνθρώπου οὐκ ἀνέβη.

28 39.19-22 prayer
ἀμίαντε Ἰησοῦ· αἰνοῦμέν σε, εὐχαριστοῦμέν σοι καὶ ἀνθομολογούμεθα, δοξάζοντές σε ... ὅτι σὺ θεὸς μόνος καὶ οὐχ ἕτερος, ᾧ ἡ δόξα καὶ νῦν καὶ εἰς πάντας τοὺς αἰῶνας τῶν αἰώνων· ἀμήν.

29 40.10-1
τοῦ κυρίου λέγοντος· ἄφετε τοὺς νεκροὺς θάπτεσθαι ὑπὸ τῶν ἰδίων νεκρῶν.

23 102.6-7 (at end of pericope)
ἀνθρώπου ἐπιστροφὴν καὶ σωτηρίαν

24 98.8-9 ὁ σταυρὸς ὁ τοῦ φωτὸς ποτὲ μὲν λόγος
καλεῖται ὑπ' ἐμοῦ

25 103.2-4 spiritual service of God
προσκυνῶμεν αὐτῷ ... μὴ δακτύλοις, μηδὲ
στόμασιν, μηδὲ γλώσσῃ, μηδ' <u>ἑνὶ ὅλως σωματικῷ
ὀργάνῳ</u>, ἀλλὰ τῇ ψυχικῇ διαθέσει

26 112.10-1 καταφεύγω ἐπὶ Χριστόν

27 106.8-10
ὅσα εἴδετε κατ' ὀφθαλμοὺς διδόμενα ὑμῖν ὑπ' αὐτοῦ,
μὴ φαινόμενα ὀφθαλμοῖς τούτοις μηδὲ ἀκοαῖς
ταύταις ἀκουόμενα

28 77.17-20 prayer
δοξάξομέν σε καὶ αἰνοῦμεν καὶ εὐλογοῦμεν καὶ
εὐχαριστοῦμεν ... ἅγιε Ἰησοῦ, ὅτι σὺ μόνος θεὸς
καὶ οὐχ ἕτερος· ᾧ τὸ ἀνεπιβούλευτον κράτος καὶ
νῦν καὶ εἰς τοὺς ἅπαντας αἰῶνας τῶν αἰώνων· ἀμήν.
94.14-6 δόξα ... αἰνοῦμέν σε πάτερ, εὐχαριστοῦμέν σοι φῶς

29 24.18
νεκροὺς νεκροῖς χαρίζεται

XIV. The Relation between the *Acts of Peter* and the *Acts of Paul*: State of the Question

WILLY RORDORF

The question of the relation between the *Acts of Paul* (*AP*) and the *Acts of Peter* (*APt*) is important for the relative dating of *APt*. It is well-known that Tertullian provides the absolute terminus for the *AP* by referring to the *AP* in his treatise *De baptismo* (17.5), dated approximately 200 AD; the *AP* must therefore have existed before then[1]. This fixed point of reference has considerable consequences for the dating of the *APt*: if it depends on the *AP*, it probably originated in the third century. On the other hand, if the *AP* depends on *APt*, we can fix the date of the writing of the *APt* in the second century, even in the middle of the second century. The swings among scholars between these two possibilities of understanding the relation between the *AP* and the *APt* – to which may be added a third, as we shall soon see – is the subject of this paper.

1. *Carl Schmidt*

In 1903, the German scholar Carl Schmidt considered the *AP* as a source for the *APt*. He advanced the following arguments to support his thesis:
1. In his *Commentary on St. John* (20.91), Origen cites a saying attributed to the Savior in the *AP* which reads, 'I am about to be

---

[1] See most recently A. Hilhorst, 'Tertullian on the Acts of Paul', in Bremmer, *AAP*, 150-63; G. Poupon, 'Encore une fois: Tertullien, *De baptismo* 17.5', in D. Knoepfler (ed), *Nomen Latinum. Mélanges A. Schneider* (Neuchâtel and Geneva, 1997) 199-205. For the date of *AP* see also Bremmer, this volume, Ch. I.3.

crucified again' (ἄνωθεν μέλλω σταυροῦσθαι). This saying which expresses a general idea in the *AP*, was used by the author of the *APt* in his composition of the famous scene, *Domine, quo vadis?*, and for the portrayal of Peter's crucifixion, replacing the unusual word ἄνωθεν with πάλιν.

2. Direct dependence is evident in the final chapter of the *APt*. After Peter's crucifixion by the Prefect Agrippa[2], Nero is angry that Peter did not suffer a punishment more cruel because some of Nero's servants had became converts to Christianity, provoking his wrath against Peter. Now, in the rest of the *APt*, nothing has been said about the conversion of any of Caesar's servants. However, in the *AP*, these servants actually appear and through their conversion provoke Nero's wrath, leading to Paul's martyrdom. Then in a vision, Nero is threatened with punishment if he refuses to release the Christians, and so he releases them. This detail is also taken over by the *APt*. For Schmidt, it is clear that the *APt* have imitated the *AP* so as to introduce Nero in the story of Peter's martyrdom, thereby harmonizing it with ecclesiastical tradition.

3. The motive for the condemnation of Peter is likewise borrowed from the *AP*. For it is because of Peter's preaching on ἁγνεία that Agrippa's four concubines and Albinus' wife deny themselves to the partners, which corresponds in fact to the fundamental preaching of the apostle in all the parts of the *AP*.

On the basis of these observations, Schmidt thought that the *APt* originated about the years 200-210[3]. But the German scholar had not said his last word. After the discovery of the Hamburg Papyrus, which he edited and which contains a large portion of the *AP*, he radically reversed his point of view.

Until 1929, he still maintained his former theory[4], but in 1930, he felt it necessary to make a 'fundamental correction'. For now he had in the Hamburg Papyrus (7.24-35), the whole passage to which Origen

---

[2] On Agrippa in the *APt* see now Karasszon, this volume, Ch. II.

[3] C. Schmidt, *Die alten Petrusakten im Zusammenhang der apokryphen Apostelliteratur nebst einem neuentdeckten Fragment* (Leipzig, 1903) 82-6; 99f.

[4] C. Schmidt, 'Neue Funde zu den alten Πράξεις Παύλου', *Sitzungsberichte der Preussischen Akademie der Wissenschaften*, Phil.-hist. Klasse, 1929, 176f.

refers in his *Commentary on St. John*. He was so struck by this passage, that he reversed his previous interpretation of the relation between the *AP* and the *APt*: It was not the *AP* which inspired the author of the *APt*, but the author of the *AP* who imitated the *APt*. Since this swing in his thinking was so radical, I will cite Schmidt word for word:

> 'Ich hatte nun den Verfasser der Quo-vadis-Szene für den Plagiator statuiert, dabei aber den Anstoss Übersehen, dass der Spruch ἄνωθεν μέλλω σταυροῦσθαι gar nicht auf Paulus zu passen schien, denn von einer Wiederholung des Kreuzestodes des Herrn in der Person des Paulus kann nach der Darstellung des Verfassers selbst keine Rede sein, da ja Paulus den Tod durch das Schwert erleidet, während Petrus durch seine umgekehrte Kreuzigung tatsächlich der Nachfolge des Herrn gewürdigt wird. Auffällig ist ferner, dass der Herr in der Antwort gar nicht auf eine Deutung seines Spruches wie seiner äusseren Traurigkeit eingeht, sondern sich mit der einfachen Aufforderung zur Reise nach Rom begnügt. Unbedingt will das στυγνὸς καὶ κατηφής auf ein trauriges Schicksal des Apostels in Rom deuten, aber es fehlt doch die Pointe, wenn unter dem ἄνωθεν σταυροῦσθαι nur im allgemeinen der Märtyrertod verstanden werden soll. So taucht der Verdacht auf, dass der Verfasser der Paulusakten jenen Spruch unter kleiner Abänderung den Petrusakten entlehnt hat.'[5]

Schmidt adds to his argument for the dependence of the *AP* on the *APt* the mention of a certain Artemon in the Hamburg Papyrus (7.19-20), who is the ship's captain and who was baptized by Peter exactly like Theon in the *Actus Vercellenses* 5; the author of the *AP* has taken over this detail of the *APt* which he knew, and changed the name of Theon to Artemon to avoid detection as a plagiarist. Schmidt also argued that the final chapter of the *APt* is likewise a source for the *Martyrdom of Paul* (*MP*); but it must be said that Schmidt's argument in this case is too feeble to merit attention here.

From 1930 onwards, Schmidt maintained his second interpretation of the evidence. In his edition of the Hamburg Papyrus, he develops it using the same arguments, situating the date of the *APt* in the years 180-190[6].

---

[5] C. Schmidt, 'Zur Datierung der alten Petrusakten', *ZNW* 29 (1930) 150-5, esp. 152 (quote).

[6] C. Schmidt and W. Schubart, *ΠΡΑΞΕΙΣ ΠΑΥΛΟΥ. Acta Pauli nach*

2. Gérard Poupon

Adolf von Harnack, followed by Léon Vouaux, was the first to advance the theory that the *Actus Vercellenses* were not a homogeneous text[7]. Above all, he thought that the first three and the final chapters of this text came from the *AP*, provoking the critique of Schmidt[8]. Harnack has been proved wrong on this point by the discovery of the Hamburg Papyrus, which allows no place for a voyage to Spain such as it is understood in the *APt* 1-3. But it is still true that the final chapter of the *APt* is difficult to understand except as a piece inspired by the *AP*. In making this observation, Gérard Poupon comes to the following conclusion:

> – si le ch. 41 est partie intégrante des Actes primitifs, ceux-ci sont postérieurs aux 'Actes de Paul', puisqu'il en est sans conteste inspiré; ce qui met en cause la thèse de SCHMIDT sur la chronologie relative des deux apocryphes;
> – si ce ch. 41 est interpolé, la thèse de SCHMIDT sur l'intégrité des 'APe' s'en trouve infirmée, le texte n'étant pas indemne de tout remaniement. C'est cette seconde hypothèse qui nous paraît la mieux fondée[9].

To support his opinion, Poupon presents a long series of arguments, of which we can only summarize a portion here. He also returns to the problem of chs. 1-3 of the *APt*. How is it that these chapters are silent about Peter and Marcellus or that, apart from Narcissus the priest, other characters who do play a role never appear in the rest of the story? Or why is it that Nero is only mentioned in chs. 1 and 41? The editorial seams between the beginning of the *APt* and the rest of the work (esp. ch. 4-6) lead to the conclusion that a later interpolator rather awkwardly attached chs. 1-3 to the rest of the story[10]. His goal

---

dem Papyrus der Hamburger Staats- und Universitäts-Bibliothek (Glückstadt and Hamburg, 1936), 127-30.

[7] A. von Harnack, 'Patristische Miszellen', in *TU* 20 (Leipzig, 1901) 102-6; L. Vouaux, *Les Actes de Pierre* (Paris, 1922) 27-33.

[8] Schmidt, *Petrusakten*, 82f.

[9] G. Poupon, 'Les "Actes de Pierre" et leur remaniement', *ANRW* II.25.6 (1988, 4363-83) 4370.

[10] Poupon, 'Actes de Pierre', 4372-4.

was to connect reminiscences from the New Testament (Acts 28.30; Rom 15.24) with the apocryphal legend, particularly the Roman tradition concerning the death of Paul.

But Poupon pushes his analysis further. Observing that in c.8 Marcellus is not yet a Christian and that in c. 10, he appears suddenly as a penitent, Poupon concludes that c.10 would have had to recount originally the conversion of Marcellus, and that the interpolator made it into a story of penitence. In this same line of thinking, the interpolator introduced the two stories of Rufina (2) and of Chryse (30), to show that the pardon from sins of the flesh is possible. The goal of these interpolations was therefore to make a plea for the second repentance. Given the controversies surrounding the pardon of adultery and of apostasy during the first decades of the third century, Poupon thinks that the alteration of the *APt* must have occurred at that time[11].

We should observe that this important work of Poupon has not yet received the attention it merits; Wilhelm Schneemelcher summarizes it but does not really take a position[12].

3. *The Position of MacDonald and its critique by Stoops*

Poupon limits himself to postulating an alteration to the *APt* at the beginning of the third century, not wanting to identify the sources used by the redactor, except in the case of *c.*41 where he sees the direct influence of the *AP*[13].

---

[11] Poupon, *ibidem*, 4375f, 4381 (date).

[12] W. Schneemelcher, in *NTA* II, 281: 'Within the frame of this introduction it is not possible to examine Poupon's thesis in detail. Many observations are undoubtedly correct, and take us further in our understanding of this work. It is however questionable whether the conclusions which Poupon draws are convincing. To put the question in another way: was an originally self-contained work (focussing on only one apostle) altered by a redactor with specific tendencies? Or are the APt to be understood as a work put together from various sources which the reviser has not always succeeded in co-ordinating?'

[13] G. Poupon tells me now also concerning chs. 1-3 of the *APt*, that he 'n'exclurait pas la possibilité d'un emprunt du remanieur aux *AP* pour étoffer son scénario "original" du départ de Paul pour l'Espagne. Il aurait pu plagier une scène de l'apocryphe aujourd'hui perdue. La rigueur dont fait preuve l'apôtre à la veille de son départ détonne' (letter of 2 October 1996).

It is not surprising then that the question of the relation between the *APt* and the *AP* has been taken up again. The American scholar, Dennis R. MacDonald, who is a fine connoisseur of *AP*[14], and who is preparing an American edition of the New Testament Apocrypha, has just taken up this question again, firstly in an article entitled '*The Acts of Paul* and *The Acts of Peter*: Which Came First?'[15], secondly in his General Introduction to the volume which will appear in print presently. He has very kindly sent me a manuscript of this chapter, dated in the Fall of 1996. In the following discussion, I will be referring to this text. Robert F. Stoops has critiqued MacDonald's above-mentioned article[16]. Since he follows the framework of this article, it seems to me simpler to speak about it with respect to the position of MacDonald.

MacDonald proposes three criteria for the determination of intertextual relations between the Apocryphal Acts of the Apostles (in this case *AP*, *APt*, *AJn*, *AA* and *ATh*). Because the importance of these criteria, I cite the passage in question:

> 1. The criterion of generative external traditions. When parallel passages exist, one of them may display reliance on antecedent literature or on oral tradition which may sufficiently account for its genesis, voiding the necessity of positing reliance on the other Acts. If the parallel in the other Acts displays no such reliance on external tradition, it may well have derived from the Acts that did.
> 2. The criterion of internal consistency. Frequently two Acts share episodes that must be genetically related, but neither of them can be traced to external traditions. In such cases one can at times determine which is the earlier by assessing which provides the episode its more native environment. This assessment may be based on motifs, characterizations, plot sequence, even vocabulary. Conversely, one can often detect scars caused by an author artlessly grafting foreign materials into the story from the other Acts.
> 3. The criterion of secondary improvement. Sometimes one of the texts seems to repair its parallel text in the other Acts. For example, one

---

[14] D.R. MacDonald, *The Legend and the Apostle. The Battle for Paul in Story and Canon* (Philadelphia, 1983).
[15] MacDonald, 'The *Acts of Paul* and the *Acts of Peter*: Which came first?', in *SBL 1992 Seminar Papers* (Atlanta, 1992) 214-24.
[16] R.F. Stoops, Jr., 'Peter, Paul, and Priority in the Apocryphal Acts', *ibidem*, 225-33.

document may contain a theologically objectionable concept which becomes more palatable in the other. More often, one Acts presents an apostle in a less than favorable light and the other does not. Insofar as tradition generally improved apostolic public relations, in such cases one often can detect the direction of dependence.

We shall now look at each of MacDonald's intertextual parallels between the *AP* and *APt*:

1. Hamburg Papyrus p. 6-7; *Actus Vercellenses* 1-4.

The scenes of departure in each of their texts (Paul's departure from Corinth; Paul's departure from Rome) show certain similarities: the Spirit announces what will happen to each one, namely martyrdom, and the brothers and sisters are deeply saddened[17]. MacDonald does not say which text he thinks is imitating the other.

Our comments will be brief: we do not have to apply MacDonald's three criteria. Firstly, the model of the two passages exists already in Acts (20.36f.; 21.10-4); we are dealing with a common literary motif of Antiquity, the 'farewell scene'[18]; secondly, if we take into account the findings of Poupon, we know that the beginning chapters of the *Actus Vercellenses* are an interpolation of the third century. So, in any case, we cannot say that the *AP* depend here on the *APt*.

Stoops' observations in this case do not call into question my conclusion[19]. He himself acknowledges that one might think that the *Actus Vercellenses* depends here on the *MP*, since it predicts the death of Paul without recounting it and Nero is mentioned only in *c*. 41 (which brings up another chronological problem: according to the *APt*, Peter supposedly arrived in Rome already during the time of Emperor Claudius). Stoops responds that Paul's death was evidently known in the oral tradition, and that the final chapter of the *Actus Vercellenses* which mentions Nero could be an addition.

---

[17] Stoops, 'Peter, Paul, and Priority', 227f, adds another point of resemblance: in both stories, the Eucharist is celebrated.
[18] E. Junod and J.-D. Kaestli, *Acta Iohannis* 2 (Turnhout, 1983) 431, note 1; P.W. Dunn, 'The influence of 1 Cor on the AP', *SBL 1996 Seminar Papers* (Atlanta, 1996) 438-54, esp. 443.
[19] Stoops, 'Peter, Paul, and Priority', 225f.

2. Hamburg Papyrus p. 7f – *Martyrdom of Paul* 1; *Actus Vercellenses* 5-7.

Paul's voyage to Rome resembles Peter's voyage to Rome on several counts: the two apostles each embark on a ship whose captain is baptized by Peter. Upon their arrivals in Italy, this captain introduces each of them to the head of the local Christian community who receives them. As soon as they each arrive in Rome, the news of their coming circulates and the faithful come to see them. It is impossible to deny the resemblances. Curiously MacDonald fails once again to discuss whether the Hamburg Papyrus or the *Actus Vercellenses* should be given priority[20]. However, Schmidt profited from the character of the baptized captain to defend the priority of the *Actus Vercellenses*, declaring that the alteration of the name of Theon to Artemon would have been necessary to hide the plagiarism[21].

Stoops comments at length on this passage to prove that the *AP* depend here on the *APt*. But his arguments do not really convince me. To begin with, it is difficult to see why the 'sharing' motif between the apostle and the captain is more at home in the *APt* than in the *AP*. Next, Stoops says that the calm which takes place during the voyage in the *APt* makes Theon's baptism possible, but in the *AP* this calm has no specific function. Moreover, in Stoops's opinion, the depiction of a sleeping Paul, who according to the *AP* is 'exhausted from fasts and watches', is a 'less than heroic presentation of the apostle'; and the effect of Paul's vision of Christ during his sleep remains obscure, whereas Theon's sleep and the vision which he receives have a specific function in the *APt*.[22]

At first one is tempted to retort that the details pointed out by Stoops manifest an effort at improving the text, which would correspond to the third criterion of dependence proposed by MacDonald. If that were the case, the dependence would go the other way! But I would not want to go so far. It seems unlikely to me that the *Actus Vercellenses* could have built upon the brief mention in the Hamburg Papyrus concerning Artemon, the captain baptized by Peter, through devising a long scene which describes the event of the baptism, changing the name to Theon.

[20] I do not see how Stoops, 'Peter, Paul, and Priority', 227, can claim that 'MacDonald feels that the story in *AcPaul* served as a source for *AcPet*.'
[21] See the literature quoted in notes 4 and 5.
[22] Stoops' additional argument that Theon's baptism in the *APt* depends on the gospel story in Mat 14.22f, seems to me too weak to be maintained.

Now in that case, would one have to accept Stoops' assessment? He writes:

> The evidence suggests that the two texts share more than familiarity with a common tradition. The number of sequential parallels in this section requires some sort of intertextual dependence. Certainly oral tradition can preserve long narrative sequences, but the parallel elements are so unnecessary to the story in *AcPaul* that it is unlikely that they would survive in oral transmission. In *AcPet* these stories constitute a carefully constructed transition from one setting to another. Either the author of *AcPet* created a narrative to explain the baptized captain and managed to distribute material from *AcPaul* over three scenes (two apostolic journeys and the encounter at the gate) with such skill that most of the dangling details found meaningful contexts, or the author of *AcPaul* borrowed from *AcPet* without paying careful attention to how the elements functioned as he constructed a travel narrative for his apostle. I find the second alternative more plausible[23].

If one excludes the dependence of the *APt* on the *AP* at this point – as I do in agreement with Stoops – would it then mean *automatically* that the author of the *AP* alludes to the episode of Theon in the *APt* which he would have known? Stoops' presentation of the problem according to which it would be necessary to choose between two alternatives leads in my mind to an impasse. *Tertium datur*. Here are the reasons for my hesitation.

a) The alteration of the name gives us reason for caution. Can we assume that we are dealing with the same person and the same story? How do we know that, in the lost portions of the *AP*, Peter's baptism of Captain Artemon was not likewise related? We should note that Peter's name appears in the Coptic version of the *AP* (ed. Schmidt, 59.7). In that case, the *APt* could depend on another tradition which was more detailed at another place in the *AP*. But this is obviously another unverifiable hypothesis.

b) On the other hand, I find that Stoops exaggerates the problems to arrive at his alternative. In particular, the resemblances of details of the apostolic voyage in the two apocryphal Acts do not seem to be sufficient to prove their intertextuality. What would be more normal than to receive a vision during one's sleep? How does that imply

---

[23] Stoops, 'Peter, Paul, and Priority', 229f.

intertextuality? And the period of calm during which extraordinary things take place – why is that necessarily a sign of intertextuality? I cannot discern in these details proof that the author of the *AP* worked 'without paying careful attention to how the elements functioned as he constructed a travel narrative for his apostle.' This author would have really been very superficial in his copying of the *APt*.

It seems much more likely to me, that the author of the *APt* and the author of *AP*, independently of one another, drew upon a common stock of oral tradition. This oral tradition would have recounted the conversion of a captain who was baptized by Peter during a sea crossing. In it would have figured a vision during sleep and a period of calm. Whereas in the *APt* this oral tradition has become the story of Theon's baptism, the *AP* only recalls the name of the baptismal candidate (which is remembered as Artemon), but keeps some of the other elements of the narrative (vision during sleep, calm), presenting them in a somewhat different context, a change which probably occurred already in the oral tradition behind the *AP*.

3. Hamburg Papyrus, p. 7; *Actus Vercellenses* 35.

The apocryphal saying of the Savior, 'I am about to be crucified again', appears in both apocryphal documents, but in contexts which are totally different. We have seen that Schmidt, after the discovery of the Hamburg Papyrus, changed his mind concerning the relation between the two Acts, precisely because of this difference in context. The discussion of this passage will therefore be especially significant.

MacDonald spends a great deal of time on this parallel, making use of his three criteria cited above:

a) According to Criterion 1, which seeks a tradition which could have been at the origin of the apocryphal saying, MacDonald points to Pauline texts or a Pauline tradition which interprets suffering or death as a continuation of the crucifixion of Christ (Rom 6.6; Gal 2.19, 5.24; Phil 3.10; Col 1.24). We should add here that the *AP* in general can be understood as a narrative interpretation of certain Pauline letters, as Peter W. Dunn has just demonstrated in his doctoral dissertation[24].

b) According to Criterion 3, which attributes to the later text the attempt to better that which appears barely comprehensible or bizarre

---

[24] P.W. Dunn, *The* Acts of Paul *and the Pauline Legacy in the Second Century* (Dissertation Cambridge, 1996); idem, 'Influence of 1 Cor'.

in the earlier text, MacDonald stresses rightly that the difference is striking: according to the Hamburg Papyrus, Paul does not think of his own death, but of the repetition of the Lord's own death, and is therefore grieved[25]; but in the *Actus Vercellenses*, on the other hand, Peter understands immediately that the saying concerns his own death and is overjoyed with his own impending crucifixion. This macabre joy seems secondary. We can add that Schmidt's argument that the point of the story is missing (i.e., that the Apostle Peter like the Lord is crucified) in the *AP*, can be turned around: the point in the *Actus Vercellenses* is made only too well!

c) According to Criterion 2, which considers which of the contextual environments appears more native, MacDonald thinks that the Hamburg Papyrus preserves the earlier environment of the story just before the beginning of the *MP*, and that the *Actus Vercellenses*, in recounting the struggle between Peter and Simon, must have pushed the episode further, so that it is situated also just before the martyrdom of Peter. Above all, the *Quo-vadis* scene seems to MacDonald to be problematic: Peter is already at Rome when he hears from Xanthippe about the plot against him. The community must really insist that he leave Rome, for he does not want to appear to be a deserter. But finally, he leaves the city and meets Jesus[26]. MacDonald points out, by the way, that the rare word δραπετεύω finds its direct parallel in the *MP* 5, which itself is impregnated with military language[27].

MacDonald's long demonstration seems to me to prove that one cannot speak of the priority of the *Actus Vercellenses* over the Hamburg Papyrus. Nevertheless, we will see that this conclusion does not

---

[25] Stoops, 'Peter, Paul, and Priority', 228, has thus misinterpreted MacDonald's position. The latter thinks that the apocryphal saying of Jesus in the *AP* focuses upon Jesus' crucifixion, and that it is only the author of the *APt* who sees in it an allusion to Peter's crucifixion. MacDonald therefore considers it an attempt at improving the text on the part of the *APt*.

[26] Stoops, 'Paul, Peter, and Priority', 231, recalls the numerous examples during the period where the flight of the bishop during persecution is seen positively.

[27] Stoops, *ibidem*, 231, stresses, however, that δραπετεύω can also signify the flight of slaves. For the military language see also J. Bolyki, 'Events after the martyrdom: missionary transformation of an apocalyptical metaphor in Martyrium Pauli', in Bremmer, *AAP*, 92-106.

imply automatically the dependence of the *Actus Vercellenses* on the *AP* either[28].

4. MacDonald reminds us that the basic plots of the two martyrdom accounts of Peter and of Paul are identical: the two apostles are arrested and led before the Roman authorities which condemn them to death, stirring up a protest from the people against the verdict; but both are nevertheless put to death, after having prayed. In the two accounts, both apostles encourage someone to faith and threaten Nero to the point where he turns away from his persecution[29], whereupon the Christians rejoice and glorify God. Despite these resemblances, however, there are also clear differences between the two martyrdom accounts. MacDonald, by referring to the first two criteria, arrives at the conclusion that the *Martyrdom of Peter (MPt)* seems to be secondary to the *MP*:

a) In accordance with Criterion 1, it is possible to detect the external sources upon which the *MP* depends, which is not the case of the *MPt*. Above all, the story of Patroclus' fall from a window (*MP* 1) shares some sort of relationship with the story of Eutychus' fall from a window in Acts 20.7-12[30]; furthermore, Barsabas Justus, who is mentioned in Acts 1.23f. and Papias (Eusebius, *HE* 3.39.9-10), appears again in the *MP* (2 and 6)[31].

b) In accordance with Criterion 2, the story of the *MP* is internally more coherent than the *MPt*. The conversion of Nero's servants is situated at the beginning of the story and becomes the reason for the apostle's martyrdom, whereas in the *MPt*, it is the preaching of ἐγκράτεια (which is certainly present in the *AP*!) which leads to

---

[28] In a letter dated September 18, 1996, Stoops wrote me that he no longer holds to the development of his argumentation, which 'was in part an effort to be as creative as Dennis in suggesting interpretations'; I will therefore not linger on it.

[29] MacDonald states in this regard: 'The motif of someone other than Jesus appearing to villains in order to rebuke them is rare in the apocryphal Acts. Here one may be quite certain of intertextual contact'.

[30] W. Rordorf, 'Les *Actes de Paul* et les Actes des apôtres canoniques. Le cas d'Eutyque et de Patrocle', unpublished paper presented at the University of Neuchâtel, June 1992.

[31] MacDonald, *The Legend and the Apostle*, 23-6.

arrest and death of the apostle, with Nero and the conversion of his servants playing only a minor and superfluous role in this affair.

For MacDonald, the priority of the *MP* to the *MPt* is not to be doubted; according to him one must even affirm that the *MPt* shows literary dependence on the *MP*. I understand well why Stoops has reacted against MacDonald's conclusion[32]. In particular, he wonders why the *MPt* has not taken up more the political aspect of the persecution which is present in the *MP*, upon which it purportedly depends. Evidently, in Stoops' perspective, this absence becomes another argument that the *MP* is later than the *MPt*; it would be the *MP* which would have introduced this political aspect, since at the end of the second century, the date of this text, the problem of the loyalty of Christians vis-à-vis the Empire was heating up, which was not the case at the time of the writing of the *MPt*.

Once again, faced with this controversy between two scholars, it seems to me more prudent to abstain from the question, 'which came first?', and to be content with scholarly ignorance: we cannot decide which one is the prior document[33].

4. *Conclusion*

Let us summarize the results of this present examination. Since neither MacDonald nor Stoops knew of Poupon's work, their studies have not been able to profit from his findings, which is regrettable. It is especially visible in their observations concerning the opening chapters and the final chapter of the *Actus Vercellenses*, which are third-century interpolations in the text according to the conclusions of Poupon.

---

[32] Stoops, 'Peter, Paul, and Priority', 231f.

[33] Stoops, *ibidem*, 232, advances two other arguments for the priority of the *APt* over the *AP*. Firstly, he argues that there is an increased focus on the person of the apostle in the *AP*, especially in the Hamburg Papyrus, p. 6 (see the critique on this point by F.S. Jones, 'Principal Orientations on the Relations between the Apocryphal Acts [*Acts of Paul* and *Acts of John; Acts of Peter* and *Acts of John*]', in *SBL 1993 Seminar Papers* [Atlanta, 1993], 499). I must say that I do not see how the focus on the apostle is more heightened in the *AP*, except perhaps by his sufferings. Secondly, Stoops compares the episode at Myra in the *AP* with the story of Peter's crippled daughter in the *APt* (p. 233). But I do not see how this comparison could lead to the conclusion that the author of the *AP* knew the *APt*.

Furthermore, MacDonald has demonstrated that the famous *Quo-vadis* scene in the *APt* is not the source for the corresponding scene in the *AP* – and here he, and not Schmidt or Stoops, is certainly right. However, here also, – contra the American scholar – I would not deduce automatically that the *APt* has copied the *AP*. I have the impression that the apocryphal saying of the Lord, 'I am about to be crucified again', developed out of the martyrdom experiences of the early Christians, where they understood that Christ suffered again in his witnesses[34]. What would be more natural than to apply this conviction to the martyrdom of the most notable apostles? One is not forced to admit a literary dependence between the *AP* and the *APt* with respect to this motif[35], although clearly the saying finds its perfect fulfillment in Peter who is crucified.

My general conclusion concerning the relation between the *AP* and the *APt* will follow this same line of thinking. If we except the final chapter of the *APt* which is, according to the opinion of a growing number of scholars, a later addition, I would say that a direct influence of the *AP* on *APt* is nowhere to be found. Granted, we cannot maintain this statement absolutely with respect to the first chapters of the *APt* (however, it speaks of a voyage of Paul to Spain, which has no place in the *AP*); but all the other parallels between the two apocryphal Acts can be easily explained by a common stock of oral traditions from which both authors have respectively drawn.

Thus, we cannot draw a conclusion from the comparison of the two documents about the dating of either the *AP* or the *APt*. Everything remains within the realm of possibilities. To shed light on these problems, we will need to resort to other kinds of criteria[36].

---

[34] Cf., e.g., W. Rordorf, *Liturgie, foi et vie des premiers chrétiens* (Paris, 1988²) 381-403 ('"Martyre" et "témoignage". Essai de réponse à une question difficile').

[35] C.M. Thomas, 'Word and Deed. The *Acts of Peter* and Orality', *Apocrypha* 3 (1993, 125-64) 153-7, arrives at the same conclusion.

[36] Peter W. Dunn (Ontario Theological Seminary) kindly translated this contribution from the French.

XV. L'Origine africaine des *Actus Vercellenses*

GÉRARD H. POUPON

La découverte du manuscrit *Vercellensis* 158 fut certainement la plus importante pour notre connaissance des *Actes de Pierre* (*APt*), même si, plus d'un siècle après, son rapport exact avec l'apocryphe pétrinien n'a pas été entièrement élucidé. Notre propos n'est pas de reprendre l'examen de cette question, mais de présenter quelques remarques qui éclairent un peu l'histoire de la traduction latine de ce texte.

Il faut se rappeler que dans le *Vercellensis* les *APt* font suite, sans titre aucun, aux *Reconnaissances* pseudo-clémentines traduites par Rufin d'Aquilée. Le manuscrit est lui-même acéphale, il comporte en revanche deux *explicit*. Voici le premier tel qu'il a été édité par Lipsius:

> *Pax omnibus fratribus et qui legunt et qui audiunt.*
> *actus Petri apostoli explicuerunt cum pace [et Simonis]. amen.*

Nous pensons que l'éditeur a eu tort de mettre *et Simonis* entre parenthèses carrées. Certes ces deux mots ne sont pas à leur place, mais cela peut s'expliquer par une distraction du scribe qui a réparé de son mieux un oubli. Il est aussi possible que l'ordre des mots ait été perturbé déjà dans son modèle. En tout cas, il est arbitraire de considérer ces deux mots comme un ajout du copiste[1]. Il est facile de rétablir l'ordre de la phrase et de lire: *Actus Petri apostoli et Simonis explicuerunt. cum pace. amen.*

Ce titre ainsi restitué ne correspond pas, il est vrai, à l'appellation traditionnelle de Πράξεις Πέτρου/*Actus Petri*, mais ce changement

---

[1] L. Vouaux, *Les Actes de Pierre* (Paris, 1922) 228 n. 1: ils sont ajoutés, "comme le prouve la place anormale de ces deux mots".

ne pourrait-il pas être l'indice que l'on a affaire à un texte remanié ou encore à des extraits[2]? Ceci correspondrait justement à l'optique du recueil, telle qu'elle apparaît dans le second *explicit* écrit en capitales: *EXPLICIT EPISTULA SANCTI PETRI CUM SIMONE MAGO*. Cet *explicit* vaut en effet pour l'ensemble formé par les *Pseudo-Clémentines* et les *APt* et centré sur les luttes entre l'apôtre et le magicien.

Mais revenons à la fin du premier *explicit* qui nous donne une indication précieuse. Ludwig Traube avait remarqué naguère que l'*explicit* de certains manuscrits contenait une formule particulière[3]. A la fin de l'*Ambrosianus* O 210 Sup on lit: *Explicit. lege cum pace*. Le *Leidensis Voss. lat.* F 58 se termine par *cum pace amen*, comme notre manuscrit, une fois *et Simonis* replacé. L'expression figure aussi dans l'Heptateuque de Lyon, dans la Grande Bible de Paris (*lat.* 11553), dans des témoins du *De trinitate* d'Hilaire de Poitiers. Et le savant émettait l'hypothèse que cette formule était d'origine africaine et que de là elle était passée en Espagne, dans le Midi de la France ainsi qu'en Italie. Or, il se trouve qu'une faute dans le *Vercellensis* vient confirmer cette hypothèse de Traube. On lit en effet au ch. 2 des *Actes*:

> *Tunc habebitis in aeterno ducem uestrum primogenitum totius creaturae et uirtutem in pace cum dominum nostrum.*

Cette phrase comporte une première faute qu'il est facile de corriger. Il faut lire: *et uirtutis*. En effet, ce passage du discours de Paul fait référence au 'premier-né de toute créature et puissance' (cf. Col.1.15 et Eph. 1.21). Mais la fin de la phrase cache une autre faute passée jusqu'ici inaperçue. Nous avions conjecturé de remplacer *in pace cum* par *Iesum Christum*. Cette phrase, dont la syntaxe et le sens sont incohérents, devient alors tout à fait limpide:

> *Tunc habebitis in aeterno ducem uestrum primogenitum totius creaturae et uirtutis Iesum Christum dominum nostrum.*
> Alors vous aurez à jamais pour guide le premier-né de toute créature et puissance, Jésus Christ notre Seigneur.

---

[2] Un argument à ajouter à ceux que j'avais mentionnés dans ma contribution à *ANRW* II 25.6 (Berlin et New York, 1988) 4372-74.
[3] L. Traube, *Kleine Schriften*, ed. S. Brandt (München, 1920) 61.

La faute du copiste s'explique par une méprise. Son modèle employait pour les *nomina sacra* des abréviations qui ne lui étaient pas familières et qu'il lui est arrivé de ne pas comprendre. C'est précisément le cas dans notre passage. La préposition de *in pace* provient de l'abréviation par suspension *IH* pour *Iesum*[4]. Quant à *pace cum*, la faute résulte d'un chrisme peut-être suivi de la désinence casuelle. Cette double correction absolument sûre est de surcroît confirmée par la tradition indirecte. En effet, l'auteur qui a écrit au IVe s. une biographie romancée d'Abercius, évêque de Hiéropolis en Phrygie Mineure vers la fin du IIe s., a plagié cinq passages des *APt*[5]. Au chapitre 13 de la *Vita Abercii* on peut lire: ἕξετε (...) στράτηγον ἡμῶν τὸν πρωτότοκον πάσης κτίσεως καὶ δυνάμεως Ἰησοῦν Χριστὸν τὸν κύριον ἡμῶν (ed. Nissen, p. 12).

Il s'avère donc que la faute du *Vercellensis*, qu'elle soit le fait du copiste ou qu'elle ait figuré dans son modèle, résulte bien d'une abréviation spéciale. On sait que les premiers traducteurs latins des textes bibliques ont simplement adopté les abréviations grecques des *nomina sacra*. Pour *Christus* il a cependant existé en plus de l'abréviation XPS qui s'imposa très tôt, une forme plus archaïque empruntée à l'épigraphie, à savoir le chrisme, ce monogramme formé par la superposition des deux premières lettres grecques: ☧ Ce signe connaîtra le succès extraordinaire que l'on sait en épigraphie, surtout après que Constantin l'eut inscrit sur ses enseignes. Mais dans les *scriptoria* son emploi est très vite tombé en désuétude. C'est que le chrisme avait deux défauts. Son format d'abord, dépassant les autres lettres, et surtout son ambiguïté sémantique, puisque cette abréviation par suspension pouvait signifier aussi bien *Christus* que *Christianus* et que l'absence de désinence casuelle compliquait encore son emploi. Celui-ci s'est néanmoins maintenu plus longtemps dans des *scriptoria* africains. On le trouve, par exemple, dans les Fragments d'évangiles du célèbre codex k de Turin (Bibl. Naz., G VII 15), provenant de l'Abbaye de Bobbio, mais certainement d'origine africaine[6]. J'en ai

---

[4] Pour cette abréviation, voir L. Traube, *Nomina Sacra. Versuch einer Geschichte der christlichen Kürzung* II (München, 1907) 151-2.

[5] Voir W. Schneemelcher, in *NTA* II, 276.

[6] C. H. Turner, 'The "Nomina Sacra" in early Latin mss', in *Miscellanea Fr. Ehrle* 4 (Rome, 1924) 74: 'Now our most important fragment of the African Old Latin Gospel, *k*, also came to its present home at Turin from Bobbio'. Turner mentionne ensuite des essais africains d'abréviation, 'after the

aussi retrouvé la trace dans un texte dont l'origine africaine ne peut être mise en doute. Il s'agit de la *Vita Cypriani*, rédigée par le diacre Pontius. On y retrouve la même faute que dans le *Vercellensis* et celle-ci a entaché toute la tradition manuscrite. Au ch. 2, 7, le biographe loue le futur évêque de Carthage d'avoir vendu ses biens pour venir en aide aux pauvres de la communauté: *Distractis rebus suis ad indigentiam multorum pacem sustentandam...* On le voit d'emblée, le texte de cette proposition à l'ablatif absolu est corrompu. Ici encore *pacem*, qui semble un intrus dans le texte, est l'interprétation erronée d'un chrisme. Cela démontre son ambiguïté sémantique. En ce cas également il a été lu *pax*. Il semble que les caractères grecs ont été pris pour les lettres latines P et X, ce qui expliquerait le passage à PAX[7]. Tous les efforts des copistes et des éditeurs modernes pour corriger le texte se révèlent désormais superflus[8]. Il suffit, en effet, de remplacer *pacem* par *Christianorum* pour que la phrase soit correcte: *Distractis rebus suis ad indigentiam multorum Christianorum sustentandam...*, 'Ayant vendu ses biens pour secourir l'indigence de beaucoup de chrétiens...'

Ces observations sur les traces du chrisme et sur la formule *cum pace* qui se rencontrent simultanément dans le *Vercellensis* renforcent la présomption de l'origine africaine du modèle des *Actus Petri et Simonis* utilisé par le copiste. C'est la même origine que celle des Fragments vieux-latins de k et de la *Vita Cypriani*.

Le manuscrit conservé dans les Archives du Chapitre cathédral de la cité piémontaise a été daté des VIe-VIIe siècle[9]. Mais l'archétype du

---

suspension used in *k*, ⳨ , had proved itself so inconvenient as to call for alteration'. Voir aussi Traube, *Nomina sacra*, 138-9.

[7] Il se peut que la proximité du chrisme et de la mention *in pace* dans des inscriptions funéraires ait favorisé leur confusion. Nombreux exemples dans *Dictionnaire d'archéologie chrétienne et de liturgie* XIII, s.v. Paix, 465-83 (H. Leclercq).

[8] Voir les nombreuses corrections proposées dans la dernière édition critique de la *Vita Cypriani* due à A.A.R. Bastiaensen, dans *Vite dei Santi* III (Milano, 1981²) 8.

[9] Voir la description codicologique dans R.A. Lipsius et M. Bonnet, *Acta Apostolorum Apocrypha* (Leipzig, 1891, 1898, 1903; reprint Darmstadt, 1959) I, XXXIII-LII; E.A. Lowe, *Codices Latini Antiquiores* IV (Oxford, 1947) 18, 37; B. Rehm, *Die Pseudoklementinen* II, *Rekognitionen in Rufins Übersetzung* (Berlin, 1965) XXXVI-XXXVII. Selon Lowe, il a probablement été écrit

modèle devait être beaucoup plus ancien, puisque l'usage du chrisme a été vite abandonné et même s'il s'est conservé plus longtemps dans les livres sacrés. Ce qui est peut-être, il est vrai, le cas des *Actus Vercellenses*, comme on le verra. Lipsius estimait que leur traducteur avait fait usage de la Vulgate et plaçait notre version au Ve siècle. Mais cet usage n'est nullement prouvé. Turner, apportant un démenti au savant allemand, n'hésite pas à la faire remonter à la fin du IIIe ou au début du IVe siècle[10]. Est-ce pure coïncidence chronologique? Cela correspond à une période de propagande intensive de la part des manichéens dans la province Proconsulaire et dans l'Afrique du Nord en général. L'intérêt des manichéens pour les Actes apocryphes est bien connu et doit remonter à Mani lui-même[11]. Un intérêt qui est aussi largement attesté chez les manichéens africains par les oeuvres de controverse de S. Augustin. Or, c'est avant la fin du IIIe siècle déjà que des missionnaires venus d'Egypte avaient prêché la nouvelle religion en cherchant à gagner des adeptes surtout dans les rangs chrétiens[12]. Il ne serait pas invraisemblable que ces missionnaires aient alors eux-mêmes emporté ce texte apocryphe dans leurs bagages et qu'ils l'aient traduit comme moyen de propagande auprès des chrétiens.

---

en Espagne. Il renvoie à A. Millares Carlo, *Tratado de paleografía española* (Madrid, 1932²) 28. C'est surtout en se basant sur des annotations marginales en écriture wisigothique qu'on a attribué une origine espagnole au manuscrit. Celles-ci sont datées du VIIIe s., mais d'autres en écriture cursive d'Italie du Nord leur sont contemporaines.

[10] C.H. Turner, 'The Latin Acts of Peter', *JTS* 32 (1931, 119-31) 119. Le caractère juxtalinéaire, voire mot à mot, de la traduction atteste aussi de son ancienneté. Voir aussi Bremmer, dans ce volume, Ch. I.3.

[11] E. Junod et J.-D. Kaestli, *L'histoire des Actes apocryphes des apôtres du IIIe au IXe siècle: le cas des Actes de Jean* (Genève, Lausanne et Neuchâtel, 1982) 40 et 78-79. Sur le témoignage des Psaumes et Hymnes manichéens voir aussi P. Nagel, 'Die apokryphen Apostelakten des 2. und 3. Jh. in der manichäischen Literatur', in K.W. Tröger (ed), *Gnosis und Neues Testament* (Gütersloh, 1973) 149-82.

[12] Voir F. Decret, *L'Afrique manichéenne (IVe-Ve siècles). Etude historique et doctrinale*, 2 tomes (Paris, 1978) I.161-77. Les origines du manichéisme en Afrique sont obscures, mais le fait que c'est en Proconsulaire qu'a été déclenchée la première persécution antimanichéenne par un décret de Dioclétien daté de 297 ou 302 laisse supposer que la secte y était déjà bien implantée et y semait le trouble.

En effet, le statut des Actes apocryphes rejetés par la Grande Eglise en faisait un instrument privilégié de polémique, un excellent cheval de bataille. En se réclamant de l'exemple laissé par les Apôtres, les manichéens pouvaient se prévaloir d'être les héritiers du christianisme authentique, tel que l'avait voulu son fondateur et tel qu'il avait été proclamé par ses envoyés. De plus, les apocryphes possédaient aux yeux des manichéens une valeur propédeutique. On sait qu'ils se reconnaissaient en particulier dans l'idéal de chasteté qui y était prôné par les Apôtres et qui apportait une caution à leur propre rejet du mariage. Quant à l'impassibilité des Apôtres devant la souffrance, elle restait un modèle à imiter pour les vrais croyants.

Cependant, à côté de ces raisons explicitement invoquées, il y en eut sans doute d'autres souterraines, non-dites. C'est celles-ci que j'aimerais esquisser très brièvement à partir des *APt*. Sans défendre un dualisme au sens strict, avec deux principes coéternels du Bien et du Mal, notre apocryphe s'inscrit dans le courant platonicien, mettant une opposition radicale entre le visible et l'invisible. Cela apparaît très nettement dans tout le discours du ch. 37, où Pierre presse ses auditeurs de se détacher du sensible, παντὸς φαινομένου μὴ ὄντος ἀληθοῦς, 'tout ce qui est apparent n'étant pas vrai'[13]. Le rejet du corps est partout diffus. Je citerai seulement l'exorcisme du ch. 8, où Pierre s'en prend au démon:

> *Tu priorem hominem concupiscentia inretisti et pristina nequitia tua et corporali uinculo obligasti.*
> C'est toi qui as pris le premier homme au filet de la concupiscence et qui l'as enchaîné par ta perversité originelle et par le lien du corps.

A entendre ces paroles, un manichéen devait se sentir conforté dans sa foi. Les tendances docètes des *APt*, ou du moins certaines formulations maladroites de leur christologie, devaient aussi agréer aux lecteurs manichéens.

Ils devaient en particulier se sentir concernés, lorsque l'apôtre interpellait ses auditeurs: Ἄνδρες, οἷς ἐστιν ἴδιον τὸ ἀκούειν, ἐνωτίσασθε, 'Hommes, dont c'est le rôle d'écouter, prêtez l'oreille' (38). Même insistance plus bas: Ὑμεῖς οὖν, ἀγαπητοί μου, καὶ οἱ νῦν ἀκούοντες καὶ οἱ μέλλοντες ἀκούειν, 'Vous donc, mes bien-aimés,

---

[13] *APt* 92.11-12: nous supprimons la virgule entre les deux membres, car ils forment sans doute une seule proposition au génitif absolu.

qui écoutez maintenant ainsi que ceux qui écouterez...' (38). Comment ne pas songer ici à la classe des auditeurs dans la secte?

Même plausible, l'origine manichéenne de notre texte latin reste évidemment une hypothèse. J'ai cru un moment, je l'avoue, que la salutation du premier *explicit* gardait une trace de cette origine:

> *Pax omnibus fratribus et qui legunt et qui audiunt.*
> Paix à tous les frères, à ceux qui lisent et à ceux qui écoutent.

Le début de la salutation, identique à celle d'Eph. 6.23, est tout à fait en harmonie avec l'ensemble du texte. Les chrétiens y constituent une communauté de frères (52 occurrences)[14], une fraternité (4 occurrences) dans laquelle il n'existe guère de différence hiérarchique. Ses membres s'adressent à l'Apôtre en l'appelant simplement: *frater* ou bien *frater Petre*[15]. Mais la fin de la salutation est surprenante avec sa division entre les lecteurs et les auditeurs. Ces derniers font bien sûr songer à la deuxième classe dans une communauté manichéenne. Mais ne serait-il pas trop hardi de voir dans les premiers une référence mal interprétée à la classe des élus?

Par ailleurs, cette salutation qui est propre au latin nous livre une information importante. Elle nous apprend que les *APt* étaient lus publiquement devant la communauté et qu'ils étaient donc considérés comme un texte sacré. Il est peu probable que cette communauté ait appartenu à l'Eglise catholique[16]. A supposer qu'il ne soit pas issu de

---

[14] Sur le titre de *frère* chez les manichéens, surtout en référence aux auditeurs, voir H.-Ch. Puech, *Sur le manichéisme et autres essais* (Paris, 1979) 268.

[15] Notons que ce n'est pas le cas dans les *Actes de Jean*. Il y a bien trois exceptions dans les *APt*, dont l'une est à écarter selon nous. Au ch. 6 Aristhon dit à Pierre: *frater et domine, sanctorum mysteriorum communis...* Mais le texte est fautif; il faut lire: *frater et domini sanctorum mysteriorum communis...* 'Frère et participant des saints mystères du Seigneur...' Un autre interlocuteur fait exception, il s'agit du patricien Marcellus, il raffole des titres et des superlatifs. Il emploie *Apostole Christi Petre* (22), *dulcissime Petre* (10), *beatissime Petre*. Enfin, les veuves aveugles qui supplient Pierre de les guérir lui disent: *domine Petre* (21). Mais n'étaient-elles pas encore païennes? La question est débattue.

[16] La hiérarchie catholique interdisait la lecture publique des Actes apocryphes, elle n'en toléra un moment que la lecture privée. On signale bien

cercles manichéens, ce texte ne peut provenir que d'une communauté dissidente. On pense évidemment aux ariens, aux donatistes ou aux priscillianistes[17].

Il est possible qu'un jour de ces menus détails, ces *Kleinigkeiten* pour reprendre le mot de Traube dans le passage auquel nous nous référions au début, permettront d'en savoir plus. Ne serait-ce pas précisément le cas de l'énigmatique *cum pace amen* dans l'*explicit* de plusieurs manuscrits[18]? Dans notre passage, il fait doublet avec la salutation qui précède. Ce fait m'incite à formuler encore une hypothèse. Ne s'agirait-il pas, comme au ch. 2 et dans la *Vita Cypriani*, de la trace d'un chrisme mal compris? Ne faut-il pas lire *cum Christo amen*? On aurait là une profession de foi chrétienne d'une extrême concision, mais ayant peut-être valeur de ralliement. Aux temps des luttes christologiques, ce pouvait être une sobre protestation de foi au Christ. La question reste en suspens. Pour pouvoir y répondre, il faudra reprendre l'examen de la liste donnée par Traube et, espérons-le, l'enrichir d'autres exemples.

En résumé, nous considérons comme quasi certaine l'origine africaine des *Actus Vercellenses*[19]. Ils ont dû servir au culte dans une communauté hétérodoxe, puis ils ont sans doute échappé à la destruction lors d'invasions barbares en Afrique grâce à leur transfert en Europe. Ils seront alors copiés avec les *Reconnaissances* pseudo-clémentines pour compléter un dossier sur la confrontation entre l'apôtre Pierre et le magicien Simon. Ce voisinage tutélaire a sans doute préservé, un siècle plus tard, l'apocryphe du funeste sort qu'auraient laissé craindre les inscriptions marginales du folio 327r: *puto quod iste hactus petri et pauli et si<mo>nis apocrifus sit*. La seconde est catégorique: *iste liber apocrifus est*. Vraiment la survie d'un manuscrit unique tient toujours du miracle!

---

quelques abus. Mais même en ce cas il serait surprenant que le manuscrit utilisé par le contrevenant ait gardé une marque de cet usage public. A ce propos, voir Junod & Kaestli, *L'histoire*, 102 qui surévaluent selon nous la fréquence de tels abus.

[17] Si le manuscrit est bien originaire d'Espagne, ce serait un argument très fort en faveur d'une provenance priscillianiste.

[18] Traube, *Nomina sacra*, 138-9 insiste sur le fait que l'expression est à distinguer de la formule *in pace*, si fréquente dans les inscriptions funéraires.

[19] Voir aussi Westra, dans ce volume, Ch. XI.

XII. Bibliography of Acts of Peter

PIETER J. LALLEMAN AND JAN N. BREMMER

Texts

Lipsius, R.A. *Acta Apostolorum Apocrypha* I (Leipzig, 1891; repr. Hildesheim, 1959).
Vouaux, L., *Les Actes de Pierre* (Paris, 1922).

Translations

Bovon, F. - Geoltrain, P., *Écrits apocryphes chrétiens* I ([Paris], 1997).
Elliott, J.K., *The Apocryphal New Testament* (Oxford, 1993).
Erbetta, M., *Gli Apocrifi del Nuovo Testamento*, II: *Atti e Leggende* (Casale Monferrato, 1966).
Klijn, A.F.J., *Apokriefen van het Nieuwe Testament* I (Kampen, 1984).
Moraldi, L., *Apocrifi del nuovo testamento* II (Torino, 1971).

Apocryphal Acts in general

Bovon, F. et al. (ed), *Les Actes Apocryphes des Apôtres* (Geneva, 1981).
—, 'Miracles, magie et guérison dans les Actes apocryphes des apôtres', *J. Early Chr. Stud.* 3 (1995) 245-59.
Elliott, J.K., 'The Apocryphal Acts', *Expository Times* 105 (1993-94) 71-7.
Kampen, L. van, *Apostelverhalen. Doel en compositie van de oudste apokriefe Handelingen der apostelen* (Diss. Utrecht, 1990).
Lipsius, R.A., *Die apokryphen Apostelgeschichten und Apostellegenden. Ein Beitrag zur altchristlichen Literaturgeschichte* II.1 (Braunschweig, 1887; repr. Amsterdam, 1967).
Plümacher, E., 'Apokryphe Apostelakten', in *Paulys Realencyclopädie der classischen Altertumswissenschaft*, Supplementband XV (1978) 11-70.

Rordorf, W., 'Terra Incognita. Recent Research on Christian Apocryphal Literature, especially on some Acts of Apostles', in his *Lex orandi – Lex credendi* (Freiburg, 1993) 432-48.
Söder, R., *Die apokryphen Apostelgeschichten und die romanhafte Literatur der Antike* (Stuttgart, 1932; repr. Darmstadt, 1968).

Acts of Peter

Cartlidge, D.R., 'Transfigurations of Metamorphosis Traditions in the Acts of John, Thomas, and Peter', *Semeia* 38 (1986) 53-66.
Deeleman, C.F.M., 'Acta Petri', *Geloof en vrijheid* 44 (1910) 193-243.
Erbes, C., 'Ursprung und Umfang der Petrusakten', *Zs f. Kirchengeschichte* 32 (1911) 497-530.
Ficker, G., *Die Petrusakten. Beiträge zu ihrem Verständnis* (Leipzig, 1903).
—, 'Petrusakten', in E. Hennecke (ed), *Handbuch zu den neutestamentlichen Apokryphen* (Tübingen, 1904) 395-491.
Flamion, J., 'Les Actes Apocryphes de Pierre', *Revue d'Histoire Ecclésiastique* 9 (1908) 233-54, 465-90; 10 (1909) 5-29, 215-77; 11 (1910) 5-28, 223-56, 447-70, 675-92; 12 (1911) 209-30, 437-50.
Jones, F.S., 'Principal Orientations on the Relations between the Apocryphal Acts', in E.H. Lovering (ed), *Society of Biblical Literature 1993 Seminar Papers* (Atlanta, 1993) 485-505.
MacDonald, D.R., '*The Acts of Peter* and *The Acts of John*: Which Came First?', in E.H. Lovering (ed), *Society of Biblical Literature 1993 Seminar Papers* (Atlanta, 1993) 623-6.
McNeil, B., 'A Liturgical Source in the Acts of Peter 38', *VigChris* 33 (1979) 342-6.
Nissen, Th., 'Die Petrusakten und ein bardesanitischer Dialog in der Aberkiosvita', *ZNW* 9 (1908) 190-203, 437-50.
Norelli, E., 'Situation des apocryphes pétriniens', *Apocrypha* 2 (1991) 31-83.
Perkins, J.B., 'The Apocryhal Acts of Peter: a roman à thèse', *Arethusa* 25 (1992) 445-7, repr. in her *The Suffering Self* (London, 1995) 124-41.
—, 'The *Acts of Peter* as Intertext: Response to Dennis MacDonald', in E.H. Lovering (ed), *Society of Biblical Literature 1993 Seminar Papers* (Atlanta, 1993) 627-33.
Poupon, G., 'Les "Actes de Pierre" et leur remaniement', in W. Haase (ed), *Aufstieg und Niedergang der römischen Welt* II.25.6 (Berlin and New York, 1988) 4363-83.

Schmidt, C., *Die alten Petrusakten* (Leipzig, 1903).
—, 'Studien zu den alten Petrusakten', *Zs f. Kirchengeschichte* 43 (1924) 321-48 and 45 (1927) 481-513.
—, 'Zur Datierung der alten Petrusakten', *ZNW* 29 (1930) 150-5.
Smith, J.Z., 'Birth Upside Down or Right Side Up?', *History of Religions* 9 (1969-70) 281-303, repr. in his *Map is not territory* (Leiden, 1978) 147-71.
Stoops, Jr., R.F., 'Patronage in the *Acts of Peter*', *Semeia* 38 (1986) 91-100.
—, 'Christ as Patron in the *Acts of Peter*', *Semeia* 56 (1992) 143-57.
—, 'Departing to Another Place: The *Acts of Peter* and the Canonical Acts of the Apostles', in E.H. Lovering (ed), *Society of Biblical Literature 1994 Seminar Papers* (Atlanta, 1994) 390-404.
Stuhlfauth, G., *Die apokryphen Petrusgeschichten in der altchristlichen Kunst* (Berlin and Leipzig, 1925).
Thomas, C.T., 'Word and Deed: The *Acts of Peter* and Orality', *Apocrypha* 3 (1992) 125-64.
Turner, C.H., 'The Latin Acts of Peter', *JTS* 32 (1931) 119-33.

Nag Hammadi Acts

Krause, M., 'Die Petrusakten in Codex VI von Nag Hammadi', in Krause (ed), *Essays on the Nag Hammadi Texts in Honour of A. Böhlig* (Leiden, 1972) 36-58.
Parrott, D.M. (ed), *Hag Hammadi Codices V.2-5 and VI...* (Leiden, 1979).
Robinson, J.M., *The Nag Hammadi Library in English* (Leiden, 1988[3]).

Index of names, subjects and passages[1]

Abercius, Life of, 13: 194; 24: 157
acclamation 108
Achilles Tatius 2.9: 8; 3.23: 11
Acta Scillitanorum 12: 4
Acts of Andrew 132; 3: 11; 34: 115; 37-9: 131; 52-3: 125; 61: 127; *Martyrium*: I.14: 114-6; II.4: 114; Coptic fragment 112
Acts of John 24: 177; 30-6: 171; 31: 16; 45: 171; 59: 16; 63: 166; 70: 166; 73: 166; 76: 166; 77: 177; 79: 175; 81: 175; 83: 175; 87: 171, 175; 87-93: 165, 168; 88: 171; 88-90: 173; 88-93: 171, 175; 90: 173, 175; 92: 171; 93: 173; 94: 173; 94-102: 164-5, 168; 95: 173; 97: 112; 97-101: 175; 98: 116, 166, 171, 173, 177; 99: 116, 130, 175; 101: 113, 173, 175; 102: 177; 103: 171, 177; 106: 171, 175, 177; 106-113: 165; 107: 171, 175; 108: 175; 109: 166, 173; 111-5: 126; 112: 177; 113: 171, 175; and *Acts of Peter* 161-77; date of 168
Acts of Nereus and Achilles 65-83
Acts of Paul 115, 125; and *Acts of Peter* 178-91; Coptic version 186; date of 178; encratism in 189; Hamburg Papyrus of 179-80; HambPap 6: 190; 6-7: 184; 7: 180, 187-9; 7-8: 185
Acts of Paul (Martyrdom), and *Acts of Peter* 180, 184, 189; 1: 185, 189; 2: 189; 3: 127; 3-5: 124; 5: 188; 6: 189
Acts of Peter 1: 101, 102, 104, 157, 164, 181; 1-3: 181-2; 1-4: 184; 1-32: 164; 1-36: 164; 2: 3, 40, 99, 136, 139, 142, 145, 154-5, 164, 170, 182, 193, 199; 3: 170; 4: 10, 15, 35, 42, 80, 89, 94, 97, 101, 155, 170; 4-6: 181; 5: 33, 45, 94, 98-9, 102, 141, 164, 180; 5-7: 185-7; 6: 40, 45-6, 99, 155-6, 164, 198; 7: 48, 105, 136, 139-40, 142, 145, 156-7, 164; 8: 4, 9, 35, 46, 94, 99, 105, 182, 197; 9: 21, 33, 46, 93, 157; 10: 10, 34, 40, 98-9, 105-6, 139, 145, 170, 182, 198; 11: 12, 34, 78; 12: 12, 34, 43, 45, 47, 94, 99, 101, 107; 13: 12, 34, 44, 107, 164; 14: 47, 49, 89, 94, 101, 107-8; 15: 12, 34, 46, 66, 94, 99, 101, 107, 170; 16: 99; 17: 7, 24,

---

[1] The editor would like to thank Geertje Huisman and Pieter Lalleman for their kind assistance in making the index.

INDEX

35, 45, 47, 94, 97-9, 104, 106, 137, 139-40, 142-3, 145; 18: 94, 97, 164, 170; 19: 5, 101, 157-8; 19-21: 4; 20: 34, 101, 109, 137, 140, 142, 158-9, 164, 166, 168, 170, 172; 20-1: 164, 167, 170; 20-2: 162; 21: 103, 172, 174, 198; 22: 3, 9, 34, 45, 47, 101-2, 129, 174, 198; 23: 35, 48, 89, 98-9, 140, 142; 23-4: 21, 94; 23-7: 162; 23-9: 21; 24: 21, 47, 159-60; 25: 108; 25-8: 34, 69; 26: 22, 78, 108, 174; 27: 4, 18, 98, 104, 108, 139-40, 145, 164; 28: 12-4, 22, 36, 44, 76, 79, 94, 97-9, 101, 108-9, 137, 139-40, 142-3, 174; 28-9: 4; 29: 3, 35, 50, 109, 160; 29-30: 98; 30: 6, 40, 50, 77, 102, 105, 170, 182; 31: 36, 44, 48, 50, 80, 89-90, 94, 97, 99; 32: 36, 48, 89-91, 101; 33: 94; 33-4: 80; 33-41: 163; 34: 23, 41, 90, 104; 35: 23, 114, 129, 187-9; 36(7): 4, 90, 92, 101-2, 127, 164, 174; 36-9: 165, 174; 36-41: 123; 37(8): 113-5, 174, 197; 37-8: 115; 37-9: 164, 167; 38(9): 115-7, 119-20, 165, 174, 176, 197-8; 39(10): 172, 176; 40(11): 35, 92, 170, 176; 40-1: 164; 41(12): 39, 102, 181-2, 184; and *Acts of John* 134, 161-77; and *Acts of Paul* 134, 178-91; and *Actus Vercellenses* 65-83, 148; African origin 195; and Bithynia 15; Coptic fragment 164, 170; date of 9, 16-8, 134, 168; encratite tendency 40; and Justin Martyr 163; and *Kerygmata Petri* 163; place of 14-6, 147; revision of 39-40; title 41, 192; *P.Oxy* 849: 76
Acts of Philip 78; 140: 120
Acts of Thomas 106: 11; 108-13: 132-3; 140: 125; 142: 128; 147: 120; 160: 127, 129; 164-8: 124
Actus Vercellenses, African origin 192-9; date of manuscript 148, 196; editions of 148-154; text of 148-60
Adam 55, 120, 129, 131
Aegeates 125-6
agentes in rebus 19
agents of censure 87, 90, 93
Agrippa 3, 6, 13, 24, 21-8, 48, 69-70, 78-9, 90-2, 107, 179
Agrippina 6, 22, 104
Albinus 6, 23, 79, 90-1, 104; wife of 179
Alexander of Abunoteichos 7
Alexandria 145, 147
Ananias 93, 95
Andrew 112, 125, 127-31, 133
angels 60
Anthologia Palatina 16.244: 7
Apocryphal Acts, and Acts (NT) 163; intertextual relations 161, 183
Apocryphon of James 128
Apollonius of Tyana 31
apostles, death of 123; suffering 197
Apuleius, *Apology* 63: 8
Aricia 9, 42, 48

Aristarchus 79
Ariston 46, 102, 198
Aristotelianism 57
Aristotle, *Poetics* 18: 85
Artemis 9
Artemon 185-7
Athena 60
Augustine 53, 145, 196; *Contra Adimanti calumnias* 17: 19; *Sermo* 215.2: 146
Augustus 13

baby 107
Balbus 15
Bar-Jesus 92
Barnabas 10; *Epistle of* 9.9: 167; 21.1: 167
Barsabas Justus 189
base narrative 81-2
bath 2
Berenice 5
Bible: *Gen* 1-3: 120; 2-3: 54; 3: 54; 3.9: 55; 19: 32; *Ex* 14: 32; *Deut* 21.23: 117; *Judg* 13: 32; 1 *Kgs* 17.17-24: 73; *Ps* 78.8: 157; *Mt* 3.7: 92; 5.38-9: 167; 7.5: 92; 7.15: 46; 7.22-3: 101; 8.22: 35; 11.19: 88; 13.33: 122; 13.37: 92; 14.22: 32, 185; 15.7: 92; 16.22: 113; 22.18: 92; *Mk* 3.22: 88; 8.34: 117; 8.38: 92; 9.39: 101; 15.13-4: 92; *Lk* 7.11-7: 71; 7.11-17: 34; 7.12: 72; 7.14: 72; 8.36-50: 95; 13.32: 92; 23.2: 88; 23.5: 88; *John* 4.29: 42; 8.44: 92; 19.26: 113; *Acts* 1.23-4: 189; 2-4: 33; 3.6: 101; 5: 33, 95; 5.1-11: 93; 5.12: 33; 5.17-26: 33; 5.30: 117; 5.41: 88; 6.11: 88; 6.13: 88; 6.14: 88; 8: 36, 95; 8.9-11: 41, 93; 8.9-13: 52; 8.14-9: 53; 8.18-19: 141; 8.20: 93; 8.22-23: 93; 8.24: 93; 10: 33; 10.39: 117; 12: 24, 33; 12.22: 27; 12.23: 26; 13.6-12: 92; 14: 10; 15: 33; 16.8: 101; 17.6: 88; 17.7: 88; 18.11: 93; 18.14: 88; 19.15: 101; 20.7-12: 189; 20.29: 46; 20.36-7: 184; 21.10-4: 184; 21.21: 88; 21.28: 88; 24.5-6: 88; 28.6: 10; 28.30: 182; 28.30-1: 39; *Rom* 2.5: 46; 6.6: 187; 12.17: 167; 15.23-4: 39, 182; *1Cor* 1.17-25: 118; 2.9: 176; *Gal* 2.19: 187; 5.24: 187; 6.12-4: 118; *Eph* 2.16: 117; 3.17: 156; 6.23: 198; *Phil* 2.8: 117; 3.10: 187; 3.18: 118; *Col*: 114; 1.20: 117; 1.23: 156; 1.24: 114, 187; 2.7: 156; 2.14: 118; *1Th* 5.15: 167; *Heb* 9.28, 10.10-8: 114; *1 Pet*: 16; 3.9: 167
black 8
Boethus 25
Bonnet, M. 150, 152-3
boule 15

Caligula 25, 26
Callimachus 166

calm, period of 187
capsa 4
Catullus 63: 62
challenge-response game 85-96
chamber pots 94
Chariton, *Callirhoe* 1.5: 15
Christ 112, 127-8; name of 12
christogram 194-5
Chryse 6, 40, 77, 102, 105, 182
Cicero, *in Verrem* 5.180: 157
Claudius 25-6, 58-60, 184
1 Clemens 21.8: 167
Clement, *Stromata* 6.127.1: 140
codex 4-5
Codex Theodosianus VI.29.1,4: 19; VIII.5.50: 19
Collyridians 62
Commodus 18
Constantine 122
consummare 160
Cornelius 117
Creed, Apostles' 135-8, 145-7; Aquileian form 146; Old Roman 135-7, 143
cross 84, 111-33; Christological function of 112; of light 113; predicates of 173; of wood 113, 117
crowd 13, 94
crucifixion head downwards 119-21
curiosi 19
Cybele 62

demons 8
denunciation 87, 95
deus, used for a human 10
Diana 9
Diocletian 196
Diognetus, Epistle to 4.6: 167
Dionysius of Corinth 16
Diotima 58
dog 34, 45, 47, 105-7
Doris 6, 22, 104
Drusiana 1, 175

Egyptians 8-9
Elijah 30
Empedocles 31

emperor, friend of, 6, 23, 26, 69, 73, 82, 90; statue of 11, 35, 106
enim 157
ennoia 58, 59
Enoch 30
Epiphanius 60
Ethiopian 8, 34
Eubola 7-8, 35, 45, 47, 104, 106
eucharist 104-5
Euphemia 6, 22, 104
Eusebius, *Historia Ecclesiastica* 3.39: 189; 4.23: 16
Eutychus 189
Eve 54-5, 58
exorcism 12
explicit 193
exstirpare 158

fabula 74-5
Falconilla 15, 17
first of the city 16
Fortunatus 166
Forum of Julius 48, 50, 69, 94, 107
frater 198
Fulgentius of Ruspe 145; *Contra Fabianum* 36.3: 146
fundari 156

gardener's daughter 40, 80
Gemellus 48
Glykon 7
gnosticism 54-62
Götz, G. 152
Gospel of Bartholomew 131
Gospel of the Egyptians 120
Gospel of Nicodemus 126
Gospel of Peter 39-42: 130
Gospel of Thomas 37: 120
Granius Marcellus 15-6
Gundermann, G. 150, 152-3

hand 13
Harnack, A. von 181
Hekate 9
Helen 59-60
Hermes 8, 10

Hermeticism 57
Hero *Spir.* 1.37: 7
Herod Antipas 25, 92
Herod the Great 24
Herodas 5: 6
Herodians 92
Herodias 25
Hesiod, *Theogony* 886ff: 58
Hippolytus 57, 60-1; 6.11-2: 61; 6.15-6: 61; 6.28.2-4: 61; *Contra Noetum* 1.7, 4.8, 8.1: 141
Homer 61
honour 86
Hymn of the Pearl 132

Icarus 111
Ignatius, *To the Magnesians* 10.1: 167; *To the Romans* 4.3: 167
inscriptions: *IGRom* 4.1094, 74-5: 10; *SEG* 32.1202: 6; 35.1523: 19
Irenaeus 57-8, 60; *Adversus Haereses* 1.23.1: 59; 1.23.2: 59; 1.23.3: 59; 3.4.2: 140; 3.16.6: 140; 4.33.7: 142, 160; 5.20.1: 141; *Demonstratio* 3: 138, 141
Isidore of Pelusium, *Epistula* 99: 158
Iulius Balbus 6
Q. Iulius Balbus 15
C. Iulius Cornutus Tertullus 16

James 24
Jerome, *Tractatus II in Psalmos* 84.13: 158
Jesus 30, 80
John 88
Joseph and Aseneth 167
Josephus 25, 27; *Antiquitates* 19: 26; *Bellum Judaicum* 24; I.7.4-5: 56
Justin 57-8; *Acts of* 138; *Apologia* I.26: 10, 58; I.60: 130; I.61.3: 142; *Dialogus* 120: 58
Juvenal 6.279, 331: 6

Kluge, F. 150
labeling process 85-96
Lactantius 53
lapsi 40, 110, 166
laughing 11, 105
Lévi-Strauss, C. 85
light 109
Linus 65, 74

Lipsius, R.A. 149-53
Longus, *Daphnis and Chloe* 2
Lucian, *Philopseudes* 13: 11
Luke 24, 53, 56, 60, 79
lynching 108
Lystra 10

magic 97-110
magus 97, 100, 102
man, first 120
Mani, Manichaeans 196-9
Marcellus 3-5, 8-13, 15, 18, 34-5, 46-7, 77-8, 81, 89, 94, 101, 105-6, 108, 129, 166, 174, 181-2
Marcion 16
marriage, age of 2
Martial 1.84: 6
Martyrium Polycarpi 12-3: 14
Martyrium Pionii 2.3: 9
Maximilla 131
Megalé Apophasis 61
megalé dynamis 60
menarche 2
Mendelssohn, H. 150
Metis 58
miracles 97-110
Montanists 62
Moses 30
Mount of Olives 112-3
mysterium(a) 57, 159-60, 165
mystikos 57
Naassenes 62
Nain 80
Narcissus 181
narrative world 84
Nature of the Archons (NHC II.4) 54
Nero 102, 104, 124, 126, 179, 184, 189-90
Nicaria 6, 22, 104
Nicolaitans 62
Nicomedia 16
Nicostratus 14-5, 69, 108-9
Ninos Col. A.III.1: 2
nomina sacra 194
Novatian 138; *De trinitate* 1.1: 145; 9.1: 142

Odes of Solomon 23: 130
Odysseus 116
On the Origin of the World (NHC II.5) 55
Origen 138, 145, 147; *De principiis* 1.pr.4-5: 144-5; *Commentarii in Iohannem* 20.91: 178-80; 32.16: 144; *Commentarii in Matthaeum ser* 33: 144; *Contra Celsum* 1.7: 144; *Fragmentum 4 in 1Cor* 144; *Homiliae in Ieremiam* 5.13.157: 144
orphans 106
Orpheus 57
Orphism 57

Papias 189
papyri: Daniel and Maltomini, *Magical Papyri* II, no. 55, 58.8-9: 12; *P.Oxy* 849: 76; 64.4432: 7
Passio Perpetuae 10: 9; 13.4: 9; 19: 126
Patroclus 189
Paul 3, 10, 95, 97, 102, 104, 105, 114, 126, 191; death of: 124, 127, 182; teaching on the cross 118
peasant's daughter 3, 103
Perpetua 9, 17-8
perstirpare 157-8
Peter *passim*; adversaries of 92; apocryphal 33-35; as second Adam 129; characterization of 32-33; cross of 111-22; crucifixion 90, 179; daughter 2, 40, 66, 80, 102, 105, 190; *martyrium* of 51, 189-90; suffering of: 114, 124, 127
Peter II of Alexandria 131
Petraeus 13
Petronius 75.11: 6
Pharisees 92
Philip 13, 25-6, 57, 79
Philo 27; *Legatio ad Gaium* 24; 32: 25
Philostratus 5; *Vita Apollonii* 1.19: 10; 3.15, 17: 11; 5.20: 7; 6.10-1: 11; 1.15: 13; 4.45: 13; 6.2: 8
pillei 14
Plato 57; *Symposion* 201d: 58; *Phaedrus* 235c: 58; *Timaeus* 36BC: 130
Pliny, *Natural History* 34.11f: 6
Plutarch, *Moralia* 815D: 14
Polycarp 13; *Epistles to the Philippians* 167
polymorphy 174-5
Pompeia Sosia Falconilla 17
Q. Pompeius Falco 17
Q. Pompeius Sosius Priscus 17

Pompey 56
Pontius *Vita Cypriani* 2.7: 195, 199
M. Pontius Laelianus 17
Pontius Pilate 92
Propp, V. 85
Pseudo-Clementines 62, 148, 192-3, 199
Pseudo-Hegesippus 65-83
Pseudo-Titus *De dispositione sanctimonii* 41, 80; 83-4: 3
Ptolemaeus 2, 103
Pythagoras 31
Pythagoreanism 57
puer 108

Quodvultdeus, *De symbolo* 1.4.35: 146; 2.3.2, 14: 146; 3.2.22: 146
Quo Vadis episode 66, 74, 129, 179, 188, 191

Recognitions, see Pseudo-Clementines
regulae fidei 134-47; monarchical and dyadic 139-40; Trinitarian 140
resurrection 13, 35, 44, 50, 69-83, 108, 174-5
retrospective interpretation 87, 93-5
Rome 185
Rufina 3, 93, 95, 104-5, 182
Rufinus, *Expositio symboli* 4-5: 146
rule enhancement 87, 93-5

Sabellianism 146
sacrificium 155
Sadducees 92
Salome Alexandra 26
Samaria 56-8
Sanhedrin 117
Sapphira 93, 95
Sappho 58
Satan 126
satyriskos 7
Saviour, gnostic 127-8
Schmidt, C. 161, 168, 178-91
scribes 92
scroll 4-5, 109
Semo Sancus Dius Fidius 10, 58
senator, young 15, 35, 70, 77-8, 94
seniores 5

Septimius Severus 18
Shechem 57
Sienkiewicz, H. 111, 114
Simon Cantheras 25
Simon Magus 2, 8-10, 14, 21, 30-1, 33, 35-38, 54-62, 65, 68, 77-82, 89-95, 97, 106, 110-1, 126; as`He that Standeth' 41; flying 11, 44, 48, 94, 100; image of 52-64; as a narrative figure, 39-51; statue of 10, 58, 98, 105; as *theios aner* 54; voice of 43
slaves, and funeral 14; manumission of 6; sex with women 6
Socrates 58
Sophia 54
soter 10
spells, for speechlesness 12
stabulum 12
status degradation ritual 87, 93-5
stauros 117
Stephen and Paul 88
Stoicism 57
storyline 74-5
Stratokles 125
Studemund, W. 149-50
Suetonius *Vitellius* 12: 6

Tertullian 4, 53; *Adversus Praxean* 2.1: 141; *Apologeticum* 13.9: 58; *De baptismo* 1: 12; 17.5: 178; *De praescriptione haereticorum* 13: 141; 36.5: 141; *De virginibus velandis* 1.3: 141
Tertullus 16, 88
Testimony of Truth (NHC IX.3) 54
Thecla 1, 125
theios aner 31-8
Theocritus 27.3, 49f: 7
theologia crucis 117
Theon 46, 98, 180, 185-7
Theophilus 25
theurgy 32
Thomas 124-5, 127-9, 133
Tiberius Gemellus 25
Tiberius 25
touching 13
Trajan 6
Transfiguration 163, 172-3
Tryphaena 15, 17
Turner, C.H. 154

urinating 11
Usener, H. 151-3
Usher, J. 135
Valentinian Gnosis 113, 123
Valentinus 113
Via Appia 42
Via sacra 100
Virgil, *Fourth Eclogue* 57
visions 101-2
volumen 5
Vossius, G.J. 135
Vouaux, L. 153, 181

widow(s) 3-5, 94, 106, 108-9
women 1-9; aristocratic 6; dark 47; *matronae* 5; and new religions 7; old 4, 171; sex with slaves 6; virgins 3

Xanthippe 3, 6, 23, 91, 104

Zeus 10, 13, 58, 60

PRINTED ON PERMANENT PAPER • IMPRIME SUR PAPIER PERMANENT • GEDRUKT OP DUURZAAM PAPIER - ISO 9706

ORIENTALISTE, KLEIN DALENSTRAAT 42, B-3020 HERENT